This book is an essential resource for researchers, policymakers and activists challenged with the task of understanding the processes of radicalisation and de-radicalisation in the British context and beyond. It questions the viability of the 'Prevent' programme, providing a nuanced, detailed and insightful account of what works or not in the context of both the concept and in the delivery of countering violent extremism programming. It facilitates a grounded social science understanding to help resolve a significant multi-faceted and multi-layered concern facing liberal democracies today and in the near future. This remarkable, brave and profound book is an indispensable intellectual contribution.

Tahir Abbas, *Royal United Services Institute, UK*

Elshimi's book represents the next step in research on (de)radicalisation, and should be essential reading for anyone who has an interest in this field. The examination of the 'Prevent' policy in *De-Radicalisation in the UK Prevent Strategy* provides welcome clarity and insight in to what's happening on the ground, policy development, and a frank and useful assessment of political discourse that marks a new and refreshing point of departure for this subject.

Jonathan Githens-Mazer, *University of Exeter, UK*

De-radicalisation in the UK Prevent Strategy

This book examines de-radicalisation policy in the UK and addresses the contradictions evident in the conceptualisation and practice of de-radicalisation.

It explores three main themes that touch upon some of the most pressing issues of our day: security, identity and religion. Situated within the Prevent strand of the UK Counter-Terrorism policy and administered by the police through the 'Channel Programme', policymakers have promoted de-radicalisation as a vital instrument in the fight against terrorism. Despite the political and legal importance of de-radicalisation as an instrument of counter-terrorism, we continue to know very little about the programme and the profile of individuals who have been de-radicalised, as well as having little or no access to data on the programme. There is also a glaring lacuna in the wider literature regarding the concept, theory, and evidence base for de-radicalisation policies. This book addresses this lacuna and, with the use of data collected from interviews conducted with 27 practitioners, this work reveals the existence of multiple conceptions of de-radicalisation and a number of conceptual features unique to the UK context. Subsequently, the book proposes that de-radicalisation in the UK would be best conceptualised as 'technologies of the self'. Seen in this way, de-radicalisation is less about tackling terrorism and radicalisation and more about the re-configuring of citizenship, the construction of a mainstream British identity, and the promotion of certain subjectivities in an era of uncertainty about British political identity.

This book will be of much interest to students of critical terrorism studies, de-radicalisation, counter-terrorism, UK politics and security studies in general.

M. S. Elshimi is a Research Analyst at the Royal United Services Institute specialising in Countering Violent Extremism. He has a PhD in Ethno-Political Studies from Exeter University, UK..

Series: Routledge Critical Terrorism Studies

Series Editor: Richard Jackson

University of Otago, New Zealand

This book series will publish rigorous and innovative studies on all aspects of terrorism, counter-terrorism and state terror. It seeks to advance a new generation of thinking on traditional subjects and investigate topics frequently overlooked in orthodox accounts of terrorism. Books in this series will typically adopt approaches informed by critical-normative theory, post-positivist methodologies and non-Western perspectives, as well as rigorous and reflective orthodox terrorism studies.

Counter-Terrorism and State Political Violence
The 'War on Terror' as terror
Edited by Scott Poynting and David Whyte

Selling the War on Terror
Foreign policy discourses after 9/11
Jack Holland

The Making of Terrorism in Pakistan
Historical and social roots of extremism
Eamon Murphy

Lessons and Legacies of the War on Terror
From moral panic to permanent war
Edited by Gershon Shafir, Everard Meade, and William J. Aceves

Arguing Counterterrorism
New perspectives
Edited by Daniela Pisoiu

States of War since 9/11
Terrorism, sovereignty and the war on terror
Edited by Alex Houen

Counter-Radicalisation
Critical perspectives
Edited by Charlotte Heath-Kelly, Lee Jarvis and Christopher Baker-Beall

Critical Perspectives on Counter-Terrorism
Edited by Lee Jarvis and Michael Lister

Researching Terrorism, Peace and Conflict Studies
Interaction, synthesis, and opposition
Edited by Ioannis Tellidis and Harmonie Toros

Hamas, Jihad and Popular Legitimacy
Reinterpreting resistance in Palestine
Tristan Dunning

Russia's Securitization of Chechnya
How war became acceptable
Julie Wilhelmsen

Ending ETA's Armed Campaign
How and why the Basque armed group abandoned violence
Imanol Murua

De-radicalisation in the UK Prevent Strategy
Security, identity, and religion
M.S. Elshimi

De-radicalisation in the UK Prevent Strategy

Security, Identity, and Religion

M.S. Elshimi

LONDON AND NEW YORK

First published 2017
by Routledge
2 Park Square, Milton Park, Abingdon, Oxon OX14 4RN

and by Routledge
711 Third Avenue, New York, NY 10017

Routledge is an imprint of the Taylor & Francis Group, an informa business

© 2017 M.S. Elshimi

The right of M.S. Elshimi to be identified as author of this work has been asserted by him in accordance with sections 77 and 78 of the Copyright, Designs and Patents Act 1988.

All rights reserved. No part of this book may be reprinted or reproduced or utilised in any form or by any electronic, mechanical, or other means, now known or hereafter invented, including photocopying and recording, or in any information storage or retrieval system, without permission in writing from the publishers.

Trademark notice: Product or corporate names may be trademarks or registered trademarks, and are used only for identification and explanation without intent to infringe.

British Library Cataloguing in Publication Data
A catalogue record for this book is available from the British Library

Library of Congress Cataloging in Publication Data
Names: Elshimi, M. S., author.
Title: De-radicalisation in the UK prevent strategy : security, identity, and religion / M.S. Elshimi.
Other titles: De-radicalization in the UK prevent strategy
Description: Abingdon, Oxon ; New York, NY : Routledge, 2017. |
Series: Routledge critical terrorism studies | Includes bibliographical references and index.
Identifiers: LCCN 2016043231| ISBN 9781138281042 (hardback) |
ISBN 9781315271361 (ebook)
Subjects: LCSH: Terrorism–Prevention–Government policy–Great Britain. | Terrorism–Prevention–Social aspects–Great Britain. | Internal security–Great Britain. | Radicalism–Great Britain. | Islamic fundamentalism–Great Britain.
Classification: LCC HV6433.G7 E57 2017 | DDC 363.325/160941–dc23
LC record available at https://lccn.loc.gov/2016043231

ISBN: 978-1-138-28104-2 (hbk)
ISBN: 978-1-315-27136-1 (ebk)

Typeset in Times New Roman
by Wearset Ltd, Boldon, Tyne and Wear

Contents

Acknowledgements		viii
	Introduction: the enigma of de-radicalisation	1
1	Radicalisation as the 'new security challenge'	20
2	The concept of de-radicalisation: an analysis of research data	51
3	An alternative concept: de-radicalisation as the 'technologies of the self'	76
4	Discursive technology (truth): the production of radicalisation	100
5	Disciplinary technology (power): surveillance, detection, discipline	125
6	Confession technologies (identity): 'salvation in this life'	156
7	A new framework for engagement	186
	Conclusion	205
	Appendix	210
	Index	212

Acknowledgements

Writing is nothing if not a lonely affair. I often found myself staggering along, tentatively and fumblingly, into what always seemed like a vast ocean of uncertainty. Writing this book could not have been done without my amazing parents, to whom this is dedicated. You have been the heartbeat that keeps everything ticking over. This is also dedicated to my beautiful and loving wife – this would not have been possible without you. And to my wonderful boys Raiyaan and Gabriel, you are my joy and light. To my brothers Ahmed and Adam, thank you for your support and engaging discussions. I'm sure we'll realise our promise to each other and get there eventually. I cannot express enough gratitude to Professor Jonathan Githens-Mazer. Thank you for believing in me, the opportunity to be your student, and support over the years.

This book is my humble attempt at understanding the changes that have occurred in my life and the world around me in the last 15 years.

Introduction

The enigma of de-radicalisation

> What we are fighting, in Islamist extremism, is an ideology. It is an extreme doctrine. And like any extreme doctrine, it is subversive. At its furthest end it seeks to destroy nation-states to invent its own barbaric realm. And it often backs violence to achieve this aim – mostly violence against fellow Muslims – who don't subscribe to its sick worldview. But you don't have to support violence to subscribe to certain intolerant ideas which create a climate in which extremists can flourish. Ideas which are hostile to basic liberal values such as democracy, freedom and sexual equality.
>
> (Prime Minister David Cameron 'Extremism' Speech, July 2015)

> We need to now be less precious about the private space. This is not about us invading private thoughts, but acknowledging that it is in these private spaces where this [extremism] first germinates. The purpose of private-space intervention is to engage, explore, explain, educate or eradicate. Hate and extremism is not acceptable in our society, and if people cannot be educated, then hate and harmful extremism must be eradicated through all lawful means.
>
> (Scotland Yard Commander Mak Chishty, in Dodd 2015)

Le problematique: what is de-radicalisation?

How do you get British citizens involved in terrorism to abandon their commitment to violence? And is it possible to divert youngsters away from terrorism before it's too late? Recent terrorist attacks in several European cities, alongside the fact that some British Muslims have travelled to Iraq-Syria in order to join Daesh, have rekindled the preoccupation of policymakers with the radicalisation of British Muslims. In response, 'de-radicalisation' has become increasingly prevalent in the UK's counter-terrorism policy as a strategy for tackling the threat of religiously inspired violence/extremism. Indeed 'de-radicalisation' has become somewhat of a buzzword amongst policymakers. In September 2014, former UK Prime Minister David Cameron announced that British jihadists returning from Iraq and Syria would be forced to attend de-radicalisation programmes to 'reverse their warped brainwashing' (Whitehead 2014). In the aftermath of the Charlie Hebdo attacks in January 2015, Cameron also championed the development of de-radicalisation in his discussion with Barak Obama at the

2 *Introduction*

White House. They discussed moving towards tackling hard-line ideologies, with American and British officials devising plans that 'will focus on ways of working with Muslim communities to challenge extremist thought and designing deradicalisation programmes' (Morris 2015). Elite policy-makers have thus conceived de-radicalisation as a vital instrument of counter-terrorism in the fight against violent radicalisation.

This greater focus on de-radicalisation in UK counter-terrorism marks a notable shift in security thinking. Following the terrorist attacks on London in 2005, the key question occupying British policymakers and public discourse at the time was: why do some young British Muslims legitimise and in some cases, adopt, violence against the state? How do young British Muslims become radicalised? In fact, governments and policymakers in Europe invested a lot of financial, political and emotional capital in order to answer the question, investing as well in counter-radicalisation projects designed to 'prevent' radicalisation. The UK government responded to the challenges of violent radicalisation through its counter-terrorism strategy (CONTEST) (HO 2006, 2009, 2011). In its efforts to win the 'hearts and minds' of British Muslims in the struggle against violent radicalisation, the strategy focused on preventing the long-term causes of radicalisation through the Prevent strand of CONTEST.

However, since 2011 Prevent has readjusted the focus of counter-terrorism initiatives towards de-radicalisation (HO 2011, 56). As an instrument of UK counter-terrorism strategy, de-radicalisation is supposed to provide the police and policymakers with a more selective, targeted and structured approach to tackling the threat of terrorism. It is also supposed to do away with the blanket and problematic approach characterising Prevent initiatives between 2006 and 2010 (see Chapter 5). In addition, since receiving Royal Assent in February 2015, the Counter-Terrorism and Security Bill has enshrined de-radicalisation in statutory law, thereby ensuring it now plays a pivotal role in the management of public spaces and the regulation of public conduct. The Act made Channel – the UK's voluntary de-radicalisation programme for people 'at risk' of radicalisation – a legal requirement for public bodies so that it is delivered consistently across the country (CTSA 2015). Schools, universities, NHS trusts, nurseries and local councils are compelled to identity 'vulnerable' and 'at-risk' individuals and report them to Channel. As the comments above by Scotland Yard Commander Mak Chisty suggest, de-radicalisation is concerned with 'private space' intervention. It is about the public effort to 'eradicate' extremism. Making de-radicalisation a legal requirement has not only expanded its operation and reach nationally, but has also further ensconced it institutionally into structures of governance in the UK.

Meanwhile, with the appointment of the new Home Secretary, Amber Rudd, in July 2016, the government announced plans to introduce a mandatory de-radicalisation scheme. This new mandatory de-radicalisation scheme will sit alongside Channel, for individuals who need more 'intensive support' (HO 2016, 16). Although at the time of writing little more has been disclosed regarding 'mandatory' de-radicalisation, it is now clear that there will be three different

Introduction 3

types of de-radicalisation schemes in the UK (in addition to Channel and 'mandatory' there are prison schemes, described in more detail in endnote 1). The focus of this book will be on Channel type de-radicalisation interventions.

De-radicalisation programmes emerged in many countries in the Middle East (ME) and Southeast Asia (SEA), and Europe in the late 1990s with the overarching objective of getting individuals and groups to move away from terrorism (Bjorgo and Horgan 2009, Ashour 2009). Many countries began responding to terrorism in innovative ways out of recognition that traditional coercive methods of counter-terrorism do not work on their own. Other factors included the counter-productiveness of repressive measures, the need for a more systematic way of managing risk and the need to reduce recruitment (Bjorgo and Horgan 2009, 1). In fact, de-radicalisation programmes targeting Jihadi terrorism were implemented before 9/11 – in places like Egypt and Algeria (Ashour 2009; 2012, 124). Such programmes were particularly associated with attempts at the reconciliation and doctrinal revision of prison inmates convicted of terrorism. It was only with the growing number of terrorist attacks globally after 9/11 that the development and concern for de-radicalisation in the ME and SEA began to mushroom. The delivery of these programmes has been implemented through a number of diverse activities that include counselling, dialogue, counter-ideology, state repressions, family involvement and aftercare (Barret and Bokhari 2009, 173–174). These programmes primarily (1) are based in prisons; (2) target convicted criminals, militants and terrorists; and (3) aim at collective groups (Bjorgo and Horgan 2009; ICSR 2010).

However, in contrast to programmes in the ME and SEA, de-radicalisation in the UK is distinguished by several key features: (1) it is aimed at 'vulnerable' youths who have not committed a crime but are deemed 'extremist'; (2) it targets youngsters; (3) interventions primarily take place outside of prisons;[1] (4) interventions require the involvement of civil society and public institutions in identifying radicalisation; and (5) it focuses on the primacy of 'Weltanschauung' or worldview in behaviour explanations of radicalisation, consequently valorising counter-ideological approaches in interventions. As mentioned by David Cameron in his 'Extremism' Speech at the beginning of this chapter, policymakers are fighting the ideology of 'Islamist extremism'. Notwithstanding the fact that the term has become a buzzword amongst policy-makers, coterminous with the growing political and legal prominence of de-radicalisation as an instrument of counter-terrorism, de-radicalisation in the Prevent strategy presents ten challenging problems to the curious mind – what I have called the 'enigma of de-radicalisation'.

The first challenge relates to the definition of de-radicalisation in Prevent. Situated under the second objective – 'supporting vulnerable people' – de-radicalisation is defined as follows:

> This area of Prevent is based on the premise that people being drawn into radicalisation and recruitment can be identified and then provided with support. The purpose of that support is to *dissuade them* from engaging in

4   *Introduction*

and supporting terrorist-related activity. This support is sometimes described as 'de-radicalisation', a term which is sometimes used to refer to *cognitive or behavioural change*: in the context of our own programmes we use it to refer to both. We seek to remove people from the influence of and from contact with terrorist groups and sympathisers, and to challenge any support they have for them.

(HO 2011, 56, section 9.4)

The above definition is taken from an updated Prevent document, whereas the initial definition of 2011 also compared de-radicalisation to crime prevention work. Notably, the analogy of de-radicalisation with 'crime prevention' is included in the summary section on page 55 in the updated version. The important point here is the opacity of this definition. To reiterate: de-radicalisation is defined as a 'support' programme aiming to 'dissuade' radicals from supporting or adopting violence and involves 'cognitive or behavioural change', which is compared to work done in crime-prevention. The confusion of Prevent's conception of de-radicalisation is also compounded when you take into consideration other terms it is associated with in the wider literature. Terms like 'rehabilitation', 're-socialisation', 'de-programming' and 'dialogue' are used to refer to de-radicalisation programmes. It is also employed interchangeably in the discourse with other terms like 'disengagement' and 'counter-radicalisation'. Such terms are used in the same context as de-radicalisation but each contains subtle differences in meaning and has subsequent policy ramifications (Horgan 2008). The definition of de-radicalisation offered by the Home Office and the fact it used in conjunction with a whole array of other terms does very little to explain what de-radicalisation is.

Second, de-radicalisation in Prevent indicates conceptual confusion. What does it actually mean? The issue surrounds whether getting someone to renounce violence entails 'cognitive' change, 'behaviour change' or both. This lack of clarity has also been exacerbated by its conflation with the idea of 'extremism', which is irrevocably a line further up the process of radicalisation and perhaps even more elusive than targeting violence directly. This muddled conception of de-radicalisation provokes a series of underexplored questions: is it possible to reverse years of cultural, religious, educational and political conditioning? Can somebody's 'worldview change' change through debate and discussion? Is it possible to dissuade people from supporting or adopting violence? Does changing a person's behaviour depend on changing their views? Is de-radicalisation really a norm free tool of governance, a means to 'protect the vulnerable' and secure a healthy identity for individuals, and a way to ensure that youngster are diverted from radicalisation?

This leads us neatly to the third problem: the de-radicalisation process itself. It isn't clear from either Prevent or the wider literature what the process of de-radicalisation looks like from beginning to end in terms of pathways out of radicalisation. Policy-makers and academics are trying to understand these processes with reference to the literature on gangs, social movements and cults (Bjorgo

Introduction 5

and Horgan 2009, 7–10). Some variables and factors leading to de-radicalisation have been identified; 'push' and 'pull' factors (ibid., 30–47), rational choice theories, the influence of counter-ideology, the influences of material based provisions, the influence of charismatic leaders, and state repression and incentives. Since de-radicalisation programmes include both material and counter-ideological components, it is difficult to evaluate what factors are the most important (Chowdhury and Hearne 2008, 16). In fact, the literature shows ideological factors play little or no role in persuading individuals to enter or leave such groups and movements (Bjorgo 2009, 36–40). This highlights the disjuncture between the largely ideological focus of current de-radicalisation programs and the factors found to motivate individuals' entry into and exit from terrorist organisations (Morris, *et al.* 2010, 6). It also reveals a poor understanding of the de-radicalisation processes.

Fourth, it is not obvious what the underlying purpose of a de-radicalisation intervention is. On the one hand, de-radicalisation is generally posited as a rehabilitative model targeted at individuals who have already crossed the line and pose a threat. It is thus underscored by the notion that 'we are going to make you good and/or better'. On the other hand, de-radicalisation sits within Prevent, whose underlying logic is 'prevention is better than cure' and suggests that 'we are here to stop you from becoming bad'. The logic of 'cure', to use the medical vocabulary of this policy domain, has been intertwined with that of 'prevention'; one is an act of reversal, the other pre-emptive.

A fifth problem is the wide ambit of concern underpinning de-radicalisation interventions. For example, the Prevent strategy exhibits a preoccupation with a future orientated temporality; something could happen in the future, which in conjunction with the immanency of the threat justifies corrective interventions in the present. This logic operates outside of juridical spaces: since those deemed 'extremist' and 'radical' have not committed a crime, have not even breached the law, the future oriented logic underpinning de-radicalisation shifts attention away from the juridical realm and towards another sphere altogether; and it is in this space of the non-juridical, one geared towards shepherding the 'Weltanschauung' of British Muslim youngsters, that the terrain of Prevent strategy and de-radicalisation intervention takes place. In other words, it targets individuals who have not even committed a crime but who merely harbour certain ideas deemed as 'extremist'. The question arises as to why – given that recruitment into terrorism, as well as acts of violence themselves, is overwhelming a group driven dynamic – UK de-radicalisation targets individuals who have not necessarily engaged in violence, who may not even have any links to wider terrorist networks?

As a result, the sixth problem relates to the disjuncture between what policy-makers say de-radicalisation is about on the one hand, e.g. 'preventing radicalisation', and what it seems to be doing on the other, e.g. policing thought crimes. It effectively moves the objective of policy-makers towards other concerns beyond only reducing the potentiality of violence: particular ideas, behaviours and practices in the temporality of the present become problematic. Religious,

6 *Introduction*

political and dissenting ideas and behaviour of religious and racial others therefore acquire greater significance, becoming objects of apprehension and existential concern, some of which has been reflected in public debates on multiculturalism, identity and immigration, amongst other issues, in a way that transcends the narrow scope of counterterrorism.

Moreover, there is no access to data that enables us to measure, evaluate or study on-the-ground programmes. There is no independent and rigorous assessment of 'Channel' in the literature. Instead there is only rudimentary information on Channel (Kundnani 2012; ACPO report 2010, HO 2011; HMG 2012; HMG 2015) and no reliable data, let alone evaluation in any form on it. The only case study of de-radicalisation interventions that could be found in the literature in the UK context is either on the Strategy to Reach, Empower and Educate (STREET) (Lambert 2011; ISD 2010; Baker 2011) or Active Change Foundation (ACF) (Rabasa *et al.* 2010, 133–136), which represent the two flagship organisations delivering interventions (With STREET no longer involved in delivering interventions through Prevent). Despite the growing prevalence of de-radicalisation, little continues to be known about these programmes

Additionally, there does not seem to be any basis or evidence for the development of de-radicalisation policies and whether they work. The lack of empirical data emerging from reports on programmes is even acknowledged in Prevent 2011(HO 2011, 61): 'There is little empirical evidence underpinning intervention work in this area here in the UK and internationally.' In addition, given the limited data available, it is also difficult to evaluate the effectiveness of these programmes. At the moment, current evaluation methods focus on something called 'recidivism rates', i.e. the number of 'ex' Jihadists who re-engage (Chowdhury and Hearne 2008, 16), but due to the lack of information and the unreliability of this measure, there have been calls, by the likes of Horgan, to find more effective ways of evaluating the success of programmes (Horgan 2009b; Horgan and Braddock 2010, 285–286). Despite the highly publicised claims for success associated with some interventions programmes, there are major barriers to even the most tentative of evaluations.

The ninth problem is the state of de-radicalisation as an area of study and research. Most of the literature, for example, is 'grey': the majority of the literature on de-radicalisation can be classified as reports that are available online but which are not published in journals or academic monographs. In fact, many of the reports online are produced by think-tanks (Demant *et al.* 2008; Rabasa *et al.* 2010; Disley *et al.* 2011; the ISD 2010; and the ICSR 2010). The UK literature on de-radicalisation has mainly been confined to think-tank reports (ICSR 2010; ISD 2010; ISD 2012), which provide a best-practice description of prison programmes. Other think-tank reports that provide comprehensive reviews are non-UK based, e.g. the RAND Corporation (Rabasa *et al.* 2010) which is an American think-tank and the Centre for International Migration and Ethnic Studies (Demant *et al.* 2008) based in the Netherlands. The only real attempts academically at conceptualising de-radicalisation have been made by John Horgan (Horgan 2008, 2009a, 2009b; Horgan and Braddock 2010; Bjorgo and

Horgan 2009) and Omar Ashour (2009, 2012). Notably, Ashour's (2009) book is the only detailed and focused case study of de-radicalisation in the field, whilst Bjorgo and Horgan's book (2009), is the first attempt in the field to provide a comparative study on the processes and programmes of disengagement and de-radicalisation. As an area of academic study therefore, de-radicalisation remains unchartered terrain.

Finally, the most surprising problem presented by de-radicalisation is the fact that there is not a single conceptual, theoretical and empirical study conducted on de-radicalisation in the UK. Even though de-radicalisation has become a centralised programme sanctioned by statutory law, there remains a marked absence of a robust conceptual framework underpinning de-radicalisation interventions, not to mention an evidence-based approach to policy development. The absence of a detailed study of UK de-radicalisation underscores how little we continue to know about the precise details of the process of de-radicalisation, the profile of individuals undergoing interventions, and the success rate of de-radicalisation interventions. The fact remains: there is not a single study on de-radicalisation in the UK.

The challenges of investigating de-radicalisation

When it comes to de-radicalisation we have seen the deep disjuncture that exists between the popular uses of the term, the way the concept is formulated, the actual programme on the ground, the process of de-radicalisation itself, and then what we know of it in the literature. Linked to this is the striking absence of an attempt to analyse and codify the rules, operations, concepts and theories of de-radicalisation. In other words, the emergence of de-radicalisation occurred without an invested concern for ontology. As a concept tied to policy objectives, de-radicalisation was formulated as a policy strategy (fight terrorism, reverse radicalism and reduce the risk of re-offending), before it was formulated as a concept. As a researcher endeavouring to study the phenomenon of de-radicalisation amidst such a fragmented and immature picture, where does one begin? How do we study it? And what are policies of de-radicalisation supposed to look like? It transpired very early on in the research process that, if I was going to do any justice to my inquiry into de-radicalisation, some heavy-lifting would be required.

This thorny state of affairs was further exacerbated by the contested, ideological, and politicised discourse on radicalisation – a new and recent knowledge domain with its own considerable research and conceptual issues. And yet it became quickly evident that no study of de-radicalisation could be undertaken without comprehending and dissecting the discursive formation of radicalisation that preceded it. For de-radicalisation shares, prima facie, similar conceptual features with radicalisation; etymologically, the 'de' that prefixes the term 'radicalisation' connotes the relationship between both concepts. More importantly, the conceptual features associated with de-radicalisation – the importance of ideology, the causal relationship between thought and action, the significance of

8 *Introduction*

identity, and the fact it is conceived as a linear process affecting individuals, bear the ontological fingerprints of radicalisation. It is therefore 'radicalisation' that is dominant in 'de-radicalisation' because it constitutes the reference point upon which it acquires its signification, since de-radicalisation cannot exist outside an understanding of radicalisation. The suturing role played by radicalisation conceptually in counter-terrorism and de-radicalisation then begged a whole range of other questions: Why radicalisation and not terrorism? What is radicalisation? Why did it not exist before? Why is radicalisation a new security challenge? What is the relationship between radicalisation and de-radicalisation?

Another challenge confronting the researcher of de-radicalisation is that it sits within the Prevent strategy, which is regarded as a controversial government policy. Amongst a whole panoply of other issues associated with Prevent, it was officially acknowledged by parliamentarians, practitioners, academics and civil society organisations to have been a muddled policy that focused its activities on intelligence gathering and counter-subversion rather than countering violent radicalisation; it wastefully expended public money on irrelevant community projects, and fostered divisions within Muslim communities, promoted envy between Muslim communities and other communities, and severed the trust between government and Muslim communities. This emotionally laden policy area presses itself upon any attempt to conduct a robust, independent and interest-free investigation. Not to mention the difficultly of securing fieldwork interviews with practitioners and stakeholders in a low-trust policy domain that is characterised by as much mistrust and suspicion as exists in Prevent.

That de-radicalisation is a Prevent initiative also makes research challenging given that it is a dynamic and constantly evolving strategy. In the space of six years (2006–11), for example, we have seen three iterations of Prevent, all of which have been accompanied by substantial changes in its approach, where the flow of resources go, terminology, and the altering profile of practitioners who are 'in' – vis-à-vis those who are 'out'. We often forget that Prevent belongs to an important and bustling policy area that has to be responsive to political events and the influx of the latest research, both of which have demonstrably been integrated into the Prevent documents more than once during its lifespan since 2006. This rapidly shifting policy domain, accompanied by a lexicographic field resembling the game of musical chairs, and supported by a hyper research area moulded by contributions from various disciplines on a one time basis, presented an external form of pressure to perpetually remain on top of developments in relation to de-radicalisation.

The last problem Prevent threw at me was that de-radicalisation is administered by the Police. Although Channel was public facing, it is nonetheless a highly confidential programme that precludes access to interventions, the names of mentors and the profiles of individuals undergoing de-radicalisation. Conducting ethnographic fieldwork to observe de-radicalisation in real-time, interview radicalised subjects to ascertain the phenomenological experience of being 'de-radicalised' or interview mentors to acquire the 'ins and outs' of de-radicalisation was consequently not a feasible option for me.

Introduction 9

So, provoked as I was by the questions highlighted in the previous section and motivated to resolve the barriers mentioned above, my research examines the ontological framework of de-radicalisation using the case study method. It does this by conducting qualitative interviews with experts and practitioners of de-radicalisation and Prevent. The rationale behind this approach was that primary data would ground my investigation and therefore enable me to deal with substance over mere conjecture, and new data over canned material. Speaking to experts with years of experience and intimate knowledge of the field behind them would also enhance the credibility of my findings. Furthermore, speaking to a wide range of experts hailing from a plethora of diverse organisations, positions, interests and political affiliations, at different levels of the policy-making process would allow me to tease out multiple interpretations in a way that goes against the conventional grain in this area, dominated as it is by binary perspectives (e.g. 'moderates' vs. 'extremists'). This would augment the usefulness, validity and purchase of my research data. My focus on ontology therefore is an attempt to say something substantial about de-radicalisation, in a way that is neglected in the literature and marginalised by policymakers.

I also decided to investigate de-radicalisation with an open mind to embracing various perspectives. What had started off as a data driven and conceptual study of de-radicalisation with a focus on policy and with a firm grounding in methodology within the disciplines of politics and international relations broadly, also quickly morphed into a theoretical thesis that drew inspiration from the disciplines of philosophy, history, sociology, anthropology and Islamic studies. Although being immersed in the literature of several disciplines proved to be an immensely enriching experience, it was in reality born out of sheer necessity. It was the only way that I could overcome many of the intellectual cul-de-sacs characterising the field of counter-terrorism and the study of radicalisation and de-radicalisation. The conceptual tools of traditional international relations and political theory, in some instances, were not particularly helpful. For example, both disciples have little ability to examine 'religion', besides its being seen as a form of ideology, like false consciousness, or a dated value system within modernisation theory. Hence I dipped into sociology, anthropology, Islamic studies and philosophy in order to understand the role of religion within the wider discussion surrounding radicalisation. As a result, the following book is replete with multi-disciplinary references and is driven by a heterodox spirit.

At this juncture it is vital to say something about my use of this strange term 'ontology'. In the case of de-radicalisation, I use the word in two ways. In the first instance, I use it in the sense of getting to the bottom of what gives something its thingness. What is this thing that we are talking about? What, also, makes the thing we are talking about, namely de-radicalisation, de-radicalisation? What has to be present for de-radicalisation to be de-radicalisation? What does it comprise? What is it that I am studying? Ontology is the most fundamental question because it starts with the basics. Before we can talk about solutions to tackling radicalisation (why) and the process of doing this (how), we need to know

10   *Introduction*

what it is that we are proposing as the solution. My concern for ontology means I am interested in the conceptual framework of de-radicalisation.

The second use of 'ontology' aligns with the use of post-structuralist ontology inspired by the likes of Michel Foucault, Jacques Derrida and Judith Butler. We can make sense of post-structuralist ontologies in contradistinction to both Realist and Constructivist conceptions of ontology. Material ontology states that what counts for something is its material existence. Interests are pre-given and fixed. According to this concept, de-radicalisation exists in the real world with fixed properties that are universally true from which we can generate universal laws about its nature, which accurately coincide with the term and concept we designate for it. In contrast, the Constructivist position, which takes its cue from idealist thinking, posits that reality is constructed primarily by ideas. It is this immaterial conception of reality that led International Relations Constructivist theorist Alexander Wendt (1999) to claim that the world is made up of ideas 'all the way down'. This position is primarily an ideational and linguistic one that would claim that the reality of de-radicalisation is constructed through language, culture and identity.

For post-structuralism however, the material is not eviscerated. The material world does exist but only acquires intelligibility and meaning through discourse. Discourse here is not just language but a framework of significations that shapes and constrains the way that people think and behave. The meaning of something only occurs in relation to a whole range of references, say the way that a hammer only makes sense in relation to nails, wood, carpenter, houses and other things too, otherwise it would be rendered an incomprehensible and useless metal object. Also, the way the hammer is discursively framed determines whether I see it as equipment used in carpentry or a weapon deployed to hit an aggressor with. With respect to de-radicalisation, post-structuralist ontology would agree that de-radicalisation exists in the real world but that the way it is framed, understood and disseminated is mediated through discourse and representation. Hence I attempt to ascertain a better picture of de-radicalisation in the UK context by finding out how it has been discursively framed and whether a coherent portrait of it emerges that would allow us to describe how it operates in the real world.

This discursive framing however does not occur in a vacuum but is shaped by history and politics, coalescing in a certain form for a particular purpose. Specifically, it is in this sense that Foucauldian ontology is considered radical because it contends that reality as we know it is the result of social practices and struggles over truth and objectivity – what he calls 'truth-games' – effectively exposing the constitutive role of power in shaping reality. This forms the philosophical background underpinning my argument in this book. Chapter 3 elaborates in greater detail Foucault's ontology and how it informs the theoretical structures of Chapters 4, 5 and 6 of this book to analyse my fieldwork data. As a result of employing a post-structuralist ontology, a crucial output of this book will therefore be a more contextualised understanding of de-radicalisation.

Indeed, one of the glaring failures of the literature on de-radicalisation is the ahistorical approach to understanding programmes, as well an overall neglect of

Introduction 11

the social-political context that allows such a phenomenon to emerge. Much of the discussion does not move beyond the domain of counter-terrorism. And yet the multifaceted challenges surrounding de-radicalisation contradict this narrow debate. Richard Jackson (2005) argues that the study of terrorism must involve analysing the discourses that give the term meaning in conjunction with the social and political institutions that produce and disseminate them, as well as the wider context that make such discourse possible, not least endowing them with traction. Echoing Jackson and inspired by post-structuralist ontology, I argue that what de-radicalisation is and what it means cannot be separated from the historical and political context in which de-radicalisation is being discussed. In fact the idea and practice of de-radicalisation impinges on multiple policy areas and issues, attested, as you will see, in Chapter 1.

Notably however my ontological investigation primarily focuses on the concept and understanding of de-radicalisation. The data elucidates how practitioners, who are involved with, work in or are familiar with the way de-radicalisation operates in Prevent, view and understand de-radicalisation. Recapitulating my argument in previous paragraphs, de-radicalisation does exist in the real world. It just exists meaningfully in the world in different ways, shaped by how it is framed discursively and how it relates to the historical and political context in which it is discussed.

However, my investigation will attempt to provide a concept and theory for making sense of the *practices* of de-radicalisation. The coordinated activities directed towards tackling the risk (distinct from threat) of radicalisation and extremism in the UK, pushed by government and affecting all society, is an evolving and constantly transforming practice. The alternative concept I propose to conceptualise de-radicalisation in Chapter 3 can be applied to describe the practice of de-radicalisation in the UK. This is because the concept and theory I outline employs a Foucauldian interpretive analytics, which presents an analytically strong framework for studying the human world; it encompasses the interconnected relationship between discourse (knowledge/power), disciplinary institutions (bodies) and subjectification (the identity of subjects). That these also sit within a theory of government makes such an analytical framework relevant and applicable to the concrete reality of our present day context. This investigation will therefore offer a more accurate and deeper way of describing the concept and practice of de-radicalisation in the UK.

Accordingly, this book is based upon research conducted for 18 months between December 2011 and May 2013, in which 27 Prevent and de-radicalisation practitioners were interviewed. The following also tries to answer a number of questions that arise from the above problematique of de-radicalisation:

- What is de-radicalisation?
- What is the purpose of de-radicalisation interventions?
- Why are policymakers concerned with what young Muslims are thinking?
- What does the hitherto non-juridical location of intervention say about the policy?

12   *Introduction*

- How can de-radicalisation interventions be justified in the absence of empirical evidence about the process of de-radicalisation?
- Why has no substantial academic work on the subject been undertaken?

Notwithstanding such objectives, it must also be explicitly mentioned that it is not the purpose of this research to investigate how de-radicalisation occurs in a positivist way and neither does it attempt to offer an explanation of the best way to de-radicalise radicalised subjects. This investigation is not, in other words, concerned with the question of process or with any normative proposal for how interventions should be improved. Those questions fall outside the scope of the book. Despite a small section at the end of this book, aimed at policymakers, that does propose an alternative framework for engagement, this section does so as a secondary by-product of my inquiry and not as an objective of my research question. It also presents a broader cursory strategy, informed by the most salient aspects of my research into de-radicalisation and political violence, rather than as a detailed breakdown of how to conduct specific interventions.

Why de-radicalisation is important

By gathering primary data and thinking rigorously through de-radicalisation conceptually, this book attempts to arrive at a more meaningful analytical framework that moves beyond the sensational headlines, the politicised discourse and the contentious claims made by commentators on the topic. Invoking the post-structuralist spirit, this book seeks to disrupt the dominant binaries characterising the discourse and implementation of de-radicalisation, e.g. Islamism vs. British values, vulnerable vs. radical, integrated vs. violent, moderate vs. extremist, cognitive vs. behavioural, etc. The dominant securitisation topos, with its positivist episteme that determines the way we think about de-radicalisation, has marginalised other crucial ways of examining it. It has relegated and closed off a world of nuance, layers and multiplicity. The following book is interested in opening up alternative spaces of thought and analysis that will prove significant to policymakers, academics and everyday citizens, not least citizens of the Islamic faith.

Consequently, given the priority invested in tackling radicalisation and terrorism in the UK, the findings of this investigation will be of great relevance to policymakers.[2] Now that the Channel programme is expanding, de-radicalisation is likely to play a greater role in counter-terrorism and in the management of public spaces against extremism. This has not hitherto been helped by the existing limitations of the Prevent conception of de-radicalisation. Moreover, the question of de-radicalisation touches upon some of the biggest, if not most pressing, concerns of our age: security, identity and religion. Yet without such an understanding on de-radicalisation, we are left with inadequate analysis that creates the condition for ill-informed policy decisions.

This research is also pertinent academically. De-radicalisation offers an account of human behaviour. De-radicalisation is premised on the notion that behavioural transformation can occur through thought reform and that agency

Introduction 13

resides in 'cognitive change'. De-radicalisation claims to be able to make a radicalised subject renounce violence, as well as have individuals re-integrated back into the 'mainstream'. Intellectually, it connotes the relationship between theory and action in terms of human behaviour, as well as the relationship between the individual and society. But, as will become evident later, research on de-radicalisation has been ideologically driven, lacks methodological integrity and credible data, and depends on an over reliance on anecdotal evidence. The need for robust, independent and fine-grained analysis has never been so pressing. Many academics and professionals in this field are therefore looking for more robust studies on de-radicalisation, something my book will provide.

The timing of this book is pertinent to citizens of all professions in public institutions. The Counter-Terrorism and Security Bill made Channel a legal requirement for public bodies so that it is delivered consistently across the country. All sectors and institutions of the state are legally obliged to deliver radicalisation awareness training, with citizens compelled to regulate the threat of 'radicalisation' and 'extremism' in their work places, as well as in their private lives. In response, many teachers, university students, civil society organisations and engaged citizens have expressed concerns about Channel and Prevent. Given that de-radicalisation poses series questions about what it means to be a citizen and transforms the way we practice our roles as citizens, many engaged citizens and diverse stakeholders outside the policy and academic world will therefore be interested in this book.

This research also provides very much needed insight for Muslims to understand a programme primarily targeting them. The production of discourses on radicalisation post 2004, the implementation of Prevent since 2006, and the growing prominence of de-radicalisation have had the Muslim population in sight. The force of this top-down gaze is evident in the government's secret propaganda efforts within Prevent. Prevent's tarnished reputation has been further besmirched by recent revelations in the press regarding the government's covert use of community groups to spread its counter-terrorism message (Cobain *et al.* 2016). This clandestine propaganda and counter-ideology strategy is spearheaded by a special Unit within the Home Office known as RICU (Research, Information and Communications Unit). Said to be inspired by the Cold War's Information Research Department (founded in 1948), RICU's work targets British male Muslims aged 15 to 39 and has received £17M in Prevent funding in 2016 (Vigo 2016). Whilst seen by government as vital to counter the propaganda efforts of Daesh, the role of RICU within Prevent nevertheless perpetuates the existing negative narrative that Muslims are being watched and subjected to all sorts of techniques. Such a deep seated perception naturally damages the trust between Muslim citizens and the government, a relationship which is very important in order to counter the appeal of Jihadi narratives.

Amidst the flurry of media headlines, public debate and implementation of policy initiatives, the agency of Muslims has either been ignored or grossly inflated. More significantly, the Muslim population in the UK occupies a position in the social imaginary of the majority that can be described as the 'infidel

14   *Introduction*

within' (Ansari 2004). The Muslim population of Britain is perceived, through the prism of an undifferentiated and conflated category of radicalisation, by policymakers, political elites and the popular media to represent a political, social and cultural problem to the nation-state. Put in other terms, elite policymakers are thus responding to the issues provoked by 'the Muslim question' (Casanova 2012). In light of the political pressure and wider cultural scrutiny on Muslims in Britain, de-radicalisation thus poses significant questions about identity, religion, citizenship and power – all of which profoundly impacts the lives of British Muslims today, as well as in the future. It is crucial therefore that sound research is produced, disseminated and shared for the purposes of public awareness. The future of the Muslim minority in European societies is poised between assimilation on the one hand and marginalisation on the other. This book should be seen as a humble intervention in that debate.

A journey through the book

The first chapter outlines the discursive paradigm that has shaped our understanding of de-radicalisation. It traces the birth and journey of the radicalisation concept. It then highlights the way Muslim identity was constructed as a problem over three decades in the UK. In particular, it identifies three critical themes that came together into a common localisation in the concept of 'radicalisation': security, identity and religion. Indeed, the intersectionality of these themes together constitutes what has been called the 'new security challenge'. Although Chapter 1 reads like a literature review, it tries instead to find the chief discursive and historical developments that enabled the idea and practice of de-radicalisation to emerge in UK counter-terrorism at a particular period in history.

Chapter 2 attempts to answer the question of my investigation using research data collated from time in the field. My aim there is to find out what 27 practitioners working in Prevent and de-radicalisation think and believe de-radicalisation is. It tries to take the Prevent conception of de-radicalisation as a point of departure and examine de-radicalisation ontologically in a more meaningful way than is articulated in the literature and by policymakers. This chapter sets out my methodology, presents the data and then analyses it. The new conceptual features that emerge from the data are examined and its implication for conceptual and policy development is assessed. This chapter makes the case for the importance of my data in deepening our understanding of de-radicalisation. It also uses primary data to ground the move towards an alternative framework of de-radicalisation.

Chapter 3 presents an alternative conception and theory of de-radicalisation. Drawing on the works of Foucault, I propose that de-radicalisation be understood through the concept of the 'technologies of the self', which is defined as that:

> …which permit individuals to effect by their own means or with the help of others a certain number of operations on their bodies and souls, thoughts,

Introduction   15

conduct, and the way of being, so as to transform themselves in order to attain a certain state of happiness, purity, wisdom, perfection, or immortality.

(Foucault 1988a, 18)

I explain what 'technologies of the self' means and how it was modified in light of the primary data gathered from my fieldwork. Other key concepts are addressed, like the 'fourfold' (the four step guide to ethical self formation), the self, and what is meant by 'technologies', as well as agency. The three technologies that constitute the technologies of the self are: discursive (Chapter 4), disciplinary (Chapter 5) and confessional (Chapter 6). The concept of the technologies of the self is then situated within the theory of governmentality. The last section deals with the way that government shapes the subjectivity of citizens: deploying concepts like the 'paradigm', 'central sphere', the 'political', 'neo-liberalism' and 'normalisation', I try to explain how the regulatory norm operates. Overall, this chapter lays the conceptual and theoretical background for understanding de-radicalisation as the technologies of the self.

Chapter 4 examines the role of discursive technology. Discursive technology is about the codification of knowledge through the claims of science and the formation of 'regimes of truth' that guide the way we think, talk and understand something. This chapter highlights how 'radicalisation' as a discourse and concept constructed the problematisation of the Muslim population. It examines the use of narratives, the legitimisation of discourse by 'experts', the search for 'root-causes', and the politicised nature characterising the will to knowledge on 'radicalisation'. More importantly, 'radicalisation' etches the discursive parameters that define the conceptualisation of de-radicalisation in the UK. It is through discursive technology that the problematisation of Muslim identity was achieved for the purposes of corrective intervention.

Chapter 5 focuses on the Prevent strategy and the Channel programme through disciplinary technology. Disciplinary technology describes the way that knowledge systems, like radicalisation, are implemented in material domains, through social institutions, programmes of intervention and by managerial experts. Disciplinary technologies seek behaviour modification and conformity amongst the population through the process of discipline and normalisation rather than through punishment. It analyses what interviewees thought of the implementation of Prevent and the impact it had on practitioners and Muslim communities. In terms of de-radicalisation, this chapter also shows how individuals who are deemed 'at risk' of radicalisation are identified, the criterion used to judge individuals bound for interventions and the normative framework guiding de-radicalisation. Through Prevent, individuals, problematic populations and the wider population are disciplined according to a norm.

Chapter 6 looks more closely at the role of confessional technology. This chapter is significant because it explores the pastoral logic governing de-radicalisation interventions and the process of subjectification. Confessional technology is rooted in the idea that concern with the welfare and wellbeing of individuals in our culture represents a secularised version of the Christian

16 *Introduction*

penance. The confessional today is re-enacted through intervention programmes and embodied in the role of the expert. This pastoral logic is evident in the extraction of knowledge from 'experts' like the Quilliam Foundation and by the transformation of individual Muslim subjectivity. The confessional dimensions of de-radicalisation interventions are highlighted: the concept of 'vulnerability', the role of mentoring, the techniques of psychotherapy, the role of dialectic dialogue and the notion of 'redemption' – are all supposed to culminate with the erasure of surfeit Muslim-ness and a transformed identity for the radicalised subject. De-radicalisation is, in the end, about 'salvation in this life'.

Finally, I explore the implications of understanding de-radicalisation as the technologies of the self in Chapter 7. I close with a section directly addressing policymakers, where I propose an alternative framework for engagement in the fight against neo-Jihadi political violence.

Notes

1 In the UK, prison de-radicalisation is managed by the National Offender Management (NOMS). Since 2007 NOMS has been trying to develop interventions targeting the drives of radicalisation (HO 2011, 88; Spalek *et al.* 2008, 45–46). According to the *Prison Service Journal*, there are two intervention programmes – Healthy Identity and Al Furqan (PSJ 2012, 31). The Healthy Identity Interventions deliver one-to-one (or two facilitators to one offender) over a number of sessions and are responsive to the individual's needs, risks, type and level of engagement and are suitable for all types of extremist offenders (regardless of cause) (NOMS 2013). Al Furqan (meaning to distinguish between truth and falsehood) is specifically suitable for Islamist offenders where ideology has become wedded with extremist interpretations of the Islamic faith. It is intended to challenge misinterpretations of Islamic texts (PSJ 2012, 32). However, the Journal concluded that the 'development and delivery of a co-ordinated, multifaceted approach to preventing terrorist offending is still in its relative infancy' (PSJ 2012, 36). Furthermore, Prevent (HO 2011) stated that 'progress has been slower' due to the lack of 'proven methodology' and the lack of a template to develop interventions from (HO 2011, 89), although national implementation was planned for 2012. One of the future goals of Prevent 2011 was 'significantly scaling up' de-radicalisation interventions in prisons. According to the NOMS summary on Healthy Identity interventions in 2013, interventions are 'available to all convicted extremist offenders in both custody and community who are assessed as suitable', with interventions being monitored and re-evaluated (NOMS 2013, 2). However, an article in January 2014 reported that 'Three quarters of all prisoners convicted of terror offences reject rehabilitation and not a single senior terror convict has engaged with the de-radicalisation programme' (Gover 2014). In short, given the lack of documentation and access to data it is difficult to assess how interventions in prison are faring.

2 One of the most influential think-tanks working in this field – the Quilliam Foundation – has acknowledged in a paper, 'In and Out of Extremism', the conceptual challenges raised in one of my articles on de-radicalisation (Quilliam 2015, 25), which at one level shows the relevance of de-radicalisation to policymakers. Elsewhere the paper also states:

> Analysing behaviour around deradicalisation is also extremely relevant for policy makers. It can indicate why people choose to adopt a particular ideology, or why they participate in high-risk activism. It also shows why people choose to deradicalise and break away from a particular ideology or organisation.
>
> (Quilliam 2015, 14)

References

ACPO (2010). *Channel: protecting vulnerable people from being drawn into terrorism. A guide for local partnership*, ACPO www.acpo/police/documents/TAM/2012/201210 TAMChannel/Guidance.pdf.

Ansari, H. (2004). *The Infidel Within: Muslims in Britain since 1800*. London: Hurst & Co Publishers.

Ashour, O. (2009). *The De-radicalization of Jihadists: Transforming armed Islamist Movements*. New York and London: Routledge.

Ashour, O. (2012). 'Post-Jihadism and the ideological revisions of armed Islamists', in *Contextualizing Jihadi Ideologies*, edited by Z. Kazimi and J. Deol,. New York, London: Columbia University Press.

Baker, A.H. (2011). *Extremists in Our Midst, Confronting Terror. New Security Challenges*. London: Palgrave Macmillan.

Barrett, R. and Bokhari, L. (2009). 'Deradicalization and rehabilitation programmes targeting religious terrorists and extremists in the Muslim world: an overview', in *Leaving Terrorism Behind: Individual and Collective Disengagement*, edited by J. Horgan and T. Bjørgo. New York: Routledge

Bjorgo, T. (2009). 'Processes of disengagement from violent groups of the extreme right', in *Leaving Terrorism Behind: Disengagement from Political Violence*, edited by T. Bjorgo and J. Horgan. New York: Routledge.

Bjorgo, T. and Horgan, J. (eds) (2009). *Leaving Terrorism Behind: Disengagement from Political Violence*. London: Routledge.

Cameron, D. (2015). *PM's extremism speech in Birmingham, July 20th*, www.gov.uk/government/speeches/extremism-pm-speech.

Casanova, J. (2012). 'The politics of Nativism: Islam in Europe, Catholicism in the United States', *Philosophy and Social Criticism*, 38: 1–11.

Chowdhury, N. and Hearne, E.B. (2008). *Beyond Terrorism: Deradicalization and Disengagement from Violent Extremism*. International Peace Institute, New York, http://ipacademy.org/media/pdf/publications/beter.pdf.

Cobain, I., Ross, A., Evans, R. and Mahmood, M. (2016). 'Revealed: UK's covert propaganda bid to stop Muslims joining Isis', *Guardian*, 2 May 2016, www.theguardian.com/uk-news/2016/may/02/uk-government-covert-propaganda-stop-muslims-joining-isis.

Counter-terrorism and Security Act 2015 (CTSA), http://services.parliament.uk/bills/2014-15/counterterrorismandsecurity.html.

Demant, F., Slootman, M. and Buijs, F. (2008). 'Decline and disengagement: an analysis of processes of deradicalisation', *International Migration and Ethnic Studies*, Amsterdam, http://dare.uva.nl/document/2/64714.

Disley, E., Weed, K., Reding, A., Clutterbuck, L. and Warnes, R. (2011). 'Individual disengagement from Al Qa'ida-influenced terrorist groups', *Rapid Evidence Assessment (REA) to inform policy and practice in preventing terrorism*, RAND Europe, Home Office, UK.

Dodd, V. (2015). 'Jihadi threat requires move into "private space" of UK Muslims, says police chief', *Guardian*, 24 May 2015, www.theguardian.com/world/2015/may/24/jihadi-threat-requires-move-into-private-space-of-uk-muslims-says-police-chief

Foucault, M. (1988). 'Technologies of the self: a seminar with Michel Foucault', edited by L. Martin, H. Gutman and P. Hutton, Amherst: The University of Massachusetts Press.

18 *Introduction*

Gover, D. (2014). 'Terrorists snub "contest" de-radicalisation programme in UK jails', *International Business Times*, 2 January 2014, www.ibtimes.co.uk/terrorists-snub-contest-de-radicalisation-programme-uk-jails-1430811.

HMG (2012). *Channel: protecting vulnerable people from being drawn into terrorism. A guide for local partnership*, ACPO, www.acpo/police/documents/TAM/2012/201210TAMChannel/Guidance.pdf.

HMG (2015). *Channel duty guidance, protecting vulnerable people from being drawn into terrorism, statutory guidance from channel panels members and partners of local panels*, www.gov.uk/government/uploads/system/uploads/attachment_data/file/425189/Channel_Duty_Guidance_April_2015.pdf.

Home Office (HO) (2006). *Countering International Terrorism: the United Kingdom's Strategy*.

Home Office (HO) (2009). *The United Kingdom's Strategy for Countering International Terrorism*.

Home Office (HO) (2011). *Prevent, CONTEST 2011*, www.homeoffice.gov.uk/publications/counter-terrorism/prevent/prevent-strategy.

Home Office (HO) (2016). *The United Kingdom's Strategy for Countering Terrorism: Annual Report for 2015*, www.gov.uk/government/uploads/system/uploads/attachment_data/file/539683/55469_Cm_9310_Web_Accessible_v0.11.pdf.

Horgan, J. (2008). 'Deradicalization or disengagement? A process in need of clarity and a counterterrorism initiative in need of evaluation', *Perspectives on Terrorism*, 2 (4): 3–8.

Horgan, J. (2009a). Individual disengagement: a psychological analysis, in *Leaving Terrorism Behind: Disengagement From Political Violence*, edited by T. Bjorgo and J. Horgan. New York: Routledge.

Horgan, J. (2009b). *Assessing the Effectiveness of Current De-Radicalization Initiatives and Identifying Implications for the Development of US-Based Initiatives in Multiple Setting*, National Consortium for The Study of Terrorism and Responses to Terrorism, www.start.umd.edu/start/research/investigators/project.asp?id=56.

Horgan, J. and Braddock, K. (2010). 'Rehabilitating the terrorists? Challenges in assessing the effectiveness of de-radicalization programs', *Terrorism and Political Violence*, 22: 267–291.

International Centre for the Study of Radicalisation and Political Violence (ICSR) (2010). *Prison and Terrorism, Radicalisation and De-radicalisation in 15 Countries*, Kings College London, http://icsr.info/wpcontent/uploads/2012/10/1277699166PrisonsandTerrorismRadicalisationandDeradicalisationin15Countries.pdf.

Institute for Strategic Dialogue (ISD) (2010). 'The role of civil society in counter-radicalisation and de-radicalisation', A Working Paper of The European Policy Planners' Network on Countering Radicalisation and Polarisation, www.strategicdialogue.org/allnewmats/idandsc2010/PPNPaper-CommunityEngagement.pdf.

Institute for Strategic Dialogue (ISD) (2012). *'Tackling extremism': de-radicalisation and disengagement'*, www.strategicdialogue.org/allnewmats/DeRadPaper2012.pdf.

Jackson, R. (2005). *Writing the War on Terrorism: Language, Politics, and Counter-terrorism*. Manchester: Manchester University Press.

Kundnani, A. (2012). 'Radicalisation: the journey of a concept', *Institute of Race Relations*, 54 (2): 3–25.

Lambert, R., (2011). *Countering Al-Qaeda in London, Police and Muslims in Partnerships*. London: C. Hurst & Co.

Morris, M., Eberhard, F., Rivera, J. and Watsula, M. (May 2010). '*Deradicalization: A Review of the Literature with Comparison to Findings in the Literatures on Deganging and Deprogramming*'. Institute for Homeland Security Solutions, www.ihssnc.org/portals/0/Documents/VIMSDocuments/Morris_Research_Brief_Final.pdf.

Morris, N. (2015). 'David Cameron and Barack Obama vow joint action against Isis in Iraq following Paris attacks', *The Independent*, 16 January, www.independent.co.uk/news/uk/cameron-and-obama-vow-action-against-isis-in-iraq-following-paris-attacks-9984510.html.

National Offender Management Service (NOMS) (2013). *Healthy Identity Intervention, Summary and Overview*, file:///F:/Personal/PhD/PhD%20Thesis%202/HII%20Summary%20and%20Overview%20Public%20April%2013%20(1).pdf.

Prison Service Journal (PSJ) (2012). 'Combating extremism and terrorism', September, No. 203, www.crimeandjustice.org.uk/sites/crimeandjustice.org.uk/files/PSJ%20September%202012%20No.%20203.pdf.

Rabasa, A., Pettyjohn, S.L., Ghez, J.J and Boucek, C. (2010). *Deradicalizing Islamist Extremists*. RAND Corporation, National Security Research Division, www.rand.org/content/dam/rand/pubs/monographs/2010/RAND_MG1053.pdf.

Spalek B., El-Awa, S. and Lambert, R. (2008). 'Preventing violent extremism in prison', *Prison Service Journal*, 180: 45–54.

Vigo, J. (2016). 'The UK's propaganda machinery and state surveillance of Muslim children', *Counterpunch*, www.counterpunch.org/2016/07/25/the-uks-propaganda-machinery-and-state-surveillance-of-muslim-children/.

Wendt, A. (1999). *Social Theory of International Politics*. Cambridge: Cambridge University Press.

Whitehead, T. (2014). 'British jihadists to be forced to attend deradicalisation programmes, says Cameron', *Telegraph*, 1 September 2014, www.telegraph.co.uk/news/uknews/terrorism-in-the-uk/11068878/British-jihadists-to-be-forced-to-attend-deradicalisation-programmes-says-Cameron.html.

1 Radicalisation as the 'new security challenge'

> A picture held us captive. And we could not get outside it, for it lay in our language and language seed to repeat it to us inexorably.
>
> (Wittgenstein 1958, 45, para 115)

> This passage quotes a 'certain Chinese encyclopaedia' in which it is written that 'animals are divided into (a) belonging to the emperor, (b) embalmed, (c) tame, (d) suckling pigs, (e) Sirens, (f) fabulous, (g) stray dogs, (h) included in the present classification, (i) frenzied, (j) innumerable, (k) drawn with a very fine camelhair brush, (l) et cetera, (m) having just broken the water pitcher, (n) that from a long way off look like flies'. In the wonderment of this taxonomy, the thing we apprehend in one great leap, the thing that, by means of the fable, is demonstrated as the exotic charm of another system of thought, is the limitation of our own, the stark impossibility of thinking that.
>
> (Foucault 2002, xvi)

In the quote above, Foucault invites us to consider the wider discursive structures – what he calls 'episteme' – that shape what is being said and done in a particular epoch rather than merely attributing it to the zeitgeist produced by authors or thinkers, or individuals in general. Taking my cue from Foucault's 'episteme', the premise of the following chapter rests on the idea that the way things are ordered and made intelligible is structured by a paradigm that governs mainstream thinking and practices. Following this logic, I claim that our understanding of de-radicalisation, in the UK context at least, emanates from the discourses on radicalisation. In other words, it is our conception of radicalisation which will allow us to arrive at a clearer understanding of how de-radicalisation came to acquire certain characteristics. Consequently, this chapter aims to (1) provide a discursive account of the major ideas and debates that lead to our current understanding of radicalisation; and (2) situate de-radicalisation genealogically within the historical and political context in which it emerges.

How did the concept of 'radicalisation' come to signify the journey undertaken by Muslims towards terrorism? How did 'radicalisation' come to eclipse our conventional understanding of 'radical' and 'radicalism'? The word 'radical' has a number of meanings, one of which is the noun: 'person who advocates thorough or complete political or social reform; a member of a political party or

The 'new security challenge' 21

part of a party pursuing such aims' (*Oxford Dictionary*). Or the adjective: 'characterised by departure from tradition; innovative or progressive' (ibid.). In modern times 'radical' and 'radicalism' were primarily associated politically with the Left, the Civil Right Movements in the United States, the Student 'Social Revolutions' of 1968 and the Feminist movement. It was not, however, only the preserve of the Left, since it was also associated with former conservative Prime Minister Margaret Thatcher in the 1980s. Being a 'radical' and 'radicalism' generally meant 'change' and 'innovation' in politics and was on the whole regarded as a positive attribute, if not a celebrated feature of democratic societies. However, today the current understanding of 'radical' has become synonymous with fundamentalism, extremism, terrorism, Al-Qaeda, Islamism, and is loosely applied in conjunction with Islam (Githens-Mazer 2010; Tahir Abbas 2005a). How did the meaning of the term 'radical' change?

Radicalisation did not exist before 2004. The term 'radicalisation' was seldom referred to in the press before 2001 but became used a lot more frequently in the media between 2005 and 2007 (Sedgwick 2010, 480). Indeed 'as late as the early 2000s, hardly any reference to radicalization could be found in the academic literature on terrorism and political violence' (Neumann 2008, 3). The changing security environment post 9/11, coupled with the severity of the attacks in Madrid (2004) and London (2005), brought a new urgency to understand terrorism. This shift in the understanding of terrorism is explained by Peter Neumann.

> Following the attacks against the United States on 11 September 2001, however, it suddenly became very difficult to talk about the 'roots of terrorism', which some commentators claimed was an effort to excuse and justify the killing of innocent civilians. Even so, it seemed obvious (then) that some discussion about underlying factors that had given rise to this seemingly new phenomenon was urgent and necessary, and so experts and officials started referring to the idea of 'radicalisation' whenever they wanted to talk about 'what goes on before the bomb goes off'. In the highly charged atmosphere following the September 11 attacks, it was through the notion of radicalisation that a discussion about the political, economic, social and psychological forces that underpin terrorism and political violence became possible again.
>
> (Neumann 2008, 4)

The advent of radicalisation as a term and concept enabled policymakers, researchers and the public to investigate the question of the 'root-causes' of terrorism. This was a welcomed development given the long neglected search for the causes of terrorism (Jackson *et al.* 2011). The Madrid attacks prompted the EU and its member states to break new ground in their approach to counter-terrorism, compelling them to delve into the mechanisms underpinning the recruitment of individuals into terrorism (Coolsaet 2010, 858). A number of policy documents expounding this new thinking in counter-terrorism were

22 The 'new security challenge'

developed in 2004. For example, the 'EU Plan of Action on Combating Terrorism' was adopted in June 2004 and by November 2004 the European Council adopted the 'Communication on prevention, preparedness and response to terrorist attacks' and the 'Hague Programme'. These documents refer to the need for identifying factors that cause people to take a path of violence and terror (Change Institute 2008, 8).

Following the 2004 Action Plan, the European Commission Directorate General (DG) for Communication published 'Terrorist recruitment; addressing the factors contributing to violent radicalisation' in 2005, which presented the initial development of a long-term EU strategy for addressing the complex factors that contribute to radicalisation and recruitment to terrorist activities (ibid.). Thereafter, that organisation adopted the 'EU strategy and Action Plan on Radicalisation and Recruitment' in December 2005 (ibid.). In this document, the concept and term of radicalisation was first defined as: the 'phenomenon of the people embracing opinions, views, and ideas which could lead to terrorism' (CEC 2005, 2). Despite Europe's long history with various forms of terrorisms for over a century (ESRC 2007, 1; Jackson *et al.* 2011), the EU document merely referred to terrorism perpetrated by Islamist inspired violence.

It was thus at the European level that preventive approaches to counterterrorism were formulated. More significantly, this new focus on the 'root cause' of terrorism situated the problem of terrorism at a stage preceding it, what came to be known as 'radicalisation'. The term 'radicalisation', as well as a strategy geared towards preventing terrorism, was further buttressed into the architecture of the EU counter-terrorism framework following the London attacks. The fact that the UK held the rotating presidency of the EU in the second half of 2005 enabled it to play a key role in shaping counter-terrorism at the EU level. It brought

> ...order to the chaos and elaborated – mirroring the structure of its own recently adopted counterterrorism strategy – an overall European Union Counterterrorism Strategy, effectively streamlining the ad hoc measures into a single framework.
>
> (Coolsaet 2010, 860)

Meanwhile, the London bombings not only provided the political impetus to firmly anchor the concept of radicalisation in the EU counter-terrorism framework, not to mention at member state level for countries like the UK, Netherlands, and Denmark in particular, but it also embedded 'radicalisation' with the 'home-grown bomber' theory (Coolsaet 2010, 869). This theory moved the focus away from the threat of international terrorism to domestic terrorism, emphasising the threat of violence posed by citizens of the Islamic faith. The narrative of the 'enemy within' represented a significant shift from the narrative accompanying the September 11 attacks, which stressed the international and foreign nature of the terrorist threat. The 'home-grown bomber' narrative had the effect of legitimising the move towards 'softer' approaches in counter-terrorism policy.

The 'new security challenge' 23

In the UK, the New Labour government made public the Home Office Counter-Terrorism Strategy (CONTEST) in 2006, which was accompanied by a new preventive approach to countering radicalisation, known as Prevent. The growing currency of the term and concept of radicalisation in this period was therefore primarily linked to the attention it was receiving in the policy world.

Following the London attacks in 2005, the then New Labour government set up working groups, called 'Preventing Violent Extremism Together' (2005), in order to investigate the causes of radicalisation. In December 2006 the EC funded three related studies in order to further understand the subject of 'violent radicalisation': motivation and desisting factors for violent radicalisation; the beliefs, ideologies, and narratives of violent radicalisation, and the socio-economic factors contributing to violent radicalisation (Change Institute 2008, 8). In the UK, in early 2007, a research project titled 'The New Security Challenge: Radicalisation and Violence – A Critical Reassessment' and funded by the Foreign Office, the Arts and Humanities Research Council, and the Economic and Social Research Council, was set up, with a pot of £2.5 million, to examine and assess the causes of radicalisation (ESRC 2007, 4). The UK government and the EC were directly sponsoring and funding research on radicalisation.

Notably, the project was nearly aborted due to the fact that a number of researchers had expressed their concerns about the potential risks of the project, particularly its connection to agencies interested in intelligence gathering on British Muslim communities (ESRC 2007, 8). According to an evaluation of the project, the legacy of the 'false start' and further issues led to the eventual disengagement of the FCO (Tilley *et al.* 2011, 1). However, by 2011, the project had produced three books, two journal special issues, and more than 40 peer-reviewed journal articles (ibid.). In effect, policy-makers stimulated the proliferation of radicalisation as a discourse, as well contributing to the legitimisation of it as an academic concept, which later dovetailed strategies of counter-terrorism.

Conceptually, radicalisation had undergone some revisions in the three Prevent iterations between 2006 and 2011. In 2006, radicalisation was defined in the Prevent strategy as a 'process whereby certain experiences and events in a person's life cause them to become radicalised, to the extent of turning to violence' (HO 2006, 9). In 2009 Prevent II defined radicalisation as: 'the process by which people come to support terrorism and violent extremism, and in some cases, then to join terrorist groups' (HO 2009, 82). The term 'violent extremism' was added in the 2009 version in order to resolve the ambiguity inherent in the 2006 definition, where 'the question of why and how the government should take an interest in thwarting radicalisation was left open' (Edwards 2015, 55). The term 'violent extremism' was perceived as the link between the radicalisation process and the turn to violence, albeit that it conflated the distinct problems of support for terrorism, ideology and terrorism itself. However, the term 'violent extremism' was subsequently abandoned in the revised Prevent strategy in 2011. Radicalisation became defined as 'the process by which a person comes to support terrorism and forms of extremism leading to terrorism' (HO 2011,

24   *The 'new security challenge'*

108). The term 'extremism' was defined as 'vocal or active opposition to fundamental British values, including democracy, the rule of law, individual liberty and mutual respect and tolerance of different faiths and belief' (HO 2011, 107–108).

Whilst the most recent formulation of radicalisation is more nuanced than it its previous articulation in 2009, it nevertheless leaves unresolved the question of how non-violent radicalism, e.g. 'extremism', leads to terrorism. Linked to this is the question of whether something that does not lead to violence, such as 'extremism', could be considered a threat (Sedgwick 2010, 484). Regardless however of the frequent revisions of radicalisation conceptually, the various definitions articulated amongst policymakers, academics and others, the explosion of discourse, the emergence of the counter-radicalisation industry and three iterations of Prevent, radicalisation still emerged as a concept with a distinct framework. This conceptual framework comprises the following features:

- Radicalisation is a 'process' experienced by individuals: despite the acknowledged complexity in some accounts, policy-makers conceived radicalisation as a 'process' and a type of 'conveyor belt' which constructed individuals as starting off as 'integrated' and non-radical and, due to mainly ideological influences, in response to an identity crisis, ending up on a trajectory that results in violence. Despite the affirmed role of groups and movements in influencing radicalisation, it is nevertheless a 'process' that affects and ends with the *individual*.
- Radicalisation is synonymous with violence: radicalisation almost always means or implies violence. The line of radicalisation is placed between political activism and violence, rather than between apathy and political mobilisation. This consequently means that political mobilisation is viewed within a security lens and therefore potentially criminalises democratic legitimate activism. It also implies violence being committed by its own citizens.
- Radicalisation is associated with Islam and Muslims: a particular conceptualisation of radicalisation took ascendency in popular use, one in which associated Islam and religion as a causal variable in the radicalisation process. Githens-Mazer critiques the dominant pejorative use of radicalisation in academia, the media and amongst policy-makers wherein radicalisation is about the 'implicit correlation between the "dangers of radical Islam" and violence' (2010a, 10).
- Radicalisation is about the direct causal relationship between ideas and violence: the concept and process of radicalisation presumed a direct relationship between ideas – particularly religious, theological and political – and action (political mobilisation and especially committing acts violence). Consequently, given the influence afforded to ideas as a prime mover in the radicalisation process (since ideas lead directly to action), Prevent prizes count-ideology as a strategy and this has led to an inordinate focus on what individuals are *thinking* rather than *doing*.

The 'new security challenge' 25

- Radicalisation minimises the role of politics: radicalisation excludes ascribing causative role or any significance to political actions taken by governments/state either domestically or internationally. Structural reasons like foreign policy, repression, war, etc. are acknowledged in some accounts (discussed as 'grievances real or perceived') but are mostly marginalised in favour of psychological and theological explanations claimed to be the 'root-causes' of the radicalisation process. Analysis is primarily focused on the 'identity crisis' and 'vulnerability' of individuals and not wider structures.

Consequently, between 2006 and 2011 the framing of radicalisation acquired salient features. Radicalisation became a loosely defined conceptual framework constructed by government officials and the media, with the help of academics to understand the processes and causal factors which lead individuals to support extremist ideas or even to support or commit violence – or 'what goes on before the bomb goes off' (Neumann 2008, 4). The framework implied the existence of a spectrum of the archetypal 'bad' and 'good' Muslim at opposite ends, or integrated on one end, and 'religious extremist/violent extremist' on the other. Along this spectrum a process occurs which leads such individuals to support or in rare cases, commit acts of violence. It is a process which the Home Office and the Foreign Office once described as the 'terrorist career path' (HO/FO 2004, 15). Radicalisation was shorthand for the process in which 'extremist' ideas prevalent amongst Muslim communities might lead some individuals to undertake acts of violence.

However, despite the prominence of radicalisation as a term and concept in this period, it suffered from a diversity of meanings (Sedgwick 2010, Awan *et al.* 2012; Githens-Mazer 2010; Githens-Mazer and Lambert 2010; Githens-Mazer 2012). Sedgwick (2010) has shown that radicalisation is used in a variety of contexts and in reference to different policy agendas: security, integration, foreign policy and private Islamic agendas. Consequently, the line can be drawn in unusual places. In McCauley and Moskelenko's (2008) definition, the line is placed between political activism and violence, with radicalisation defined as the 'dimension of increasing extremity of beliefs, feelings and behaviours in support of intergroup conflict and violence'; whereas Githens-Mazer (2010) situates the line between apathy and political activism, defining radicalisation as 'collectively defined, individually felt moral obligation to participate in direct action'. Moskelenko and McCauley's definition therefore situates political activity within the process towards terrorism, whereas radicalisation for Githens-Mazer is the transition towards action and not violence. Another striking example of where the line can be placed in unusual places is gleaned from Denmark, where a Danish newspaper remarked that since Danish culture is not religious, 'reducing Muslim religiosity is therefore a triumph for integration' (2010, 490). Sedgwick notes that on this basis the normal practice of Islam may be classified as 'radical'. This expansive understanding of radicalisation is the by-product of the fact that radicalisation conceptually was intertwined with issues of integration,

26 *The 'new security challenge'*

social policy, multiculturalism and the representation of minority groups (Coolsaet 2010, 870).

Besides suffering from a diversity of understandings, 'radicalisation' was beset by a number of other problems. Some of these include the facts: that the concept espoused a linear narrative instead of seeing the trajectory as complex phenomenon accommodating equafinality and multifinality factors (Githens-Mazer 2010); that it explains radicalisation but not terrorism (Richards 2011, Kundnani 2012); that it stigmatises and criminalises Muslims (Githens-Mazer 2010, 2012, Lambert 2011, Kundnani 2009, Baker-Beall *et al.* 2015); that it has proven to be practically inoperable (Heath-Kelly 2013; Githens-Mazer 2012); and that there was no evidence supporting the transition of 'radicalised' groups and individuals to violence (Dalgaard-Nielsen 2010).

Given the various problems inherent in the conceptualisation of radicalisation, some have questioned its utility and purpose. Richards (2011, 144) posed the poignant question: 'If it is terrorism that we are concerned with, then where is the additional benefit of investigating radicalization as a *process*, over and above becoming a terrorist as a *process*?' Githens-Mazer also asks whether radicalisation is a made up 'securitising' label designed to 'other' Muslims and maintain a non-Muslim hegemonic status quo (2012, 10). And Heath-Kelly advises that caution should be exercised with respects to the accuracy of the radicalisation concept to explain the actual process of radicalisation in the real world (2013, 397).

It is important, then, to note in this section that the production of radicalisation as a discourse and its sudden emergence as a concept and term was instigated by political and social elites at the EU level and adopted by a number of countries, trickling down and becoming disseminated in a plethora of spaces: politics, the media, academia, various public institutions and civil society. The by-product of this wide and extensive collaboration between various areas and levels in the governmental and social spheres is that the concept acquired a number of distinctive features that have come to dominate our understanding of radicalisation and the type of policies needed to counter it. Ultimately, however, the instability and inconclusiveness of this concept of radicalisation provokes the following question: why did policymakers invest so much in the concept?

The new security paradigm: securitisation and the radicalised other

The first major theme that is crucial to understanding the 'new security challenge' confronting Britain since 2005 is the concept and practice of 'security'. How did the domestic radicalisation of British Muslims, alongside the ubiquitous spectre of 'extremism', come to occupy such a menacing presence in security thinking and in the national imaginary? What, in simple terms, constitutes a severe security threat?

The concept of 'security' is paradoxical and complex (Jarvis and Holland 2015, 2). It is both a descriptive and a normative term, denoting a desirable goal

The 'new security challenge' 27

that actors such as states, communities and individuals want to achieve. At the same time 'security' makes us less safe and is capable of terrible acts: the use of violence, incursions into civil liberties, and the incurring of huge opportunity costs (Jarvid and Holland 2015, 2–3). For Jarvis and Holland, the complexity of 'security' is borne out by the fact that it is not immediately obvious to 'whom or what we are referring when we think about, discuss, or seek to achieve security' (3). Conventionally, the concept of security is concerned with how states interact with one another. By the 1990s however, the logic governing security thinking during the Cold War period gave way to new ideas and political realities, like the concepts of 'new wars', 'Responsibility to Protect' and humanitarian interventions. The referent object of security therefore expanded to include non-state actors, like individuals and communities, and wider issues besides national security, like the environment, food and poverty (Booth 1991).

During this period the concept of security was reconceptualised by the Copenhagen School in Security Studies beyond the narrow concepts of state and military security, in a way that also transcended the concern with states as sole actors.[1] Stemming from the speech act theories of J.L. Austen and John Searle, the school advanced the argument that security is the outcome of a 'speech act' rather than an objective condition (Buzan *et al.* 1998). According to this argument security threats do not exist independent of its representation. Thus the School argues that there are choices made about what becomes a security issue and this is invariably contingent on something being labelled as such. Securitisation theory, in short, outlines how a certain issue or group is transformed by an actor into a matter of security. The School defines securitisation as:

> The discursive process through which an intersubjective understanding is constructed within a political community to treat something as an existential threat to a valued referent object and to enable a call for urgent and exceptional measures to deal with the threat.
>
> (Buzan and Weaver 2003, 491)

The process of securitisation is an intersubjective process, which means that the meaning of the security threat is neither an objective nor subjective reality but one contingent on an audience receiving the 'speech act' and how it chooses to perform it in everyday life. All securitisation acts involve four components (Barry *et al.* 1998):

- A securitising actor/agent: an entity that makes the securitising move/statement, normally a state official/representative.
- An existential threat: an object (or ideal) that has been identified as potentially harmful.
- A referent object: an object (or ideal) that is being threatened and needs to be protected.
- An audience: the target of the securitisation act that needs to be persuaded and accept the issue as a security threat.

28 *The 'new security challenge'*

Stuart Croft (2012) has developed a post-Copenhagen theory of securitisation in which a number of the key elements of the school's concept are relaxed and other elements are added. Instead of just a process initiated by a speech act, Croft expands the securitising move to include texts and symbols (2012, 80). Second, the speech act does not merely have to be confined to the state as agents of securitisation but is in fact undertaken by a wider base of political, social and cultural elite, primarily located in London, across various institutions and professions (Croft 2012, 81–83). Third, Croft expands the notion of 'audiences' (the target group that needs to be persuaded), so that instead of being reduced to by-standers, the audience 'performs various roles that are crucial to the politics of securitisation' (including resisting securitisation) (2012, 83). The fourth pillar relates to the outcome of a successful securitisation move: if accepted by an audience it legitimises the use of extra-ordinary measures to defend the threat-ened interest of the group (Croft 2012, 84). More important for the success of securitisation is the way in which wider society re-enacts and performs securiti-sation, which in effect 'co-produces the new social-reality' (Croft 2012, 85).

The 'new security' paradigm adumbrated in these pages has all the hallmarks of Croft's post-Copenhagen securitisation theory. The securitisation move began with the 'war on terror' in the aftermath of the 9/11 attacks on New York, developed further after the Madrid attacks in 2004, and was propelled by the London attacks in 2005. As highlighted in the previous section, it was initiated by speech acts made by political and social elites through key institutions like the EU. The speech act has been accompanied by a discursive explosion (more below), which has in turn, been adopted and performed by the media, academics, civil society, cultural figures, everyday society and individuals (Chapters 4–6). Taken together, the securitisation of Muslim identity has consequently led to the reconfiguration of collective identity and what it means to be a British citizen. The remainder of this section and chapter elaborates in great detail how Muslim identity becomes securitised.

An important starting point for identifying the establishment of a new security paradigm was the 9/11 attacks on the Twin Towers in 2001. The American administration responded with the 'Global War on Terror' (GWT). Analogous to its counterpart nomenclature that preceded it (i.e. the 'Cold War'), which struc-tured the mainstream security dynamics of inter-state politics for decades, the GWT has become the international policy narrative describing and legitimising the security practices of nation-states post 2001. The GWT narrative essentially conceives the world as its stage and postulates the existence of a ubiquitous, evil and omnipotent enemy. In the words of Roselle *et al.*, the GWT 'sets out states as protecting individuals from non-state actors known as terrorists in a battle for security' (2014, 76).

Under the pretext of conducting the GWT, the US and Britain have gone to war in Afghanistan (2001) and Iraq (2003), and have consistently intervened in Somalia, Yemen and Pakistan through the use of drone attacks; it has also legiti-mised the expansion of greater surveillance techniques, the securitisation of boarder control, the rolling out of new technologies for the regulation of the population, extraordinary rendition flights, expansive and penetrating domestic counter-terrorism policies and the suspension of habeas corpus, and has been associated with the controversial images of the Guantanamo Bay concentration camp, as well as torture centres like Abu Graib in Iraq. Besides legitimising the globalisation of violence and the expansion of the machinery of War globally (Reid 2009), the GWT effectively subjugated all domains (education, health, charity, etc.) – even the banal and the mundane, such as carrying toiletries with you whilst passing through an airport – to the politics and logic of securitisation.

However, central to understanding the practice of unrestricted conflict, the flouting of domestic law, the expanding power of nation state sovereignty and the extensive infrastructure accompanying the GWT, is the concept of the 'state of exception'. The works on the 'state of exception' (Schmitt 1985; Agamben 2005; Butler 2006; Huysmans 2008) asks questions about the limits of law, when exceptional practices are justified, and the general problem of limits (Huysmans 2008, 167). Limited by space to address this debate, we refer here only to the progenitor of the idiom of the exception – Carl Schmitt. In Political Theology, Schmitt defined the sovereign as 'he who decides on the exception' (Schmitt 1985, 5). For Schmitt the state of the exception determines the authority and place of sovereignty, compelling the 'decision' to appear in its absolute purity. Politics for Schmitt is predicated on the decision of the sovereign against the norm or rule. Given the unpredictability of the emergency scenario, it is futile for legal positivism, or the norm, to establish what can be done beforehand. Schmitt also believed that the exception was more important than the norm, for the exception defines the norms (1985, 15). Notably, Schmitt emphasised that the exception is by definition exceptional and cannot be transferred into a permanent state. For Benoist (2013), Reid (2009) and Agamben (2005) however, the 'GWT' made the exception a permanent state of affairs.

The politics of 'state of the exception' is justified on the grounds of averting a crisis, catastrophe and an exceptional circumstance. Such a logic was encapsulated in Donald Rumsfeld's famous 'unknown unknowns' speech (Rumsfeld 2002), as well as Tony Blair's proclamation in the aftermath of the London bombings that the 'rules of the game had changed' (Blair 2005). Importantly, the 'state of the exception' helped established the condition for a particular form of governance centred on pre-emptive policies. For Massumi (2007), 'preemption is not prevention': 'Prevention operates in an objectively knowable world in which uncertainty is a function of a lack of information, and in which events run a predictable, linear course from cause to effect' (ibid.). He continues: 'Prevention has no proper object, no operational sphere of its own, and no proprietary logic. It is derivative. It is a means toward a given end.' In other words, prevention presumes the objective existence of something before intervention and only makes sense within the domains of different policy domains (economics, health, etc.).

Pre-emption however operates according to a different logic. Whilst prevention and pre-emption strategies are both concerned with risk, it is the 'uncertainty' of the future which distinguishes them from each other. Massumi (2005)

30 *The 'new security challenge'*

argues that the uncertainty of the future shifts the rationale for decision-making from what is known, quantified and understood to the realm of the imagination, catastrophe and the worst-case scenarios. This risk-governed rationale differs therefore from the logic of other political decision-making, such as prevention or rational calculation, in the way it acts on the basis of uncertainty and probability. It does not matter whether the spectre of the catastrophe actually occurs, but it is instead sufficient for the potentiality to exist in order to justify pre-emptive action. This is how 'uncertainty' becomes tied up with 'futurity'. According to Massumi therefore, the emerging aim of security governance is to police the future by anticipation so as to bring about a 'future perfect' liberated from the ominous spectre of always-imminent catastrophe (2005, 6). The conceptual lens through which the idea of security is understood has thus been temporalised, with an imagined fear of the future providing justification for sovereign action under the pretext of security, thereby rendering the present as the site of intervention.

It is this pre-emptive logic that has provided the intellectual and 'scientific' justification for policies of community intervention and counter–terrorism. The discourse on 'new terrorism' is a case in point. 'new terrorism' is associated with academics like Walter Laqueur (1999), Quintan Wiktorowicz (2005) and Peter Neumann (2008).[2] The concept of 'new terrorism' argued that Al-Qaeda inspired terrorism witnessed in the attacks of 9/11, Madrid, and the London bombings was qualitatively different to previous patterns of violence in four main ways (ESRC 2007; Jackson *et al.* 2011, 165). First, unlike the old terrorism of the IRA or ETA which focused its operations within territorial boundaries, new terrorism was transnational and operated across borders. Second, organisationally new terrorism was horizontal in structure and based on loose networks, whereas old terrorism was hierarchical. Third, in terms of personnel, new terrorism was comprised of amateurs, whilst old terrorists were more professional. Lastly, new terrorism was driven by ideology based on religious fanaticism divorced from political goals, whereas, again, old terrorism, epitomised by groups like the Red Brigade and Baader Meinhoff, is presented as being motivated by clear political objectives.

The discourse on 'new terrorism' was influential in shifting the conceptual boundaries of what constituted an existential threat, as well as being linked to the legitimisation of counter-terrorism policy. Basia Spalek (2011) traced the impact of the 'new terrorism' discourse on many fronts: Muslims distrusting the government, increased counter-terrorism powers, creation of suspect communities, human rights abuse, Muslims being viewed as fifth column and the problematisation of Muslim identities (194–195). Similarly, Heath-Kelly (2013) also attributes the emphasis in the Prevent's strategy's focus on religious ideas and vulnerability to the 'new terrorism' literature (399). Meanwhile, the London attacks in 2005 were explained in terms of the 'new security challenge' posed by 'new terrorism', now embodied by home-grown terrorism (ESRC 2007). As seen in the last section, this led to the preoccupation in Britain with 'preventing root-causes' of terrorism, which was couched in the concept 'radicalisation'. It was

The 'new security challenge' 31

the success of discourses like 'new terrorism', governed by the political imperative to manage the risk of existential threat emanating from it, that lay the groundwork for the emergence of radicalisation and preventive approaches to countering terrorism.

A melange of discourses aspiring to investigate and codify the 'truth' of radicalisation emerged post 2005, bringing a vast tapestry of knowledge domains, experts, institutions and organisations into common localisation. Indeed one of the distinguishing features of the way that knowledge developed during this period, in conjunction with multiple other discourses, was the dominance of the natural sciences over the social science in the theories, language, tools and methods deployed to construct a predictive and explanatory model of radicalisation. There was, for example, a preoccupation with 'root-causes', 'process' and the use of various 'models' said to explain and predict radicalisation (Moskalenko and McCauley 2008; McCauley and Moskalenko 2009, Sageman 2008, Wiktorowicz 2005, Haqq Baker 2011). Despite their differences in emphasis and degree, all models nevertheless posited a causal relationship between thought and action within a linear process which Muslims undergo en route to violent radicalisation. The production of discourse on radicalisation reached its zenith in 2010 (Richards 2011; Sedgwick 2010; Kundnani 2012), culminating in a body of knowledge with its own theories, models, experts and concepts.

Another effect of radicalisation discourses was that the 'radical' existed in a type of transcendental and eternal way, prefiguring their historical, social and political context. The production of the 'radical' rendered him a threat and danger irrespective of the existence of an actual threat/danger. The existence of the radical, through discursive production, enabled the *possibility and potentiality* of radicalisation and the perpetual perception of an immediate and imminent threat, divorced from the reality of actual attacks by radicals (Heath-Kelly 2013, 407–408). Indeed, radicalisation had been conceived within a particular framework and process – one which took as its starting point the paradigmatic law abiding citizen, and placed at the polar end of the spectrum the paradigmatic violent Muslim radical. The potentiality for violence by implication therefore resided within every British citizen of Muslim faith.

Similar to Wittgenstein's quote at the beginning of this chapter about the 'picture' captivating Western thinking, the accounts of radicalisation have been built upon the threat of 'ideology'. The dominant conception of radicalisation, which is embedded in Prevent, posits that ideology leads to violence and that it is thus ideology that constitutes the main security threat. It is a formulation that holds that ideas and beliefs not only explain behaviour but can also predict it. And it is based on a foundationalism that dichotomises the mind and body and reduces identity and religion to a list of propositions and statements. More importantly, it is a result of downloading the Islamist ideology, to use a software metaphor, that the perceived Muslim potentiality for violence is activated. This is why, like Wittgenstein's picture, security thinking became captivated by ideology.

32   *The 'new security challenge'*

Integral to understanding the notion of the *potential* seed of violence that lies dormant within the British Muslim mind and which can become activated, as at the flick of a switch, alongside policy imperatives to countering radicalisation, is the idea of 'risk'. Awan *et al.* rightly alert us to the pertinence of asking 'how and why some processes or threats become understood as risk and some do not' (2012, 9). In the case of radicalisation, Gutkowski (2011) asks us to differentiate between the *risk posed* and *threat posed* by radical Islamism. Thus what is under consideration in the discourse production of radicalisation is not the threat of an imminent attack *but several stages removed*: the risk of radicalisation spreading among a population (Gutkowski 2011, 347). It is explicitly *risk* and not *threat* that has preoccupied policy-makers.

The most famous theorist of risk is Ulrich Beck (2008). He argues that risk is a feature of modernity, a 'side effect' of the advances made in modernity. These risks, defined as a systematic way of dealing with hazards and insecurities, which can be transformed into catastrophe, are seen as an objective reality of modernity, an externality impacting global societies. Specifically, 'risk' is used to indicate the possibility of danger or harm and is constituted by three major properties: probability, uncertainty and futurity (Mythen and Walklate 2006, 381). We saw earlier with Massumi how important 'uncertainty' and 'futurity' was in the formulation of risk assessment and the implementation of pre-emptive policies post 9/11. In the case of radicalisation, however, we have something *different.* For example, Githens-Mazer emphasises the substantial gap between the reality of the security threat and perception of that threat. He reminds us that the actual threat of violence from Muslim communities in Europe is statistically negligible. There are

> ...probabilistically higher dangers involved in driving too fast, drinking too much, not looking both ways when crossing the street, or falling asleep with a cigarette in our hand.
>
> (2012, 10)

In contrast to Beck's theory on risk therefore, what we have with radicalisation is not simply a case of managing risk out there in the world, but rather a case of socially constructing risk. Hence we turn here to the social construction theories of Mary Douglas (1992). Douglas argues that risk is a modern approach to the way in which traditional communities and societies addressed threats to their cohesion and values. According to Douglas, risk is seen as a socially constructed phenomenon that reflects the norms and cultural values of a particular tribe, group or society. Risk, in other words, is a cultural artefact. It is this vital distinction between objective risk and the social construction of risk that enables us to understand the securitisation of Islamist radicalism in the production of radicalisation discourses. Besides Githens-Mazer, other security scholars have noted the central role that the social construction of risk has played in shaping the knowledge production of radicalisation. Heath-Kelly (2013), for example, views radicalisation in terms of 'performativity', in that it 'produces the effects it

The 'new security challenge' 33

names' (2013, 395). She argues that knowledge on radicalisation produces a possible counterfactual to terrorism by inventing a narrative about transitions to militancy, one that allows security mechanisms to perform interventions into the supposed production of terrorism (Heath-Kelly 2013, 397). In other words, radicalisation is produced as a discourse in order to justify governmental interventions.

To summarise: the way security has been understood and practiced evolved in the years leading to 9/11. Using Croft's post-Copenhagen theory of what and how an issue or group become a security threat, I argued that the 'GWT' and events like 7/7 created the conditions for the emergence of a new security paradigm called 'radicalisation'. Central to the development of radicalisation has been the entrenchment of pre-emptive logic in structures of governance and the implementation of policies. Such a logic has been aided by the rationale of the 'state of the exception', the severity of which is reinforced by the social construction of risk. The risk of Islamist radicalism has, at its heart, the narrative that Islamist ideology, coupled with the precariousness of Muslim identity (more below), can trigger the path towards violence. Security thinking has, in other words, been captivated by the risk posed by Islamist ideology. It is this contextual background that not merely impinges on other domains (e.g. identity and religion) but which creates the conditions of possibility for de-radicalisation to become an idea and practice of counter-terrorism.

The integration agenda and the politics of belonging: the 'death of multiculturalism' and problematic Muslim identity

The second cluster of issues is concerned with political, social and categorical identity. Here, political multiculturalism must be distinguished from social, as well as normative multiculturalism. Social multiculturalism denotes the fact that Britain today is a multicultural society (which is not the matter being discussed in public debate), whereas normative multiculturalism signifies the ideal of celebrating and promoting diversity and plurality. By contrast, Political multiculturalism refers to government strategies to manage difference (Modood 2005; Parekh 2006). Political multiculturalism in Britain developed in an ad hoc way. The arrival of migrants to the UK was a consequence of labour migration, the arrival of families joining migrant workers, as well as the arrival of political asylums. The initial model of integration, formulated by the Home Secretary Roy Jenkins in 1966, was based on the gradual socialisation of racial and ethnic groups from the Commonwealth countries into wider society. Integration was defined by Jenkins as 'not a process of flattening out uniformity but of cultural diversity, couple with equal opportunity in an atmosphere of mutual tolerance' (Rex 1996, 236–237). Initially the integration of immigrants into Britain merely focused on providing immigrants with language and employment skills in order to bolster their economic opportunities. The move towards political multiculturalism was developed through local government, particularly in the 1980s by promoting the celebration of diversity in schools and of festivals, what Ali

34   The 'new security challenge'

Alibihai-Brown called 'sari, somosa, and steelband' (2000, 17), whilst nationally it was responsive to political and social events in the country.

However, a number of critical events over three decades have led many to question the viability of political multiculturalism: the Brixton Riots (1981), the Rushdie Affair (1988), the Northern Riots (2001), Danish cartoons (2006) and the Charlie Hebdo attacks (2015). In particular, the Rushdie Affair revealed the beginning of the disillusionment with multiculturalism, producing new fault lines in its wake. It led, for example, to the lamentation by Roy Jenkins that 'we might have been more cautious about allowing the creation in the 1950s of a substantial Muslim community here' (Parekh 2006, 301). This episode was seen to have created polarisation between the liberal and cultural elites and some British Muslims, in which the 'cultural difference' of Muslims became the subject of questions (Rai 2006; McRoy 2006; Brighton 2007, 7).

Of all these incidents, the Northern Riots were also especially important because they brought to light the failure of multiculturalism as a model for managing multi-ethnic/religious communities in Britain. They introduced into the political lexicon, through the publication of the Cantle Report, the concept of 'community cohesion' and the notion that communities were living 'parallel lives' (Cantle 2001, 9; Thomas 2007). The Cantle Report identified the Asian communities as not being adequately integrated, recommending that a 'greater sense of citizenship', 'common elements of nationhood' and the use of the 'English language' would need to be forged by the 'non-white community' (2001, 10–13). These events culminated in arguments promoted by some political and media elites calling for the 'death of multiculturalism' in Britain.

Whilst the viability of political multiculturalism was questioned during these events, it was not until the attacks on London in 2005 that political multiculturalism became securitised. Multiculturalism was identified as one of the causes of radicalisation amongst British Muslims. It was blamed for creating segregated communities, undermining a cohesive national identity and promoting a type of relativism with respect to values (Mirza *et al.* 2007). The integration agenda, which confusingly encompasses concerns about immigration, the emergence of neo-nationalism and the management of diversity (Sedgwick 2010; Coolsaet 2010), became integrated into the security agenda (the threat of Islamist ideology and home-grown terrorism) in the media, the discourse on radicalisation and the Prevent policy. David Cameron's speech at Munich in 2011 marked the success of this logic, further entrenching the notion that multiculturalism and political identity function as a galvanising agent that produces the security challenge (Cameron 2011).

In the democratic age, multiculturalism poses obstacles to coexistence because it concerns the divisive issue of the political identity of the state. Charles Taylor (2011) brings to light the paradox of liberal democracy: that despite being considered as the philosophy of inclusion (rule of the people, by the people, for the people), it also excludes certain citizens, minorities and identities in its pursuit of a high degree of cohesion. Taylor shows how in the modern period the new collective agency of 'the people' was created and how popular sovereignty

The 'new security challenge' 35

needs to have a personality (2011, 124–125). In order to remain viable, states seek to create a feeling of common belonging. The modern state has a political identity: 'To form a state, in the democratic era, a society is forced to undertake the difficult and never to be completed task of defining its collective identity' (Taylor 2011, 131). Political identity is crucial for the cohesiveness and integrity of the nation state.

There is thus a sort of dialectic between state and nation. It is not just that nations strive to become states; it is also that modern states, in order to survive, strive to create a national community. The process of creating a national community has been written about by historians like Anderson (1983), Hobsbawm (1983) and Ernst Gellner (1983). Their accounts reveal the constructed nature of the nation, the development of the nation-state in line with the growth of capitalism, homogenisation of language and the printing press. In the twentieth century, nationalism, an extension and feature of the nation state, has proved to be the most popular ideology, and most successful surrogate to religion (in terms of a unifying grand narrative) (Eagleton 2014). This is why, explains Taylor, democratic states need a healthy degree of patriotism, a strong identification with the polity and a willingness to give oneself for its sake. This explains why nation-states have focused on cultivating citizenship over a host of other poles of identity, like the family, class, gender and religion. This may be promoted either through a direct assimilationist model like French republicanism, or fostered in more indirect ways, like British multiculturalism, which renders other modes, such as religion, outside the operation of public life (Taylor 2011, 90). It is in this way that the task of defining political identity, a necessary feature of the nation-state, creates exclusions in democratic societies.

If we are to make sense of the cacophony of voices denouncing multiculturalism as a source of social and political tensions, then we must consider the ideas of political liberalism. John Gray (2000) identifies two faces of liberalism – 'universalist' and 'modus vivendi', also referred to by Bhiku Parekh as 'proceduralist' and 'civic assiminalionist' (2006, 199). For Gray, 'universalist' liberalism is inhospitable to difference, insists on the uniform application of the rules defining rights and is suspicious of collective goals; whereas the second mode of liberalism is a project that seeks peaceful coexistence between different regimes and ways of life. British multiculturalism primarily belongs to the second liberal regime. However, the Muslim presence in the UK, as a result of 'modus vivendi' liberalism, is seen as hindering national and community unity. It is therefore the task of 'universalist' liberalism to curb Muslim difference in order to ensure a common political identity is possible.

Indeed, political elites in the UK have indicated a preference for 'universalist' liberalism, encapsulated by David Cameron's (2011) 'muscular liberalism' and underlined by the promotion of 'British values' in public institutions and counter-terrorism policy. Part of the problem, however, according to Charles Taylor is that 'universalist' liberalism cannot accommodate 'what the members of distinct societies really aspire to, which is survival' (Taylor 1994, 61). In the case of 'liberal multiculturalism, tension arises when particular demands are met

36 *The 'new security challenge'*

at the expense of a unified nation and when separate communities develop little attachment to the nation. A second source of tension arises when a disconnection occurs between the identity of nation (based on common ethnicity, language and history) and the legal and political dimensions of citizenship.

It is with the second tension that the narrative about the failure of Muslims to integrate takes place. In contrast to the 'death of multiculturalism', this narrative confusingly conflates questions about immigration on the one hand with concerns about religion, ethnicity and culture (all reductively merged), on the other hand. A stereotype developed post 9/11 in Europe that equated the 'immigrant' with Muslim, further entrenching the image of that Muslim as different and a foreign outsider (Roy 2002). This second sub-narrative moved the focus beyond the limitations of citizenship and towards a different boundary of difference: culture. According to this argument, despite being citizens, Muslims are perceived as being culturally different and therefore cannot be accepted as part of the nation – until their beliefs and practices are reformed.

This logic is reflected in the language of public discourse and Prevent policy, exemplified by the array of perpetually shifting signifiers attributed to Muslims – between the binary 'moderate' and 'extremist' and 'vulnerable' and at-risk', to 'fundamentalist', 'violent radical' and violent 'extremist', all of which are synonyms for surfeit Muslim difference. Such signifiers are also connected to the association of British Muslim communities with a wide range of social ills perceived by many to be disrupting community and national cohesion: the repression of women, the practice of Female Genital Mutilation (FGM),[3] homophobia, sex trafficking (Roberts and Hurst 2015),[4] extremism in faith schools,[5] proliferating birth rates and a drain on welfare resources, etc. The message being produced and disseminated – and then internalised by the mainstream majority – is that Muslims are disrupting the cohesiveness of the British nation.

As mentioned above, the narrative about the failure of Muslims to 'integrate' had its origins in the Rushdie Affair. This episode in the history of British multiculturalism was a catalyst for the move away from the category of 'Black' to the category of 'Muslim' (Rai 2006; McRoy 2006; Brighton 2007). In fact, throughout most of the post-war era, Muslims in Europe were defined primarily by race and ethnicity. The ascendancy and predominance of the 'Muslim' category in describing diverse immigrant and diaspora populations in Europe can be attributed to (1) European Integration in the 1990s, which had to define itself against Islam in the making of a common European identity (Casanova 2012); (2) domestic efforts by the Labour government to promote and encourage the creation of a single body of Muslim representation in the 1990s (Ansari 2004; Rai 2006; McRoy 2006) (3) the political and media response to 9/11 that compressed Muslims into a monolithic category of the 'Muslim community', despite the vast ethnic and racial diversity, class disparity and socio-cultural differences amongst Muslims; and (4) globalisation which played a pivotal part in creating new spaces, lifestyles and transnational networks for a global community of Muslims ('Ummah') (Roy 2002).

The 'new security challenge' 37

Although a complex topic to be addressed properly here, a couple of points on globalisation must nevertheless be made. The significance of globalisation stems from the challenges it poses to the nation-state in areas relating to the control of information, people, capital, goods and the distribution of power. In terms of shaping Muslim categorical identity, globalisation allows ethnic diasporas in Europe to maintain strong social, cultural and political relations with their countries of origin (Roy 2002; Rai 2006; McRoy 2006). It is also crucially able to make and unmake social and political realities, so that what happens in Palestine impacts London and the political dynamics of Bangladesh influence the power struggles unfolding in Tower Hamlets (Briggs *et al.* 2006, 55). The narrative here argues that minorities have managed to hold on to older identities, as well as creating other newer identity synthesis, without developing affiliation and allegiance to the British mainstream political identity. Over the last 30 years a dominant perception emerged that minorities were increasingly identifying with a global Muslim identity. Paradoxically, however, many diasporic communities have adopted the 'Muslim' category, despite the top-down construction of the category and attempts to racialise Muslims by political and media elites. The result, according to Sayyid and Tyrer is that Muslim identity is problematised:

> In turn, Muslims are frequently represented as an awkward presence, interrupting the closure of the nation because of an assumed lack of shared symbolic grounds between Muslims and the 'host' nation. The solution offered with increasing regularity takes the form of attempts to tame or erase the difference that is seen as tearing the nation apart.
>
> (2012, 354)

Nevertheless, the dominant narrative about Muslim populations being problematic due to problems of identity made its way into accounts of radicalisation. For example, Olivier Roy (2002) treats Islamism as a cultural, social and political phenomenon in which individuals seek to reconstruct a lost identity in a hostile and confusing world. The adoption of a globalised transnational Islam by second and third generation Muslims is accompanied by the abandonment of the traditional culture of their parents. Oliver Roy explains this phenomenon in terms of 'de-culturalisation' (2009, 117–147). The cultural displacement experienced by the Muslim diaspora in Europe has thus been construed in terms of 'identity crisis'; in other words, many young Muslims do not feel like they belong to Europe or, by the same token, their countries of origin. This leads to them appropriating 'purer' forms of religiosity which do away with cultural and national markers. This process is exacerbated by the 'de-territorialisation' of Islam (Roy 2009, 18), which became reconfigured through globalisation and resulted in the formation of alternative identities, with loyalties beyond the state.

Furthermore, social movement theories also emphasise the importance of identity, meaning and belonging in accounts of radicalisation, particularly articulated by Marc Sageman (2008) and Quintan Wiktorowicz (2005). Their works

38   *The 'new security challenge'*

have been influential, inspiring the radicalisation model used by the Intelligence Division at the New York Police Department and the FBI, as well as being directly linked to extensive surveillance of Muslim populations in America by the NYPD with the assistance of the CIA (Kundnani 2012). Wiktorowicz sits on the US Nation Security Council and is also largely responsible for drafting the counter-terrorism strategy for Obama's administrations in 2011 to prevent violent extremism, which has been inspired by the experience of Prevent in the UK.[6] Both Sageman and Wiktorowicz formulated a model that combines psychological, theological and social factors in the analysis of radicalisation, known as the 'bunch of guys' theory. The theory is predicated on the notion that radicalisation is a phenomenon that happens amongst networks of friends.

Specifically, Sageman identifies four stages to this process: (1) moral outrage; (2) enabling interpretation; (3) personal experience; and (4) mobilising network. The first stage of moral outrage is in response to a perceived injustice; the second relates to the framing of political events within a narrative, e.g. there is a war against Islam (Sageman 2008, 75–81); the third relates to personal experiences of discrimination, which is understood as a manifestation of the grievances afflicting Muslims globally (Sageman 2008, 83); and finally the existence of a group of people who share their experience and grievance and who 'can help them cross the line from venting their anger to becoming terrorists' (Sageman 2008, 84). According to this model, radicalisation begins with the individuals who try to understand the world through a particular narrative that pits them in identity camps, which is then internalised and reinforced by a social group. Crucial to stages (1) and (2) is identification with Islam and the Muslim 'Ummah' and the feeling of despair and outrage with regards to Muslim suffering in a plethora of conflicts globally, whilst (3) problematises the identity further, which is then recalibrated at stage (4). In order for stages (1) and (2) to occur there must be what Benedict Anderson (1983) calls 'imagined communities', or the emotional, imaginative and intellectual investment of individuals into a collectivity that is constructed. In other words, it is the affiliation of British Muslims with other Muslims globally that is considered problematic for UK political and social elites.

Meanwhile, the narrative of problematic Muslim identity became embedded in Prevent. This was strikingly demonstrated by the fact that the delivery of the Prevent strategy until 2011 was delegated to the Department for Communities and Local Government (DCLG). It was unreservedly clear, and later proved to be problematic, that British counter-terrorism was being executed through a department of government responsible for delivering the Community Cohesion agenda. This, if anything, was testament to the fact that the logic of security and identity had intermeshed in the eyes of policymakers. But, as I have argued here, the intertwining of the integration and security agendas had its roots in the problematisation of identity in Britain as far back as the 1980s.

Such arguments are made by security scholars like Shane Brighton and Heath-Kelly. Brighton (2007) situates Prevent within the historical development of domestic multiculturalism. Amidst the backdrop of the loss of a cohesive

The 'new security challenge' 39

British identity, precipitated by the decline of empire, religious affiliation and the shifting socio-cultural changes of the past decades, events like the Rushdie Affair and Northern Riots were framed as 'crisis' by political elites (Brighton 2007, 12–13). Brighton thus argues convincingly that Prevent signified the reworking of political multiculturalism in the UK. Heath-Kelly (2013) also makes the connection between British Muslim communities being produced as the problematic 'Other' during events like the Rushdie Affair and the Northern Riots in 2001 and narratives linking Muslim communities to violent disorder, and its persistence as a discourse in Prevent (2013, 409). The fact that Prevent anchors the problem of radicalisation in the identity crisis of the British Muslim and promotes 'British values' as a panacea further reinforces the argument that the problematisation of Muslims was shaped by discourse surrounding multiculturalism and integration.

I have thus argued in this section that the problem of the integration agenda has been articulated in terms of a failure of multiculturalism on the one hand and the inability of Muslim to 'integrate' on the other. I have also implicitly explained the move towards the categorisation of 'Muslim' as an attempt by government to racialise and problematise Muslim identity in order to manage and curtail perceived excess, which is represented as threatening liberal democratic values, as well as disrupting the unity of the nation. This constructed narrative of problematic Muslim identity made its way in the conceptualisation of radicalisation and the implementation of Prevent.

Islam as the orientalised other and the de-privatisation of religion: the 'Muslim question' within the context of the secular in Europe

The final set of issues impacting our understanding of what became problematic to policymakers relates to the role of religion in modern public life. The dominant theory that explains modernity and religion in the West has been the secularisation thesis. This scholarship is complex and cannot be rehearsed here.[7] However, noteworthy is the fact that the secularisation thesis is both descriptive and normative (Asad 2003, 181). Descriptively, it states that as societies industrialise and modernise, religious belief declines. In terms of normativity it states that in order for 'society to be modern it has to be secular and for it to be secular it has to relegate religion to non-political spaces' (Asad 2003, 182). To avoid confusion, I draw on Casanova's (1994) tripartite distinction of this thesis: (1) increasing structural differentiation of social spaces resulting in the separation of religion from politics, economy, science and so forth; (2) the privatisation of religion within its own sphere; and (3) the declining social significance of religious beliefs, commitments and institutions.

Casanova holds that (1) and (3) hold true whereas the same cannot be said of (2). We are witnessing what Casanova calls the 'de-privatisation' of religion and the re-emergence of religion in the public space. Whilst Casanova considers the 'de-privatisation' of religion a global phenomenon, visible with the rise of

40 *The 'new security challenge'*

Pentecostalism in South American, Evangelical Christianity in America and Christianity in China, many commentators view the presence of Islam and Muslims in Europe as disrupting the narrative about secularisation and the decline of religion. This perception is set against the empirical reality that there is little sign of religious revival in Western Europe if we exclude the influx of new immigrant religions (Casanova 2008, 101).

The role of the secular in European consciousness and history must be stressed. According to Casanova, the 'secular' nature of the modern European state and the 'secular' character of European democracy serve as one of the foundational myths of contemporary European identity (2008, 109). For Charles Taylor, the modern West's normative order was established from the seventeenth century onwards as it moved away from 'cosmic-religious' order to a new 'bottom up view of society', which stresses (1) the rights and liberties of its members; (2) the equality among them; and (3) the principle that rule is based on consent (2011, 318). What Taylor therefore describes as the 'modern moral order' (intermeshed with Enlightenment ideals, particularly liberal ideas and values), political identity, democracy and the modern nation state is associated with the European history of secularisation.

Importantly, modernity, at one point synonymous with the West, was associated with the decline of religion and being modern entailed moving beyond religion. Indeed, for Asad, secularism is not merely about the confinement of religious belief and practice to a private space where its threat to political stability and the 'liberties of free-thinking citizens' is mitigated, but rather 'builds a particular conception of the world and the problems generated by that world' (2003, 191–192). In a sense, Asad teases out the analogy between secularism, the nation-state and nationalism and the way religion operates, indirectly and paradoxically showing the 'religious' nature of the 'secular' in Europe (2003, 191–195).

The presence of Muslims in European societies amidst wider security challenges since 9/11, continual immigration and rampant globalisation has been interpreted by European societies as not only a social challenge but as a threat to its secular shibboleths, not least paradoxically its Christian heritage. This is provoked by the growing visibility of religious symbols like the veil, the growing presence of Muslims in urban cities, and the political mobilisation of Muslims over issues regarding free speech and foreign policy. This tension between secular critique on the one hand and the protection of the sacred on the other has acquired an almost ritualised re-occurrence in public discourse in response to crisis events like Rushdie (1988), the Danish Cartoons (2006), and Charlie Hebdo (2015). Also, this perception has been exacerbated by Muslim mobilisation in response, inter alia, to the Afghanistan War, the Iraq War, Gaza protests (2009), and the Palestinian issue, amongst others. The overall perception and feeling is of an expansive and encroaching Muslim presence. In terms of a sociological and political reality rather than as faith, Muslim identity poses problems for secular, Christian and Liberal Europe. Parekh argues that there is now a widespread perception that:

The 'new security challenge' 41

...Muslims are collectivist intolerant, authoritarian, illiberal and theocratic and that they use their faith as a self-conscious public statement, not quietly held personal faith but a matter of identity which they must jealously guard and loudly proclaim, not only to remind them of who they are but also to announce to others what they stand for.

(2006, 180–181)

In addition, Islam represents the Other of Western secular modernity (Casanova 2008, 108; 2012). For Roy (2009), the hostility to Islam in France is rooted in the belief that Islam cannot be integrated into secular and liberal society. This notion has its basis in the idea that religion is rooted in a particular culture and must therefore be curbed and contained. The message being generated in discourses, the media and the social imaginaries of Europe is that Islam is anti-modern, fundamentalist, backward and barbaric. This discourse on Islam has been built upon three elements (Casanova 2008 109; 2012; Roy 2009, 42):

1   A theological-political distinction between 'civilised' and 'barbaric' religions, that is, between religions that are compatible with enlightenment principles and liberal democratic politics and religions that are grounded in traditions that resist the progressive claims of the Enlightenment philosophy of history, liberalism and secularism;
2   A nativist, anti-immigrant posture that postulated the unassailability of foreign immigrants because of their illiberal and uncivilised social customs and habits, supposedly grounded in their traditional religion; and
3   Transnational attachments and loyalties to either a foreign religious authority (i.e. the papacy) or to a transnational religious community (i.e. the umma) that appear incompatible with republican citizen principles and the exclusive claims of modern nationalism.

The response to the orientalisation of Islam in the public sphere has differed depending on the place and context. Examples include banning the veil in schools in France, banning minarets in Switzerland, the growth of right wing parties in many European countries, the rise of Gilt Wilders in the Netherlands, the emergence of PEGIDA in Germany (PEGIDA stands for 'Patriotic Europeans against the Islamisation of the Occident', and is, according to the BBC (2015), a German anti-Islam political organisation founded in Dresden in October 2014), the rise and fall of the English Defence League (EDL) in the UK, the rising popularity of UKIP and the promotion of 'British values' in public institutions, amongst many others.

In addition, the problematisation of the Muslim presence has been instrumentalised politically. This is exemplified by the way that politicians stoke the flames of anti-Muslim prejudice in order to win votes and appeal to a growing constituency of anxious voters;[8] the way that the liberal elite invoke the fundamentalist threat in order to stop the transmission of illiberal, fundamentalist and patriarchal customs to younger generations (Casanova 2012); the manner in

42   The 'new security challenge'

which the media regularly conflate issues and spin stories in order to sell papers; the way that anti-Muslim prejudice has galvanised various groups of the far right, evidenced by the activities of the EDL, the works of right-wing think-tanks,[9] the Oslo attacks by Andres Breivik in 2011, and the political success seen with UKIP in Britain (according to BBC Election 2015, UKIP received almost 4,000,000 votes and a 12.6 per cent of the share of the vote in the elections of 2015). More importantly, the anxiety directed towards Muslims has been primarily driven by the mainstream and not just by the fringe, encapsulated by Baroness Warsi's speech on islamophobia, in which islamophobia had passed the 'dinner-table test' (Batty 2011). In short the spectre of Islam within Europe has provoked various reactions and is being employed as a pretext for the fulfilment of heterogeneous political, social and cultural objectives.

What makes intolerant liberalism justifiable is the notion of teleological liberal secularist assumptions built into a notion of modernity that one set of norms is enlightened and progressive and the other is dark and backwards. A European narrative of progress is uncomfortable with looking in the mirror and seeing its past return. In one sense the vocal and visible Muslim presence is perceived as a throwback to the Middle Ages in Europe:

> At a more diffuse level, the Islamic revival signals a cultural anxiety in the West. The West sees in Islam the distorted mirror of its own past. It marks the rebirth of the God they had killed so that Man (sic) could live. The Islamic resurgence marks the revenge of God; it signals the return of faith, the return of all that puts into question the idea of the progressive liberation of humanity.
>
> (Sayyid 2015, 4)

Part of the anxiety in Europe comes from the implicit fact that being modern is no longer associated with being Western. There is a global trend towards what Taylor (2011) and Casanova (2008) refer to as 'multiple modernities', that is, that every society, culture and tradition seeks to negotiate a modernity in its own image and in a way compatible with its way of life, instead of the previously held assumption that all societies have to follow the trajectory of the West en route to modernisation. Even a champion of the Enlightenment and secular modernity like Jürgen Habermas now speaks of a 'post-secular age' in which secular reason must learn to become 'aware of what is missing' in secularity which the reason of faith, oxymoronically, provides space for. For Habermas, secularisation now 'functions less as a filter separating out the contents of traditions than as a transformer which redirects the flow of tradition' (Habermas *et al.* 2010, 18). In other words, the de-privatisation of religion in Europe is seen to have derailed its conception of modernity. This argument draws on current global trends in which Western modernity is challenged by globalisation, the rise of new powers in Asia and the diversity of European society. The notion of multiple modernities effectively decentres the West as the bastion of universal values and severs the link between the West and modernity.

The 'new security challenge' 43

With this in mind, it is important to turn to the connection between the role of the secular, the perceived threat of Islam and counter-terrorism in Britain. Using Prevent as a case study, Stacy Gutkowski (2011) shows how political and cultural secularity has contributed to perceptions of risk. Secular ideas consequently helped make the following problematic suppositions seem plausible (Gutowksi 2011, 358):

- Religious identity (rather than evidence of extremism) was a useful and unproblematic way to identify a diverse Muslim population, bringing it under surveillance;
- Religious narratives, doctrine and law are static entities that can be instrumentalised for security purposes; and
- There is a 'slippery slope' between mainstream Islamic ideas and radical extremism, particularly for young men.

Gutkowski also crucially highlights the position of religion in relation to secularism and liberalism, supported by assumptions like the natural separation of politics and religion, and that religion is a kind of personal 'idiosyncrasy' with an 'irrational' hold over people (2011, 349). Concomitantly important in defining religion as risky is the perception of religion by the political liberal tradition, the historical experience of British colonialism with non-violent and violent religions, and the increasing non-religiosity among the white mainstream from the 1960s onwards (ibid.). She therefore argues that a by-product of this secular orientation, is something she calls the 'ambivalence of the secular', which has 'exaggerated the extent to which radical ideas have taken hold among Muslims' and that 'moderate Islam could be co-opted into managing the spread of radical ideas' (Gutowski 2011, 35). It is thus the secular liberal context of Europe that has determined what is seen as 'risk' and which has shaped the representation of the radicalisation threat in security discourses and counter-terrorism policy in the UK.

As a result, the construction of problematic Muslim communities and the threat posed by the spectre of Islam has shaped the production of discourses on radicalisation. Specifically, it has resulted in the privileging of theology and ideology as causal factors in accounts of radicalisation and in the focus of Prevent on Islamist ideology and 'extremism' and the religious rehabilitative models deployed in de-radicalisation interventions (PSJ 2012; Bjorgo and Horgan 2009; Ashour 2009). Such examples point to the primacy of beliefs and ideas in the conceptualisation and understanding of human behaviour. Indeed, the notion that beliefs are a doctrine or set of rational precepts is a feature of Enlightenment thought on religion. Thinkers of the Enlightenment attacked religious doctrine, assuming that religious behaviour is a result of religious beliefs, which will cease to exist once the belief is refuted. The fallacy in this thinking has been proven historically, since there many reasons religions exist for people outside of rational precepts: as a social glue, as myth, as cult, religion as an aid to survival, and religion as sublimated violence (Scruton 2006, 121–128). The

44   *The 'new security challenge'*

point is that the by-product of this thinking is that individuals are defined in solely religious terms, the conflation of religion and personal identity into a categorical identity (à la 'British Muslims'), and that 3,000,000 Muslims constitute a single subjectivity.

Consequently, this discursive development inscribes causal power onto Islam and Muslim subjectivity and links it with propensity to violence, as well as identifying it as the source of problematic identities, not to mention troublesome practices incompatible with life in modern Britain. As a result, the solution to 'radicalisation' and 'integration' becomes an issue that needs to be addressed in theological and psychological terms. Indeed, the preoccupation with theological reflections in Muslim political activity is itself an integral component of de-radicalisation intervention. Since the security and integration threat is understood and analysed in terms of identity and religion, then the logical solution for government and civil society is to intervene in the religious life of Muslims. Hence we see the call, in some quarters, for a 'reform of Islam' as well as the promotion of 'moderate Muslims' in Prevent, evidenced below in a speech by Prime Minister David Cameron in July 2015.

> Now the third plank of our strategy is to embolden different voices within the Muslim community. Just as we do not engage with extremist groups and individuals, we're now going to actively encourage the reforming and moderate Muslim voices. This is a significant shift in government approach – and an important one.

With respect to reforming Islam the history and experience of Christianity in the British context provides a normative blueprint for the type of Islam that would be accepted in the UK. Both Casanova (2006, 23) and Taylor (2007, 2011) show how Protestant Christianity is implicated in the development of secular modernity. For policymakers the remoulding of Islam to suit British political, social and cultural spaces would ideally take the shape of Anglican Christianity – private, non-political, institutionalised. And it would also entail, as is clear from the emphasis on 'shared values' in Prevent, compatibility with liberal values of equality, human rights and democracy. The British experience of the secular and religion prescribes a normative template for the indigenising of Islam in Britain.

To recapitulate my argument in this section, constructions of Islam as a foreign entity, transnational in scope, politically ambitious, and possessing a fanatical hold on its adherents have been shaped by the European experience of religion, the secular and modernity. The de-privatisation of religion as a result of immigration and globalisation in recent times has challenged European societies with respect to the place of religion in public and social life. These explain the fashion in which the threat of Islam has been imagined, as well as the attempt by elites to remake and domesticate Islam in an image palatable to European realities.

Notes

1 The Copenhagen School is an approach to the study of Security, which is considered a sub-discipline of International Relations. The mainstream approaches are Realism, Liberalism and Constructivism, which together form a broad family of shared ideas. Other approaches are considered 'critical', in both the sense of emphasising the importance of 'emancipation' and the sense of encouraging reflection and re-examination of assumptions and limitations governing how we think and do security. Besides the Copenhagen School, these other approaches include the Welsh School, Feminist approaches, the Paris School and Post-Structuralism. Due to space limitations, I cannot explicate the differences between these schools and approaches. For more see Buzan and Hansen (2009); and Jarvis and Holland (2015).
2 A number of scholars (Jackson *et al.* 2011; Spalek 2011; Lambert 2011) are critical of the categorisations of 'old' and 'new terrorism'. They argue that there are similarities between what was called old terrorism and new terrorism and believe that the validity of New Terrorism is hampered by its link to counter-terrorism policy.
3 PM David Cameron explicitly mentions the practice of FGM in relation to young British Muslim girls in his Extremism Speech in Birmingham 2015 (Cameron 2015).
4 The Rochdale sex trafficking gang was a group of men who preyed on under-age teenage girls in Rochdale between 2005 and 2013. Twelve men were originally charged. Of the nine men convicted, eight were of British Pakistani origin and one was an Afghan asylum-seeker.
5 There were allegations concerning Birmingham schools arising from the 'Trojan Horse' letter sent to Birmingham City Council in November 2013. Operation 'Trojan Horse' refers to an organised attempt by a number of associated individuals to introduce an Islamist or Salafist ethos into several schools in Birmingham (Clarke 2014).
6 In August 2011, the White House revealed its strategy for countering radicalisation, entitled 'Empowering Local Partners to Prevent Violent Extremism'. Wiktorowicz has been described as the 'chief architect' of this strategy (Vidino and Hughes 2015, 18).
7 The debate on the secularisation theory is complicated by different uses of definitions, concepts, empirical evidence, type ('weak secularism' as in the UK vs. 'strong' secular states like France) and contexts (the theory does not apply in the same way to the United States, for example, which was established as a secular state, unlike European states, but which predominantly remains socially religious, in contrast to Europe where religious belief has declined). For more see Bruce (2002, 2011) Taylor (2007, 2011); Casanova (1994, 2006, 2008); and Talal Asad (2003).
8 In the build up to the 2015 General Election in the UK, Nigel Farage, Leader of UKIP, in an interview with Trevor Phillips, equated the fear of immigration with some British Muslims who were described as a 'fifth column' (Mason 2015). In addition, Afzal Amin, a Conservative candidate in North Dudley, was suspended after being caught by the *Mail on Sunday* trying to arrange with the EDL a fake demonstration outside the mosque, which would then be called off after his intervention (Watt and Mathew 2015).
9 Spin Watch Reports examine the work and funding of two right-wing think-tanks in the UK – the Centre for Social Cohesion (now Henry Jackson Society) and the Policy Exchange. The reports reveal their links to global transnational counter-Jihadi movements and show that the arguments advanced by these think-tanks are a reversion to counter-subversion strategies of the Cold-War era (Mills *et al.* 2011).

References

Abbas, T. (2005). *Muslim Britain: Communities Under Pressure*. London: Zed Books Ltd.

46 *The 'new security challenge'*

Agamben, G. (2005). *State of Exception*. Chicago: Chicago Press.

Anderson, B. (1983). *Imagined Communities: Reflections on the Origin and Spread of Nationalism*. London: Verso Books.

Ansari, H. (2004). *The Infidel Within: Muslims in Britain since 1800*. London: Hurst & Co Publishers.

Asad, T. (2003). *Formations of the Secular: Christianity, Islam, and Modernity*. Stanford: Stanford University Press.

Ashour, O. (2009). *The De-radicalization of Jihadists: Transforming armed Islamist Movements*. New York and London: Routledge.

Awan, A., Hoskins, A. and O'Loughlin, B. (2012). *Radicalisation and Media: Connectivity and Terrorism in the New Media Ecology*. Abingdon: Routledge.

Baker, A.H. (2011). *Extremists in Our Midst, Confronting Terror. New Security Challenges*. London: Palgrave Macmillan.

Baker-Beall, C., Heath-Kelly, C. and Jarvis, L. (2015). *Counter-Radicalisation: Critical Perspectives*. Abingdon: Routledge

Batty, D. (2011). 'Lady Warsi claims Islamophobia is now socially acceptable in Britain', *Guardian*, 20 January 2011, www.theguardian.com/uk/2011/jan/20/lady-warsi-islamophobia-muslims-prejudice.

BBC (2015). *Elections 2015*, www.bbc.co.uk/news/election/2015/results.

BBC (2015). *Why are thousands of Germans protesting and who are Pegida?*', 13 January 2015, www.bbc.co.uk/newsbeat/article/30694252/why-are-thousands-of-germans-protesting-and-who-are-pegida.

Beck, U. (2008). *World at Risk*. Oxford: Polity Press.

Benoist, A. (2013). *Carl Schmitt Today: Terrorism, 'Just' War, and the State of Emergency*. London: Arktos.

Bjorgo, T. and Horgan, J. (2009). *Leaving Terrorism Behind: Disengagement from Political Violence*. New York: Routledge.

Blair, A. (2005). *Prime Minister's Press Conference, 5 Aug. 2005*, http://webarchive.nationalarchives.gov.uk/20060715135117/number10.gov.uk/page8041.

Booth, K. (1991). 'Security and emancipation', *Review of International Studies*, 17: 313–326.

Briggs, R., Fieschi, C. and Lownsbrough, H. (2006). *Bringing it home, community-based approaches to counter-terrorism*, DEMOS, www.demos.co.uk/files/Bringing%20it%20Home%20-%20web.pdf.

Brighton, S. (2007). 'British Muslims, multiculturalism and UK foreign policy: "integration" and "cohesion" in and beyond the state', *International Affairs*, 83 (1): 1–17.

Bruce, S. (2002). *God is Dead: Secularization in the West*. Oxford: Wiley-Blackwell.

Bruce, S. (2011). *Secularization: In Defence of an Unfashionable Theory*. Oxford: Oxford University Press.

Butler, J. (2006). *Precarious Life: The Power of Mourning and Violence*. London and New York: Verso Books.

Buzan, B. and Hansen, L. (2009). *The Evolution of International Security Studies*. Cambridge: Cambridge University Press.

Buzan B. and Wæver O. (2003). *Regions and Powers: The Structure of International Security*. Cambridge: Cambridge University Press.

Buzan, B., Wæver, O. and De Wilde, J. (1998). *Security: A New Framework for Analysis*. Boulder, CO: Lynne Rienner.

Cameron, D. (2011). *PM's speech at Munich Security Conference*, www.gov.uk/government/speeches/pms-speech-at-munich-security-conference.

The 'new security challenge' 47

Cameron, D. (2015). *PM's Extremism Speech in Birmingham, July 20th*, www.gov.uk/government/speeches/extremism-pm-speech.

Cantle, T. (2001). *Community Cohesion: A Report of the Independent Review Team*, London: Home Office, http://resources.cohesioninstitute.org.uk/Publications/Documents/Document/DownloadDocumentsFile.aspx?recordId=96&file=PDFversion.

Casanova, J. (1994). *Public Religions in the Modern World*. Chicago: University of Chicago University Press.

Casanova, J. (2006). 'Secularisation Revisited: A Reply to Talal Asad', in *Powers of the Secular Modern: Talal Asad and his Interlocutors*, edited by D. Scott and C. Hirschkind. Stanford: Stanford University Press.

Casanova, J. (2008). 'Public religions revisited', in *Religion: Beyond a Concept (Future of the Religious Past)*, edited by Hent de Vries. Fordham: Fordham University Press.

Casanova, J. (2012). 'The politics of nativism: Islam in Europe, Catholicism in the United States', *Philosophy and Social Criticism*, 38: 485–495.

Commission of the European Communities (CEC) (2005). *Terrorist Recruitment: Addressing the Factors Contributing to Violent Radicalisation*, Brussels, http://eur-lex.europa.eu/legal-content/EN/TXT/PDF/?uri=CELEX:52005DC0313&from=EN.

Change Institute (2008). *The Beliefs, Ideologies and Narratives of Violent Radicalisation*. Report for the European Commission. London: The Change Institute, www.changeinstitute.co.uk.

Clarke, P. (2014). *Report into Allegations Concerning Birmingham Schools Arising From the 'Trojan Horse' Letter*, www.gov.uk/government/uploads/system/uploads/attachment_data/file/340526/HC_576_accessible_-.pdf.

Coolsaet, R. (2010). EU counterterrorism strategy: value added or chimera?', *International Affairs*, 86 (4): 857–873.

Croft, S. (2012). *Securitizing Islam: Identity and the Search for Security*. Cambridge: Cambridge University Press.

Dalgaard-Nielsen, A. (2010). 'Violent radicalization in Europe: what we know and what we do not know', *Studies in Conflict and Terrorism*, 33: 797–814.

Douglas, M. (1992). *Risk and Blame: Essays in Cultural Theory*. Abingdon, Oxon: Routledge.

Eagleton, T. (2014). *Culture and the Death of God*. New Haven: Yale University Press.

Edwards, P. (2015). 'How (not) to create ex-terrorists: prevent as ideological warfare', in *Counter-Radicalisation: Critical Perspectives*, edited by C. Baker-Beall, C. Heath-Kelly and L. Jarvis. Abingdon: Routledge.

ESRC (2007). *New Security Challenges: 'Radicalisation' and Violence – A Critical Reassessment Specification*, www.esrc.ac.uk/ESRCInfoCentre/Images/Specification_tcm6-18574.pdf.

Foucault, M. (2002). *The Order of Things*. Abingdon: Routledge.

Gellner, E. (1983). *Nations and Nationalism*. New York: Cornell University Press.

Githens-Mazer, J. (2010). *'Rethinking the Causal Concept of Islamic Radicalisation'*, Committee on Concepts and Methods Working Paper Series, www.concepts-methods.org/Files/WorkingPaper/PC%2042%20Githens-Mazer.pdf.

Githens-Mazer, J. (2012). 'The rhetoric and reality: radicalization and political discourse', *International Political Science Review*, 33 (5): 556–567.

Githens-Mazer, J. and Lambert, R. (2010). 'Why conventional wisdom on radicalization fails: the persistence of a failed discourse', *International Affairs*, 86 (4): 889–890.

Gray, J. (2000). *The Two Faces of Liberalism*. Cambridge: Polity Press.

48   The 'new security challenge'

Gutkowski, S. (2011). 'Secularism and the politics of risk Britain's prevent agenda, 2005–2009', *International Relations*, 25 (3): 346–362.

Habermas, J., Reder, M., Schmidt, J., Brieskorn, N. and Ricken, F. (2010). *An Awareness of What is Missing: Faith and Reason in a Post-Secular Age*. Cambridge: Polity Press.

Heath-Kelly, C. (2013). 'Counter-Terrorism and the counterfactual: producing the "radicalisation" discourse and the UK PREVENT Strategy', *British Journal of Politics and International Relations*, 15: 394–415.

Hobsbawm, E. (1983). *The Invention of Tradition*. Cambridge: Cambridge University Press.

Home Office (HO) (2006). *Countering International Terrorism: The United Kingdom's Strategy.*

Home Office (HO) (2009). *The United Kingdom's Strategy for Countering International Terrorism.*

Home Office (HO) (2011). *Prevent, CONTEST 2011*, www.homeoffice.gov.uk/publications/counter-terrorism/prevent/prevent-strategy.

Home Office/Foreign Office (HO/FO) (2004). *Young Muslim and Extremism*, http://tinyurl.com/dx65b.

Huysmans, J. (2008). 'The jargon of exception – on Schmitt, Agamben and the absence of political society', *International Political Sociology*, 2: 165–183.

Jackson, R., Jarvis, L., Breen-Smyth, M. and Gunning, J. (2011). *Terrorism: A Critical Introduction*. London: Palgrave Macmillan.

Jarvis, L. and Holland, J. (2015). *Security: A Critical Introduction*. London: Palgrave Macmillan.

Kundnani, A. (2009). *Spooked! How Not to Prevent Violent Extremism*. London: Institute of Race Relations, www.irr.org.uk/pdf2/spooked.pdf.

Kundnani, A. (2012). 'Radicalisation: the journey of a concept', *Institute of Race Relations*, 54 (2): 3–25.

Lambert, R. (2011). *Countering Al-Qaeda in London, Police and Muslims in Partnerships*. London: C. Hurst & Co.

Laqueur, W. (1999). *The New Terrorism: Fanaticism and the Arms of Mass Destruction*. Oxford: Oxford University Press.

Mason, R. (2015). 'Nigel Farage: British Muslim "fifth column" fuels fear of immigration', *Guardian*, 12 March 2015, www.theguardian.com/politics/2015/mar/12/nigel-farage-british-muslim-fifth-column-fuels-immigration-fear-ukip.

Massumi, B. (2005). 'The future birth of the affective fact', Conference proceedings: *Genealogies of Biopolitics*, http://browse.reticular.info/text/collected/massumi.pdf.

Massumi, B. (2007). 'Potential politics and the primacy of preemption', *Theory & Event*, 10, 2.

McCauley, C. and Moskalenko, S. (2009). 'Measuring political mobilisation: the distinction between activism and radicalism', *Terrorism and Political Violence*, 21: 239–260.

McRoy, A. (2006). *From Rushdie to 7/7: The Radicalisation of Islam in Britain*. London: Social Affairs Unit.

Mills, T., Griffin, T. and Miller, D. (2011). *The Cold War on British Muslims: An Examination of Policy Exchange and the Centre for Social Cohesion*, SpinWatch, www.thecordobafoundation.com/attach/SpinwatchReport_ColdWar12.pdf.

Mirza, M., Senthilkumaran, A. and Ja'far, Z. (2007). *'Living Apart Together': British Muslims and the paradox of Multiculturalism*, Policy Exchange, www.policyexchange.org.uk/images/publications/living%20apart%20together%20-%20jan%2007.pdf.

Modood, T. (2005). 'Foreword', in *Muslim Britain: Communities Under Pressure*, edited by T. Abbas. London: Zed Books.

Moskalenko, S. and McCauley, C. (2008). 'Mechanisms of political radicalization: pathways toward terrorism', *Terrorism and Political Violence*, 20 (3): 415–433.

Mythen, G., and Walklate, S. (2006). 'Which thesis? Risk society or governmentality', *The British Journal of Criminology*, 46 (3): 379–398.

Neumann, P. (2008). *Old and New Terrorism: Late Modernity, Globalization and the Transformation of Political Violence (UT – Understanding Terrorism)*. Cambridge: Polity Press.

Oxford Dictionary, www.oxforddictionaries.com/definition/english/radical.

Parekh, B. (2006). *Rethinking Multiculturalism: Cultural Diversity and Political Theory*. London: Palgrave Macmillan.

Prison Service Journal (PSJ) (2012). 'Combating extremism and terrorism', September, No. 203, www.crimeandjustice.org.uk/sites/crimeandjustice.org.uk/files/PSJ%20September%202012%20No.%20203.pdf.

Rai, M. (2006). *7/7: The London Bombings, Islam and the Iraq War*. London: Pluto.

Reid, J. (2009). *The Biopolitics of the War on Terror: Life Struggles, Liberal Modernity and the Defence of Logistical Societies*. Manchester: Manchester University Press.

Rex, J. (1996). 'Ethnic minorities in the modern nation state', *Working Papers in the Theory of Multi-culturalism and Integration*, file:///C:/Users/dell/Downloads/doc_dinamicas_1.pdf.

Richards, A. (2011). 'The problem with "radicalization": the remit of "Prevent" and the need to refocus on terrorism in the UK', *International Affairs*, 87 (1): 143–152.

Roberts, G. and Hurst, P. (2015). 'Rochdale child sex grooming: 10 men charged after new police investigation', *Mirror*, 2 March 2015, www.mirror.co.uk/news/uk-news/rochdale-child-sex-grooming-10-5258851.

Roselle, L., Miskimmon, A. and O'Loughlin, B. (2014). 'Strategic narrative: a new means to understand soft power', *Media, War & Conflict*, 7 (1): 70–84.

Roy, O. (2002). *Globalised Islam: The Search for a New Ummah*. London. C Hurst & Co Publishers Ltd.

Roy, O. (2009). *Secularism Confronts Islam*. New York: Columbia University Press.

Rumsfeld, D. (2002). *'There are Known Knowns'*, www.youtube.com/watch?v=GiPe1OiKQuk.

Sageman, M. (2008). *Leaderless Jihad: Terror networks in the Twenty-First Century*. Philadelphia. University of Pennsylvania Press.

Sayyid, S. (2015). *A Fundamental Fear, Eurocentrism and the Emergence of Islamism*. London: Zed Books.

Sayyid, S. and Tyrer, D. (2012). 'Governing ghosts: race, incorporeality and difference in post-political times', *Current Sociology*, 60 (3): 353–367.

Schmitt, C. (1985). *Political Theology, Four Chapters on the Concept of Sovereignty*. Cambridge, MA: MIT Press.

Scruton, R. (2006). *A Political Philosophy: Arguments for Conservatism*. London: Bloomsbury Publishing Plc.

Sedgwick, M. (2010). 'The concept of radicalisation as a source of confusion', *Terrorism and Political Violence*, 22 (4): 479–494.

Spalek, B. (2011). '"New terrorism" and crime prevention initiatives involving Muslim young people in the UK: research and policy contexts', *Religion, State and Society*, 39: 2–3.

50 The 'new security challenge'

Taylor, C. (1994). 'The politics of recognition', in *Multiculturalism*, edited by A. Gutman. New Jersey: Princeton University Press.

Taylor, C. (2007). *A Secular Age*. Cambridge: Harvard University Press.

Taylor, C. (2011). *Dilemmas and Connections*. Cambridge: Harvard University Press.

Thomas, P. (2007). 'Moving on from "anti-racism"? Understandings of "community cohesion" held by youth workers', *Journal of Social Policy*, 36 (3): 435–455.

Tilley, N., Bouhana, W. and Braithwaite, A. (2011). *Evaluation of the ESRC/FCO/AHRC New Security Challenges: Radicalisation and Violence – A Critical Assessment Initiative*, www.esrc.ac.uk/_images/EC_Executive_Summary_NCSRV_tcm8-22040.pdf.

Vidino, L. and Hughes, S. (2015). *Countering Violent Extremism in America*, Centre for Cyber & Homeland Security, the George Washington University, https://cchs.gwu.edu/sites/cchs.gwu.edu/files/downloads/CVE%20in%20America%20.pdf.

Watt, N. and Taylor, M. (2015). 'Tory candidate accused of EDL plot expected to be forced out within days', *Guardian*, 22 March 2015, www.theguardian.com/politics/2015/mar/22/tory-candidate-afzal-amin-accused-of-edl-plot-urged-fess-up-go-now.

Wiktorowicz, Q. (2005). *Radical Islam Rising: Muslim Extremism in the West*. Lanham, MD: Rowman and Littlefield.

Wittgenstein, L. (1958). *Philosophical Investigations*. Oxford: Basil Blackwell.

2 The concept of de-radicalisation

An analysis of research data

My research uses the case study method, which is defined as:

> An empirical inquiry about a contemporary phenomenon (e.g., a 'case'), set within its real-world context – especially when the boundaries between phenomenon and context are not clearly evident.
>
> (Yin 2009, 18)

Accompanying the case study method is the qualitative interview approach to data collection and a semi-structured style to interviews. In semi-structured interviews the interviewer generally has a list of questions and discussion prompts, but the order in which they are asked can vary in each interview. The interviewers may ask additional questions and probe beyond the questions on their lists. It is the balance between some consistency in questioning and some flexibility to probe further during the interview that attracted me to the semi-structured approach.

Accordingly, my research of de-radicalisation is based upon 27 semi-structured interviews I conducted between December 2011 and May 2013. Participants were identified for their expertise and knowledge on Prevent and de-radicalisation from across a cross section of bodies and organisations. This included Prevent Engagement Officers, Police Officers, a de-radicalisation intervention provider, think-tank analysts, academic researchers, Muslim organisations that received Prevent funding, community activists, Prevent practitioners and a former counter-terrorism officer. This targeted sample was the most effective way of collating data on a phenomenon that is under studied, misunderstood and lacking in rigorous methodology. The number of individuals to be interviewed was determined primarily by the time available for fieldwork, access to interviewees and the quantity and quality of the data obtained. At 27 I stopped once I felt that I had interviewed sufficient diversity of participants and could identify a number of trends and patterns to begin answering my research question. The result was over 30 hours of recorded interviews and over 300 pages of transcribed interviews.

As one of the conditions for agreeing to be interviewed, participants signed a statement of confidentiality stipulating that their names would not be mentioned.

52   *Analysis of research data*

However, participants agreed to be referred to by their position/organisation/ company, even if the attitudes and opinions expressed in the interviews was their own. In fact, the data analysis throughout the book employs the title of the person's occupation and not their names. I have also anonymised the occupation of interviewees to protect their names given that many of the interviewees were at the forefront of work on Prevent and de-radicalisation. The high profile status of my interviewees, illustrated in Table A.1 in the Appendix therefore enhances the results of the data, particularly with regards to its reliability, relevance and usefulness.

During interviews I asked all of the 27 participants the question: what is de-radicalisation? The data provides a more nuanced and complex picture of what de-radicalisation entails conceptually. So, starting with definitions, my research revealed that there were over 28 ways of referring to de-radicalisation by interviewees, which included:

(1) de-legitimisation, (2) disengagement, (3) disaffiliation, (4) dissuasion, (5) re-education, (6) counter-ideology, (7) brain washing, (8) counter-brain washing, (9) counter-radicalisation, (10) counter-subversion,(11) rehabilitation, (12) reintegration into mainstream, (13) de-programming, (14) re-programming, (15) re-balancing, (16) desisting, (17) empowering, (18) detox, (19) thought-control, (20) behaviour change, (21) cognitive change, (22) propaganda, (23) supporting vulnerabilities, (24) de-construction, (25) disaffection, (26) reversing radicalism, (27) pacifying and (28) de-nazification.

In the first instance the various definitions of de-radicalisation confirm the contested nature of de-radicalisation as highlighted in the literature. The significance of having a myriad of ways to define de-radicalisation will be explored in the next section. The second picture that emerges from the data is the existence of nine conceptual pillars constituting the framework of de-radicalisation according to interviewees. De-radicalisation is thus comprised conceptually of the following:

1   Cognitive change
2   Behavioural change
3   Process/journey of change experienced by the individual
4   Programmes of interventions
5   Expertise and knowledge
6   Political remit
7   Young people
8   Radicalisation
9   Individual-level interventions.

The first four conceptual features that came through the data neatly align with the conceptual framework expressed in the literature and in Prevent. The data

Analysis of research data   53

extends what we know about de-radicalisation as encapsulated by conceptual features 5–8. In particular, conceptual features like *expertise and knowledge, political remit, young people as targets and its relationship with radicalisation discourse*, are explicitly unique to the UK context in comparison to conceptualisation of de-radicalisation elsewhere.

Third, the data reveals four different conceptual interpretations of de-radicalisation. These include

1   Counter-violence (renunciation)
2   Counter-ideology/extremism (non-violent)
3   Re-integration of individuals into mainstream society
4   Youth empowerment.

The four concepts also correspond to four policy areas:

1   Counter-terrorism
2   Counter-subversion
3   Community cohesion
4   Crime-prevention.

Of the four conceptions of de-radicalisation expressed in the data, two were not articulated in the literature. The first is the understanding of de-radicalisation connecting 'counter-ideology/counter-extremism' (whilst 'counter-ideology' and 'counter-extremism' are terms with distinct meanings, they are nevertheless employed interchangeably by interviewees, and so I have grouped these terms together) to a wider policy of counter-subversion. The understanding of counter-ideology/counter-extremism has been associated solely with counter-terrorism policy and not counter-subversion. Second, the data reveals an understanding of de-radicalisation connecting 'youth empowerment' with crime-prevention. Whilst de-radicalisation has certainly been referred to in relation to crime prevention, something the Prevent strategy itself confusingly does, it does not however frame this understanding directly in terms of empowering/developing youth. Both conceptions open new ways of viewing de-radicalisation, bringing more explicitly to the fore the central role of the logic of discipline and pastoral power in conceptions of de-radicalisation. It is in this way that the data extends further what we previously understood as de-radicalisation from the literature and Prevent strategy. Taken altogether, the data challenges what we know of de-radicalisation, moving our conceptual lens beyond parsimonious accounts of de-radicalisation in which it is perceived as a signifier for 'moving away from violence' and thus only as an instrument of counter-terrorism. Instead the data suggests that another way perhaps of understanding de-radicalisation, besides conventional concerns with terrorism, is to view it as having more complexity – as being concerned with wider political and governmental objectives relating to reconstructions of the state, identity and citizenship. This significance of the data will be analysed in greater detail in subsequent sections.

54 *Analysis of research data*

Bewitched by language: the many faces of de-radicalisation

Fieldwork data revealed that there were over 28 ways of referring to de-radicalisation by interviewees. The sheer diversity of definitions relating to de-radicalisation and its association with other terms provokes a number of questions: how do we account for the plethora of terms associated with de-radicalisation? Why did some struggle to define it? And why did some 'experts' working in the field of counter-terrorism feel it was sufficient and permissible not to define it? Would practitioners in other fields tolerate the same laxity with respect to key terms and concepts in their knowledge domain? If not, why is there a discernible resignation to the use of vague and ambiguous terminology in this field?

First, the data confirms the findings articulated in the wider literature that there are various definitions of de-radicalisation. As captured in Table A.2 in the Appendix, there are eight main definitions identifiable in the literature. Of the eight definitions, the Prevent conception of de-radicalisation is the most confusing, whilst the definition of de-radicalisation offered by think-tanks emphasises an expansive view of de-radicalisation in which radical individuals have to embrace Western values as a necessary prerequisite for successful de-radicalisation. This is contrasted with Ashour's definition which places de-radicalisation within the history and politics of Islamist movements at the collective level, whereas all the other definitions seem to place de-radicalisation as an intervention designed for individuals. Horgan defines it in two ways, revolving around the desire to 'reduce risk'. In addition, Quilliam's definition of de-radicalisation was not an official definition but one found in a written interview between a researcher and a Quilliam analyst (Johnson 2009, Appendix). It is used because it shows another understanding of de-radicalisation, one relating to the hermeneutics of the Islamic tradition, which is a theologically focused definition. It is interesting that at the global and UN level, member state governments show a reluctance to use the term 'de-radicalisation' and prefer the term 're-integration'. A significant contribution of my fieldwork data therefore when compared to the literature is that it not only confirms what is articulated there but that it underscores the true extent to which the term is contested and ill-defined. The various definitions of de-radicalisation convey that the term *means different things to different people.*

This, however, does not explain how the meaning of de-radicalisation is secured in spite of the aforementioned terminological labyrinth. To do this I want to examine the semantic logic that underpins the search for objective and precise meanings of words, what Charles Taylor calls the 'designative theory' of language. The designative semantic logic works by ascribing names to objects in the world. It makes the meaning of words clear and is concerned with tracing relations between sentences and their truth conditions (Taylor 1995, 220–221). It came into its own in the seventeenth century with Descartes, Bacon and Hobbes, where a meaningful view of the universe was abandoned in favour of an objective view of the world (Taylor 1995, 224). According to Taylor, this theory

Analysis of research data 55

of language is suited to the canons of modern science (1995, 220–221). However, since language is not just about ascribing terms to corresponding objects in the world, it is clear that the designative theory of language does not take us very far and we have to look elsewhere for explanations. The fact that de-radicalisation is associated with so many other ideas confirms this. As with the term de-radicalisation, the word itself does not seem to be important in designating the phenomenon of de-radicalisation in the world. Consequently, a different semantic logic is needed in order to understand the vague meaning of de-radicalisation, the inability to pin it down and its diverse associations.

Ludwig Wittgenstein's philosophy offers a different route. In *Philosophical Investigations* (1958), Wittgenstein introduced the concepts of 'language-game' to designate forms of language simpler than the entirety of a language itself, 'consisting of language and the actions into which it is woven' (7), and connected by family resemblance or 'Familienähnlichkeit'. The concept was intended 'to bring into prominence the fact that the speaking of language is part of an activity, or a form of life' (Wittgenstein 1958, 23) which gives language its meaning. Some examples are needed to illustrate the profound importance the concept 'language-games' has for understanding the conundrum of de-radicalisation in terms of meaning. Wittgenstein urged his interlocutors to consider examining what all the various 'games' that are played have in common:

> Consider for example the proceedings that we call 'games'. I mean board-games, card-games, ball-games, Olympic Games, and so on. What is common to them all? – Don't' say: 'There must be something common, or they would not be called "games"' – but look and see whether there is anything common to all. – For if you look at them you will not see something that is common to all, but similarities, relationships, and a whole series of them at that.
>
> (Ibid., 66)

The things we call 'language games' are indeed related to one another, but they do not all share a defining characteristic. If we examine all the things we call games, we will not find any one feature in common, but simply a number of relationships between kinds of games. Wittgenstein calls the similarity between different kinds of games a 'family resemblance' because a family is also distinguishable by certain similarities in features, but is not defined by any one or number of those features. The notion of family resemblance is fruitful in trying to make sense of the fact that de-radicalisation is associated with so many other terms, like radicalisation, extremism and terrorism. On the one hand, it is clear from the data that interviewees found the existence of many terms, as well as the lax application of those various terms in relation to de-radicalisation, problematic; on the other hand, the notion of 'family resemblance' suggests – in contrast to the designative theory of language – that exact definitions are not required for meaning to be secured. Instead, as Wittgenstein shows, use comes before the individual meaning of the word. In other words, we know what a word means

56 *Analysis of research data*

not because there is some fixed meaning attached to it with which we are familiar, but because we know how to use that word in certain contexts. This is expressed by the following interviewee:

> I'm going to take a hard line view. For me I think de-radicalisation is about empowerment ... what you are trying to do I guess ... well it's a good question. I'm just going to say empowerment because you can get into difficult territory otherwise.
>
> (Interview 7, Academic and Prevent practitioner)

What seems at first glance to be pointing to the notion of de-radicalisation as a confusing and misleading term also suggests, upon closer inspection, that the meaning of de-radicalisation can be secured without having to define it. The word 'empowerment' is a concept that can take on countless other meanings and associations. To say therefore that de-radicalisation is 'empowerment' is to connote any number of meanings (e.g. subjects undergoing intervention gain more confidence, skills, access to resources, improved mental health, better literacy, etc.). However, as a result of the language 'games' that interviewees played, the meaning of de-radicalisation in connection with 'empowerment', rather than merely signifying an attempt to evade the necessity of defining and explaining the term, actually makes sense in the context of youth development, probation services and mentoring – an area of work this interviewee specialises in.

With the notion of 'language games' and 'family resemblance' in mind, we can situate the status of de-radicalisation with respect to meaning more clearly. De-radicalisation as term, word and idea belongs to its own language game: it makes sense in the context in which it is employed, which for interviewees means the policy domain of counter-terrorism. Every single word of the 28 words/phrases has a unique and different meaning and yet each shares similar connotations/meanings. In the context of radicalisation, particularly the radicalisation of young British Muslim men, it is acknowledged or understood, without any precise definitions, what is broadly meant by de-radicalisation, as articulated below:

> I mean there's a problem with the terminology and even people in the Channel Project would say that they don't like the word de-radicalise because they are not trying to de-radicalise people. People use the term in different ways so it's important to realise that people that use the term are probably saying we are trying to move someone down from a violent extremist angle away from violence.
>
> (Interview 10, Investigative journalist)

In the context of de-radicalisation therefore the general meaning pertains to getting individuals away from violence using discursive debate and education; and as the data highlights this phenomenon can be expressed in a multitude of

Analysis of research data 57

ways. However, an important matter to consider besides the plethora of terms denoting de-radicalisation by practitioners in this policy domain is the fact that confusion enveloping the term remains a glaring problem for practitioners, evidenced by the fact that four of the interviewees openly stated that they did not know the meaning of de-radicalisation. This is shown by the following respondents, both of whom attempted a definition but conceded the ambiguity of de-radicalisation as a term.

> So de-radicalisation … I don't know what it means, I'd be surprised if anyone even knows what it means.
>
> (Interview 18, former Chair of community organisation)

> Yeah I know but I don't know much about it. I don't know why the government doesn't take a more humanist approach to all this instead of seeing young Muslims as statistics.
>
> (Interview 5, Director of company funded by Prevent)

There are indeed indications in the literature that there is some reluctance to embrace current definitions of the term de-radicalisation. It is significant, for example, that the Office for Security and Counter-Terrorism (OSCT) at the Home Office commissioned a review in 2011 of de-radicalisation, titled 'Individual disengagement from Al-Qaeda influenced terrorist groups' (Disley *et al.* 2011). It deliberately chose not to use the word 'de-radicalisation'. Moreover, in a literature review conducted for the International Centre for Counter-Terrorism, Alex Schmid highlighted the fact that governments prefer to use terms like 'rehabilitation' and 'reintegration'.

> The term 'de-radicalisation' is generally avoided by governments when it comes to winning back the 'hearts and minds' of those who became violent radicals or terrorists. The Global Counterterrorism Forum (a new multilateral forum consisting of 30 member states spearheaded by the US and Turkey) used, in its recent *Rome Memorandum*, the terminology of 'Good Practices for Rehabilitation and Reintegration of Violent Extremist Offenders' as did the Roundtable Expert Meeting and Conference on Rehabilitation and Reintegration of Violent Extremist Offenders, co-organised by ICCT – The Hague and UNICRI, in their paper *Core Principles & Good Practices*.
>
> (Schmid 2013, 49)

Coming back to the observation regarding the confusion pinned to the concept of de-radicalisation, whence, one has to ask, does it emanate? An immediate and obvious starting place is the conflation of de-radicalisation with concepts and discourses of other knowledge domains. The following statement highlights the confusion surrounding the concept of de-radicalisation, which is being complicated by two different concerns – 'extremism' and 'terrorism'.

58 *Analysis of research data*

> So the problem is when you have that approach and you use the term de-radicalisation, you could easily say that what you are trying to do is make someone not extreme. In order to deal with the threat of terrorism you have to tackle all radical and extremist thinking. That becomes problematic because how then do you define extremist and radical thinking (?) ... We need to focus on the issue of terrorism rather than the issue of extremism per se because the language of extremism is muddying the waters.
>
> (Interview 10, Investigative journalist)

The respondent believes that the language of 'extremism' rather than 'terrorism' is 'muddying the waters'. The confusion surrounding the meaning of de-radicalisation is also noted in the literature by John Horgan (2008). Horgan has identified a plethora of terms that are used in the same context as de-radicalisation and yet contain subtle differences in meaning and subsequently pose different policy ramifications. For example, terms like 'rehabilitation', 'desists', 'de-legitimisation', 'socialisation', 'de-programming' and 'dialogue' are used to refer to de-radicalisation programmes. It is also employed interchangeably in the discourse with other terms like 'disengagement' and 'counter-radicalisation'. This, again, was reflected in the fieldwork data. A good example of this loose and interchangeable use of terms is the way that, for many, the term 'violence' was used synonymously with the term 'terrorism', as well as other concepts like 'extremism', 'non-violent extremism' and 'violent radical'. By the same token, de-radicalisation is used by interviewees in some instances in the same sense of 'counter-ideology', 'disaffiliation' and 'counter-brainwashing'.

Other preliminary reasons for the definitional quagmire de-radicalisation finds itself in include the fact that many policymakers lack the knowledge to tackle radicalisation, the fact that policymakers have alternative political objectives to accomplish, and the fact that ambiguous definitions and terms can still function practically, as demonstrated through Wittgenstein's 'language games' and 'family resemblance'. This semantic logic is a better way to understand definitions than the designative logic, because it is based on grouping common features under the same term rather than concentrating on the veracity of the word to its designative phenomenon in the world. In the end, this section has demonstrated that despite terminological and conceptually opacity, the underlying meaning of de-radicalisation is secured in the 'language games' played in the policy world of Prevent.

The conceptual framework of de-radicalisation

There are four main understandings of the concept of de-radicalisation, which include:

1   Counter-violence (renunciation)
2   Counter-ideology/extremism (non-violent)

3   Re-integration of individuals into mainstream society
4   Youth empowerment.

The first interpretation views de-radicalisation as a way of getting radicalised and militant individuals to abandon their use/support for violence. The data conveys that 16 interviewees, almost 60 per cent of the sample, believed the de-radicalisation signified a move 'away from violence'. This also represents Prevent's conceptions of de-radicalisation and essentially aims to reduce the risk of violence committed on British soil by intervening in the worldview of the militant before they cross the line. The following respondent explains the logic underpinning this predominant interpretation of de-radicalisation.

> It's just reversing radicalism and getting extremist ideas out of people's heads and especially violent extremist. Many committed terrorists in countries like Saudi Arabia and Egypt have admitted their path was wrong and have publicly recanted.
>
> (Interview 25, Quilliam analyst)

This view of de-radicalisation is posited as a solution to the security threat posed by transnational terrorism, which security thinking post 7/7 believes is primarily motivated by a perverse and dangerous ideology. The assumption underlying cognitive change in conceptions of de-radicalisation is that the justification for violence by militants is sanctioned by a particular ideology; de-radicalisation is therefore about dislodging the theoretical construct behind it. In other words, ideology and/or a set of particular ideas are a causal factor in pathways towards terrorism. Hence whilst de-radicalisation purportedly aims to achieve behavioural change, i.e. to stop terrorism, behaviour change is considered secondary to cognitive change. It is in this sense that de-radicalisation is presented as a strategy that seeks to tackle the ideas that lead to violence:

> De-radicalisation, to do it, you need to be able to deconstruct the ideas that formed in that person's mind and give him a better way of understanding the proof and evidences that led him to those thoughts. Plus we have to give him an alternative to taking that course of action.
>
> (Interview 23, Director of prison intervention provider)

The second interpretation presents de-radicalisation as an attempt to counter the ideology of extremism in a broad sense and not just the way it is deployed by militants seeking to justify violence:

> Having said that, it's equally possible to see de-radicalisation has been part of the process that is not at all concerned about people's behaviour or about moving people away from violence, whether it's gang violence or extreme violence, but it's more about de-radicalising people from this ideology.
>
> (Interview 17, former Head of counter-terrorism unit)

60   *Analysis of research data*

In contrast to the first conception of de-radicalisation, an alternative view of counter-ideology, one that emphasises the political, social and cultural threat of such ideas, was articulated by a number of interviewees. This alternative interpretation suggests that the theological-political framework underpinning 'violent-extremist' ideology (outlined in the next section), is re-framed and represented as the framework underpinning the ideology of 'non-violent extremists'.

> The Salafis, some of the Brotherhood groups, Hizb-el-Tahrir, basically preached in this country for many years that a good Muslim cannot integrate and be a loyal citizen of this country; cannot serve in the military or the police because that's allegiance to a Kufr system or man-made laws; so a lot of these Islamist ideas are holding back Muslims in this country and also it kind of builds up rage, with an over emphasis on foreign policy.
>
> (Interview 25, Quilliam analyst)

This interpretation of ideology is more expansive than the first because it is not only concerned with tackling the threat of violence. It is an interpretation that consequently bought many individuals and groups into the category of 'extremism'. The category 'extremist' encompassed 'non-violent' individuals, as well as violent individuals on the cusp of radicalisation towards terrorism. Indeed this new categorisation was introduced with the second revision of Prevent in 2009. It was not merely violence therefore that was problematic but also issues like 'integration', 'citizenship' and 'loyalty' to Britain. Instead of terrorism therefore this expansive focus on ideology belongs to a strategy of counter-subversion. As a result, with this interpretation of 'worldview' in mind, it became feasible to conceive of a more substantial conception of de-radicalisation, one preoccupied with the purging of political and social spaces of these theological and political ideas in the UK. A former representative of the National Association of Muslim Police (NAMP) draws an analogy between de-radicalisation and the 'detox' of certain ideas.

> I look at it in my head as it being like going to a detox clinic and getting cleansed and you come out and I'm not now on drugs or alcohol or anything. Look, this is not as simple as that ... To answer your question, a journey to radicalisation and backwards, where to a point you are considered by the government to be a saint and don't pose a threat and you hold Islamic values that are compatible with the Prevent strategy.
>
> (Interview 16, Representative of NAMP)

The third interpretation of de-radicalisation evident in the data sees it as a programme designed to re-integrate individuals to the political and social mainstream. Unlike the two previous conceptions, this view of de-radicalisation is less about moving away from radicalisation and extremism and more about emphasising the move towards the mainstream. This view is encapsulated by a retired Police Officer who has served on the Prevent Delivery Board:

Analysis of research data 61

I think the agenda is to stir disaffected young people into the mainstream viewpoint. Getting them to sign up to those elusive British values we were talking about, getting them to sign up to liberal secularism.

(Interview 24, former Chief Inspector and Prevent Board member)

This understanding of de-radicalisation focuses on changing an individual's 'worldview' and moves the concern of policy-makers beyond violence. It suggests that de-radicalisation in the UK shows a greater concern than programmes in the ME and SEA with the adoption of values and norms by individuals undergoing intervention. A closer examination also indicates that this understanding of de-radicalisation is more about the socialisation of individuals, not only into mainstream society, but also towards a political mainstream view. It is therefore a conception that seeks a more substantial transformation in the individual and suggests that in the UK context, it is a necessary but not a sufficient condition to get violent individuals to renounce violence as part of the de-radicalisation process. In other words a necessary and sufficient condition for de-radicalisation to occur entails both abandoning violence, as well as adopting the values and norms of wider society. Two respondents expressed this holistic conception of de-radicalisation in the following ways:

It's almost like mind control, thought control, it's about your thought, your beliefs, your understanding is wrong and we will put you through something that will actually make you have the correct thoughts. It brings us back to the idea that what we are trying to achieve here is a version of Islam that is palatable to a British political mindset.

(Interview 11, Academic)

So you spoke about British values earlier on; if you feel someone isn't well integrated and believes Britain is the enemy and that kind of narrative and that's somebody you consider to be radical, then de-radicalisation is about pacifying this person to try and make him understand that actually, Britain and the West doesn't have a problem with Muslims and British society and values are great.

(Interview 26, Forward Thinking analyst)

The fourth conception of de-radicalisation is preoccupied with youth development and empowerment, in addition to crime prevention strategies. In fact, as seen earlier on, the data indicates that nine interviewees mentioned youngsters in relation to de-radicalisation. This amounts to a third of interviewees and suggests that this feature is unique to the UK context in comparison to de-radicalisation in the ME and SEA For example, here is a Senior Prevent Officer discussing de-radicalisation in terms of crime rehabilitation:

As Police Officers … we've begun a process of holding that persons hand, picking them up, and walking with them; to places where they can get

62   *Analysis of research data*

voluntary experiences, be mentored, and meet people outside his universe of reference; he's never met anybody outside a community other than his own and if he was radicalised, well that's de-radicalisation.

(Interview 22, Senior Prevent Officer)

As indicated in the statement, this view of de-radicalisation has a tenuous link with tackling terrorism and violence at the level of ideas. Another example is also shown below by a community activist, who not only talks in terms of youth empowerment and crime prevention, but also interestingly evokes other phenomena, like extremism and political violence, in her definition of de-radicalisation:

Ideally it's about making disenfranchised young people make the right choices. Deradicalisation could be about any route. So in this instance it should be about becoming extremist Muslim and going to fight wars abroad and stopping that. But it should be about giving young people choice and money should be pumped out, you know, to help them staying out of gangs.

(Interview 13, former Vice-Chair of community organisation)

This conception of de-radicalisation indicates a greater preoccupation with crime prevention strategies than counter-terrorism strategies. In the Prevent strategy for example, de-radicalisation falls under 'supporting vulnerable' individuals and the relationship between preventative approaches to crime and youth empowerment is evident in the police run Channel project. This view of de-radicalisation indicates a pastoral logic, one that extols the importance of caring for 'vulnerable' individuals and 'extremists', and providing them with support, education and resources to overcome radicalisation.

In summation, the data shows that there are multiple understandings of de-radicalisation in the UK context: one concept of de-radicalisation relates to the renunciation, through thought-reform, of violence only; a second conception situates de-radicalisation as part of an attempt to domesticate Islam by suppressing extremism and promoting a more liberal version of Islam in public spaces; the third conception emphasises the need to have individuals adopt the political and social values of the country for a successful de-radicalisation to occur; and the fourth conception situates de-radicalisation within the preventative framework of youth empowerment, probation services and crime prevention. Whilst the data corroborates the overall fact regarding the contested conceptual framework of de-radicalisation presented by Prevent, it expands our understanding of de-radicalisation by bringing to light two other conceptions of de-radicalisation not articulated in the literature.

The role of counter-ideology in de-radicalisation

Almost 89 per cent of interviewees believed that 'cognitive change' in the form of counter-ideology or counter-extremism was a central feature in the

Analysis of research data 63

conceptualisation of de-radicalisation. Given that there is no criminal liability for possessing a particular state of mind, why is the UK's counter-terrorism policy placing particular emphasis on the threat of certain ideas? An immediate answer, argued in Chapter 1, is that the new security paradigm is predicated on the idea that behaviour change (whatever the outcome) is dependent upon cognitive change. In other words, the realm of ideas is conferred with agency, becoming the locus for human behaviour in accounts of radicalisation and de-radicalisation. Another way to put it is that de-radicalisation is an account of human behaviour in which human action in the real world is determined by ideas, beliefs and values. Without delving into the philosophical veracity of such a proposition here, this section is more interested in what ideas actually constitute a threat to policymakers and why. According to interviewees 23 and 25, these ideas are linked primarily to concepts and rulings found in Islamic Jurisprudence surrounding, in no particular order:

1   Jihad ('struggle', but in this context violent struggle)
2   Takffir (rendering someone a non-believer or 'infidel')
3   Khalafa (Islamic political institution akin to a Sultanate)
4   Ummah (General Community of Muslims)
5   Sharia (Islamic Law).

Notably, the majority of interviewees did not go into this much detail. As articulated by almost 50 per cent of interviewees, this type of technical language and specialist knowledge highlights the important role that expertise and knowledge play in constructions of de-radicalisation and the Prevent strategy more generally, an area that will be addressed in Chapters 4 and 6. Nevertheless, according to the data, the five point theological-political formulation above forms the constitutive block of the ideology of violent militants. I am limited by space to elaborate further here; however, Ashour (2012) interestingly identifies eight pillars of violent takffiri ideology, in which he distinguishes between arguments made by militants in Muslim majority countries and militant individuals amongst the Muslim diaspora in the West: (1) 'alhakamiyya', the idea that legislation belongs to God and (2) 'ridda' (the charge of apostasy, or 'takfirr)', which is used pejoratively to de-legitimise pretty much anyone, including Muslims. Both (1) and (2) legitimise (3) Jihad (meaning 'struggle' but in this context holy war); (4) the visibility of change (that change only comes by the bullet and the failure of other means) and (5) the inevitability of conflict between good and bad. Pillars 1–5 form the ideological-political frame legitimising violence in Muslim countries. The other three (6–8) apply to Muslims as minorities in Western societies: (6) defensive jihad (to undertake war as self-defence); (7) 'ahkam al dar' (dividing the world into two camps – the abode of Islam vs. the abode of War); (8) al wala' wa a bara' (loyalty and animosities, pledging allegiance to your group and leader).

In any case, a major component of de-radicalisation programmes is the use of counter-ideology and theological discussions with inmates. Theological dialogue

64 *Analysis of research data*

is predicated on the idea that militant extremists follow an incorrect understanding of Islam (the eight pillars mentioned above) and a crucial dimension therefore of de-radicalisation intervention has been religious doctrinal revision. Here, de-radicalisation in Egypt was distinguished for its pioneering work on theological doctrinal revision in the 1990s. The whole process involved dynamic interaction between inmates and charismatic leaders and discussions with Al-Azhar (the leading Islamic institution in the World) imams. Notably, the comprehensive de-radicalisation of the Islamic Group (IG) in 2007 was accompanied by the publication of 25 volumes of doctrinal revisions. Similarly, the de-radicalisation of Al-Jihad in 2007–08 resulted in the publication of two books by former Al-Qaeda ideologue and Emir (leader) of al-Jihad Dr. Sayyid Imam al-Sharif (Ashour 2012, 124).

Similar to the counter-ideological efforts in programmes in the ME and SEA, the Prevent strategy's conception of de-radicalisation, shared in fact by some of the interviewees, is that this 'worldview' causes violence and must consequently be challenged. However, as confirmed by the data, many interviewees believed that the focus on ideology was not merely confined to the problem of violence but applied also to the perceived problem of the subversive threat posed by Muslim mobilisation, the threat to community cohesion as a result of illiberal values and the inability of 'vulnerable' Muslim youth to effectively think through ideology and make the right choices. In other words, ideology is represented as a pervasive and penetrating force that guides the action of both the radicalised Muslim and the Orientalised Muslim. This type of agency is transferred not merely to ideology but also to Islam more generally. And this is where de-radicalisation in the European context differs to how it is understood in other parts of the world.

There is, therefore, an important caveat to consider about discussions on 'cognitive change' in the literature. It is not always clear what is meant by 'cognitive change'. On the one hand there is unequivocal agreement that at a policy level it entails changing attitudes towards violence. On the other hand, there is also recognition that, conceptually, de-radicalisation is about the softening of views and attitudes with respect to issues like democracy and women's rights, which are important to 'reintegrate into mainstream society'. For example, whilst Rabasa *et al.* (2010) and Demant *et al.* (2008) do not advance a conceptual framework for de-radicalisation, the authors of both reports nevertheless stress the significance of a particular type of 'cognitive change', one entailing belief change on issues like democracy and women's rights. Rabasa *et al.* and Demant *et al.* therefore present an expansive view of de-radicalisation, one in which substantial 'cognitive change' occurs when participants in these programmes not only abandon violence but also embrace the views and norms of the host society.

In contrast, both Ashour and Horgan, who write about prison de-radicalisation, conceptualise de-radicalisation as being about getting violent takfirri jihadists to abandon violence. In fact Ashour explicitly states that de-radicalisation in Egypt is not about changing attitudes towards democracy and other norms, claiming that many de-radicalised groups still uphold

Analysis of research data 65

'misogynist, homophobic, xenophobic, and anti-democratic views' (Ashour 2009, 6). Cognitive change, therefore, does not entail the adoption of liberal values and norms that has become associated with de-radicalisation in the European context (Demant *et al.* 2008, 13; Rabasa, *et al.* 2010, 2). Consequently, Horgan's and Ashour's studies on de-radicalisation suggest a disjuncture between de-radicalisation as a notion (changing their view on a whole range of issues) and actual de-radicalisation as practice (merely getting them to stop violence).

An important and striking question arises from the focus on counter-ideology which dominates interviewees' understanding of de-radicalisation in the data and in the Prevent policy generally: de-radicalisation is predicated on the idea of a quick fix – the undoing of years of social and behavioural conditioning that has led an individual person to harbour certain views or engage in terrorist activities. Is this linear process of moving from a violent state to a non-violent state through re-education feasible?

Examining three different accounts of exit from violence will help us with this difficult question. First, based on interviews with terrorists, Horgan identifies two factors of disengagement – psychological and physical. Psychological factors include (Horgan 2009, 21–22):

- Disillusionment arising from incongruence between the initial ideals and fantasies that shape a person's initial involvement and their subsequent experiences with the reality of what is entailed by involvement – in other words, the mismatch between the fantasy and the reality;
- Disillusionment arising from disengagement over tactical issues;
- Disillusionment arising from strategic, political or ideological differences;
- Becoming burned out;
- Changing personal priorities.

Whereas physical factors include (Horgan 2009, 25):

- Voluntary exit from the movement
- Involuntary exit from the movement
- Involuntary movement into another role
- Voluntary movement into another role
- Involuntary exit from the movement altogether
- Experiences stemming from psychological disengagement that acts as a catalyst for physical disengagement across points 1 to 4 above.

Also, arrest, imprisonment and death are identified by Horgan as the most dramatic examples of physical disengagement (ibid.). These psychological and physical factors can therefore become linked, or occur independently, or converge. Moreover, a salient point about this process is that the occurrence of these factors does not necessarily lead to complete and total disengagement; it may lead instead to 'role change' (Horgan 2009, 26). In this instance the individual

66 *Analysis of research data*

may renounce violence but remain active with the group's activities in another way or role, and uses the example of a known IRA militant who moved away from a militant role to a political role in Sinn Fein (ibid.). An interesting point about Horgan's disengagement process is the absence of ideology as a motivating factor in disengagement, which is a notable area of contention in the literature and de-radicalisation programmes.

Meanwhile, Tore Bjorgo (2009) draws on interview data (50 individuals) in order to shed further light on disengagement processes but from the perspective of right-wing extremism. Bjorgo makes a distinction between 'push' and 'pull' factors (2009, 36–40). 'Push' factors include:

- Negative social sanctions that may cause some to reconsider their affiliation. These may range from parental scolding and social isolation to criminal persecution and harassment or violence by militant anti-racists (Bjorgo 2009, 36);
- Loss of faith in the ideology and politics of the group or movement;
- A feeling that 'things are going too far' (Bjorgo 2009, 37);
- Disillusionment with the inner workings and activities of the group;
- Losing confidence, status and position in the group (Bjorgo 2009, 38); and
- A feeling of exhaustion and that they can no longer take the pressure.

'Pull' factors in contrast refer to factors attracting the person to a more rewarding alternative. These include:

- A longing for the freedoms of a normal life (Bjorgo 2009, 39);
- Activists feeling they are getting too old for what they are doing;
- Activists caring about career prospects and personal futures; and
- Establishing a family with new responsibility for spouse and children (Bjorgo 2009, 40).

Moreover Bjorgo believes that 'how' questions are more useful than the 'why' questions when trying to persuade an individual to leave an extremist or violent group (2009, 42). He identifies three main strategies to facilitate disengagement: individuals need to make a public break with the group and therefore renounce the attitudes and ideologies it represents (ibid.); breaking with the group without breaking the ideology (2009, 43); third, a quiet and gradual withdrawal. Interestingly, Bjorgo concludes the following:

> Anti-racist campaigns with a focus on ideology and values – the favourite measure of politicians who 'want to do something against racism and right-wing extremism' – are not likely to have much effect in terms of preventing youths from joining racist groups or of inducing anyone to quit such groups.
>
> (2009, 48)

As a result of the stress on behavioural approaches to the understanding of disengagement, the role of counter-ideology as a factor in disengagement is

Analysis of research data 67

disregarded. The behaviour over cognitive approach has been translated into real life through the EXIT programmes in Scandinavian and other European countries (Norway, Sweden, Finland, Germany and the Netherlands) that deal with right-wing extremism, a project Bjorgo has influenced and been involved with (2009, 47).

The previous two accounts of pathways out of violence have been about disengagement. The only real attempt to understand the process of de-radicalisation directly, therefore, has been that of Omar Ashour (2009). Ashour's study is based on case study examination of collective de-radicalisation efforts in Egypt and Algeria and uses comparative qualitative research that combines content analysis and interviews (2009, 17). His analysis shows that the de-radicalisation process relies on the dynamic interplay between the following factors:

- State repression: this incorporates a range of actions by the state to bring about political quiescence – restrictions on free speech, violation of rights, such as torture and imprisonment, as well as state sponsored terror in the form of assignations, civilian slaughters and mass-murders (Ashour 2009, 14–15).
- Selective inducements (material incentives: refers to explicit or implicit socio-political/socio-economic incentives to Islamist movements, which include ceasing systematic torture or offering a power-sharing formula for participation in the government (Ashour 2009, 15).
- Social interaction with significant others: refers to internal and external interactions with individuals and groups within and outside their own group and with others and takes place mainly in prisons (ibid.).
- Involvement of influential leaders in the process: only leaders/leadership are seen by the majority of followers as pious, theologically knowledgeable and preferably with a history of 'struggle' could cast legitimacy on the de-radicalisation process. Leaders have a considerable influence over followers (Ashour 2009, 15–16).

Ashour states that a combination of all these factors played a role in the de-radicalisation of Islamic Jihad and Islamic Group in Egypt (2009, 102–109). Despite providing the most detailed case study of de-radicalisation in the field, Ashour's work is context specific to Egypt and Algeria. A factor like state repression, for example, is not transferable into de-radicalisation programmes in the UK. In addition, whilst it is clear that counter-ideology played a role in the collective de-radicalisation efforts in Egypt, Ashour's analysis actually demonstrates a more complex picture in which other influences, particularly structural political factors, played a greater role in the de-radicalisation process.

The scant and limited examination of processes, factors and pathways of de-radicalisation in the research field unanimously concludes with three critical points: first, since de-radicalisation programmes include both material and counter-ideological components, it is difficult to evaluate what factors are the most important (Chowdhury and Hearne 2008, 16). Second, the literature shows

68   *Analysis of research data*

that ideological factors play little or no role in persuading individuals to enter or leave such groups and movements (Bjorgo 2009, 36–40). In fact, Horgan and Bjorgo prefer to emphasise disengagement, a behavioural focus, over de-radicalisation, which focuses more on cognitive change. Ashour does consider ideological revisionism and de-legitimisation an integral feature of the de-radicalisation process but, based on the four chief processes that he identifies are needed for successful de-radicalisation, it is clear that counter-ideology plays a limited role in contrast to state repression, selective inducements and the role of leaders. This fact was strikingly corroborated by the findings of a study of 145 people across four European member states on behalf of the European Commission, published by the Change Institute in 2008 (one of the very few empirical studies done in radicalisation studies). The report − 'Beliefs, ideologies and narratives of violent radicalisation' − concluded that developing and promoting counter ideologies is unlikely to suffice in itself (2008, 140) and that:

> ... there is little, if any, historical evidence that ideology, whether radical, violent or otherwise, can be defeated solely by the employment of a counter-ideology. More often ideology collapses or comes to be seen as redundant as its explanatory power comes into question in the face of accumulating evidence that it is unable to explain.
>
> (Change Institute 2008, 143)

Finally, one reading actually points to the fact that material provisions are more influential than counter-ideology in the de-radicalisation process, exemplified by Abuza's (2009) review of de-radicalisation programmes in Indonesia, Malaysia and Singapore targeted at Jimaah Islamyia (JI) militants. He conveys that many of those 'de-radicalised' remain committed to the goals of JI in establishing an Islamic state and the imposition of Sharia (Bjorgo and Horgan 2009, 194). He observed that those detainees completing de-radicalisation programmes still had a commitment to Sharia and maintained their 'cognitive radicalism' (Abuza 2009, 211). Perhaps more interesting is the fact that many segments of society would 'not think JI did anything wrong in the first place' (Abuza 2009, 194). Abuza writes about how providing support for detainees' families had a dramatic impact on detainees involved in de-radicalisation programmes, leading the overseers of the programme to conclude that the 'economic aid, however, is ultimately more important than religious arguments in changing prisoners' attitudes' (ibid.). The evidence, in short, emanating from reports of de-radicalisation programmes in different parts of the world strongly demonstrates the futility of counter-ideology on its own in leading to successful de-radicalisation.

Why, then, does Prevent adhere to the notion that counter-ideology is the saving grace of counter-terrorism? After all, the first pillar of Prevent is countering ideology (HO 2011, 43−54) and, as we have seen, de-radicalisation (which forms the second pillar of Prevent) is also synonymous with counter-ideology. There is limited space here to discuss the prominence of ideology, despite its acknowledged limited role in both the radicalisation and de-radicalisation

Analysis of research data 69

process, but an answer to this conundrum is adumbrated in Chapters 4–6. In the meantime, a few brief suggestions regarding the ubiquity of ideology in security thinking will suffice for now: first, it enables policymakers to problematise a foreign ideology instead of its own structural and political issues; it distances and delegates the responsibility for finding solutions to the problem of radicalisation away from government and onto civil society and individual level therapeutic interventions; it justifies interventionist policies in the theological and political lives of Muslims in society so as to transform their behaviour within British society, and it enables the expansion of governmental remit and intervention beyond terrorism and into other spheres of life, leading to an enhanced degree of control and order. The problematisation opened up by placing ideology at the heart of counter-terrorism policy is aptly summarised by the investigative journalist:

> Is it your views on women? Or your views on democracy? Or your views on foreign policy? Or is it your views on domestic policy? Or is it your views on violence? … they're saying it's not just about terrorism and violence, it's about all these other things that somehow make you vulnerable to the violent part.
>
> (Interview 10, Investigative journalist)

As this statement implies, the focus of de-radicalisation has moved far away from terrorism. The next section elaborates the implications of the data in more details.

The implications of multiple conceptions of de-radicalisation

What are the implications of having four different conceptions of de-radicalisation in the data? And what does it mean in terms of understanding the ontological framework of de-radicalisation? It reveals three important elements to consider: (1) de-radicalisation in the UK suffers from definitional and conceptual confusion; (2) de-radicalisation as an intervention indicates a disarrayed policy logic at the heart of the UK counter-terrorism strategy; (3) the data shows the limits of the inductive method in understanding de-radicalisation, suggesting both an academic and policy imperative to find an alternative conceptualisation of de-radicalisation

Regarding conceptual confusion, the data corroborates findings in the literature that de-radicalisation as a term and concept 'meant different things to different people'. John Horgan, for example, critiques current understandings of de-radicalisation for failing to distinguish between cognitive and behavioural dimensions of de-radicalisation (2008; Bjorgo and Horgan 2009). De-radicalisation is predicated on the reorientation of the 'worldview' and the cognitive shift of detainees taking part in such programmes (Bjorgo and Horgan 2009, 5). However, one aim of de-radicalisation is to get armed Islamist groups to renounce violence, which is in fact a behaviour change, also known as

70   *Analysis of research data*

'disengagement'. Unlike de-radicalisation, disengagement does not require a change of ideals or views but only the renunciation of violence. He therefore argues that the most significant problem with current assumptions about de-radicalisation is the failure to divorce behavioural and cognitive dimensions conceptually. In other words, it is based on the misleading assumption that 'radical views predict radical behaviour' (ibid.). Instead, Horgan argues that the relationship between behaviour and cognition and how they interact is more complex than previously understood. Contrary to misconceptions, research demonstrates that, more often than not, extremist views are acquired after an individual joins a group and not before (ibid.). Based on the principle that behavioural changes can and do occur before changes to the views of militant individuals, Horgan emphasises the need to focus more on disengagement.

Meanwhile, this confusion between cognitive-behavioural factors is avoided by Omar Ashour (2009). Ashour situates de-radicalisation as a process of relative change which occurs at the collective level within Islamist movements (2009, 5). It does not thus address the strict conceptual separation between behaviour and cognitive variables as a process at an individual level. Instead Ashour distinguishes three different levels of de-radicalisation (ibid.: 6):

1   Behavioural: refers to groups abandoning the use of violence.
2   Ideological: relates to the de-legitimisation of violence.
3   Organisational: refers to the demobilisation of members and can only occur after the first two levels are achieved.

In contrast to Horgan, Ashour is more open about the potential of cognitive change in inducing a more 'substantive' level of de-radicalisation through the delegitimising of violence in counter – ideological provisions. In addition, Ashour's conceptualisation encompasses three dimensions (ibid.):

1   Pragmatic: refers to behavioural de-radicalisation without ideological change.
2   Substantive: this encompasses both behavioural and ideological changes.
3   Comprehensive: this occurs when de-radicalisation happens at all three levels.

Indeed the categorisation of different types and levels is useful as a framework to understand de-radicalisation since it does away with problematic dichotomy in the cognitive-behavioural formulation. Ashour offers a conception that does not presume a causal relationship between cognitive and behavioural variables at an individual level. However, the challenge with Ashour's conceptual understanding of de-radicalisation is that it is context specific. De-radicalisation in Europe, for example, appears to be concerned with processes at the individual level and does not occur amidst the same influences inherent to Egypt and Algeria, e.g. repression by the state in processes of de-radicalisation, and thus questions arise regarding the transferability of his framework.

Analysis of research data   71

So Horgan avoids the concept because it confuses policy whilst Ashour's conception of de-radicalisation is referring to a different dynamic to that articulated in the UK context. My fieldwork data reaffirms this confusion but to a more radical degree. But which of the four interpretations of de-radicalisation accurately embodies the idea and practice of de-radicalisation in the UK? Could all four interpretations be valid? It is in this way that de-radicalisation represents a conceptual confusion. The conceptual confusion surrounding de-radicalisation does not get us closer to a coherent and robust conceptual framework that enables academics to understand the phenomenon properly or even allows policymakers to build an effective policy.

There are two suggestions in the data explaining the confusion about de-radicalisation: the role of experts in formulating concepts of de-radicalisation and the impact the concept of radicalisation has had in the way that de-radicalisation developed. For example, eight interviewees mentioned the role of think-tanks in formulating de-radicalisation. Of the eight, six identified the Quilliam Foundation as a key player in shaping de-radicalisation; the other two respondents mentioned the Policy Exchange. This is interesting because de-radicalisation as a policy and idea was not the by-product of Quilliam's work and yet, for six of the interviewees, de-radicalisation is explicitly associated with them. The association of de-radicalisation with the work of Quilliam nevertheless shows the success of Quilliam in being able to position itself as an 'anti-extremism' think-tank, as well as the fact that de-radicalisation connotes counter-ideology; and Quilliam's work has primarily focused on counter-ideology. More will be said on this in Chapter 6. Below, interviewees make the link between de-radicalisation and the influence of the Quilliam Foundation.

> ...you know, people like Quilliam think that you could re-programme these people in a different way, like denazification...
> (Interview 24, former Police Chief Inspector and Prevent Delivery Board member)

> De-radicalisation is the word often used by Majid Nawaz at Quilliam. It's the journey backwards after you've gone on the path of being radicalised but then...
> (Interview 16, Representative of NAMP)

I think it was clear that de-radicalisation, from a government's perspective was to intervene with people whose ideological heart lies in more retribution action against British policy interests. This was defined for instance by Quilliam, and they managed to shift the definition to be wider than it was originally.

> (Interview 2, Director of an organisation countering terrorism on campus)

Meanwhile, the second factor explaining the confusion of de-radicalisation is exemplified by the importation of the ideas, theories and language of radicalisation, which had predated the emergence of de-radicalisation as a policy in 2011.

72 *Analysis of research data*

Indeed, as illustrated in the second section of this chapter, seven interviewees mentioned radicalisation in conjunction with de-radicalisation. This shows that for more than 25 per cent of the interviewees, de-radicalisation was understood in relation to radicalisation, a relationship which will be explored in Chapter 4.

Despite the discernible relationship between both concepts, each has its origins in different genealogies. As enumerated in the introduction of this book, most of the literature on de-radicalisation is based on work undertaken in other places before 2006, as well as according to completely different contexts. De-radicalisation in the ME and SEA was concerned with terrorism and not radicalisation. However, in contrast to the ME and SEA, the UK conceptualised the 'new security threat' posed by transnational terrorism in the register of 'radicalisation', with the UK government sponsoring the codification of radicalisation as a body of knowledge to accompany its move towards preventative approaches in counter-terrorism. By 2011, the discourses on radicalisation had formed into a body of knowledge with its own theories, experts and concepts. Chapter 1 explicates how the discourse on radicalisation encompassed a number of concurrent discursive formations, which included the security discourse, the integration and identity discourse, and discourses on Islam and Muslims, amongst others.

The by-product of the discursive explosion on radicalisation was a particular thinking that shaped the formation of de-radicalisation interventions in the UK. This includes the primacy of tackling the ideology of radicalised subjects, the fact that it targets individuals, the existence of a linear process and the importance of identity. Hence while the definition of de-radicalisation in Prevent 2011 adopts the language found in the literature that conceives de-radicalisation in terms of 'cognitive' and 'behavioural' change, in reality, de-radicalisation interventions through Channel indicate a greater affiliation with the thinking produced by radicalisation discourses. This explains some of the confusion surrounding de-radicalisation that is evident in the data. The influence of radicalisation theories on de-radicalisation is articulated by the former President of a student society:

> De-radicalising people – what a stupid and horrible thing to do; if you are talking about radicalisation as someone becoming extremists then you need to know what makes an extremist in the first place and is going to go on and be a terrorist. As far as I understand it there's no roadmap to say that A+B+C+D equals terrorist. Actually quite the opposite; I guess this deradicalisation process, which you have noted here, and perhaps Prevent is trying to do, relies on there being this conveyor belt to a person becoming a terrorist.
>
> (Interview 3, former President of a student society)

Now, the second significant implication of the data is that the four interpretations of de-radicalisation highlights the fact that de-radicalisation is a muddled policy. As explained in the Introduction to this book, the conflation of several policy domains is manifested in Prevent's conception of de-radicalisation: a policy

Analysis of research data 73

designed to 'reverse radicalism' is situated in a preventive strategy and then compared to crime prevention. Similarly, the four interpretations correspond to four different policy domains and agendas: the first interpretation of de-radicalisation, getting individuals to abandon violence, fits with the counter-terrorism agenda. This is motivated by the need to secure the lives of citizens, manage the backlash against Western military involvement in Muslim-majority lands, and the implementation of risk-management strategies and institutional resilience building.

The second interpretation, where de-radicalisation is about counter-ideology in a broad sense, in which Salafi and Islamist ideas and practices are purged from public spaces, coupled with the promotion of 'moderate Islam', fits in with a strategy of counter-subversion. This interpretation views political and religious Muslims as subversive elements within the UK that need to be disciplined and controlled. Here analogies with the counter-subversion of the Communists and the Trade Union movement in Britain during the Cold War can be made. In the Introduction to this book I briefly mentioned the role of RICU in Prevent. What is striking, amplifying the confusion surrounding the idea of de-radicalisation even further, is that RICU's work is associated with 'attitudinal and behavioural change', with one of its objectives said to be a 'reconciled Muslim identity' (Cobain *et al*. 2016). Despite, therefore, being separate programmes altogether with distinct remits – RICU's work is focused on counter-narrative and public communication (ideas), whereas Channel is about 'supporting vulnerable people (people) – both are associated with the same end goals of de-radicalisation interventions.

The third interpretation of de-radicalisation, which conceives it as a policy designed to re-integrate individuals into mainstream society, relates to the community cohesion agenda. This interpretation is a complex one given that it brings together a number of issues and concerns regarding the integration of Muslims in Britain and the political and national identity of Britain. Hence problems related to immigration, anti-EU sentiments amongst the public and the rise of a neo-nationalism are conflated into the integration agenda. As part of the discourse of the integration agenda, the position of Muslims vis-à-vis the majority is debated, their loyalty is questioned, and norms and values acquire greater significance in discourse and social and political practice. This interpretation consequently places emphasis on the adoption of British values and norms by Muslims.

The last interpretation of de-radicalisation stresses the development of youth, which relates to work done in crime prevention. The onus in crime prevention is on the pastoral care of youngsters through mentoring, courses and relationship building. Since the majority of those deemed radical in the UK are youngsters, the aim of this policy logic is to prevent them from becoming radicals further up the line. These policies often involved the probation services, parents and a number of other agencies.

Ultimately, the data shows that de-radicalisation as a policy exhibits a tangled logic in which it performs the functions of counter-terrorism, counter-subversion,

74 *Analysis of research data*

community cohesion and crime prevention altogether. Insofar as de-radicalisation encompasses all four logics, then it is clear to see that it represents an incoherent policy that moves the concern of policymakers far beyond terrorism.

The last significant implication of the data is that it reveals the limit of the inductive method. De-radicalisation suffers from poor definition and is conceptually confusing: is it, in other words, about tackling violence, ideology, identity, crime or the management of risk? This is also complicated by conflicting policy logics: is it governed by the objectives of counter-terrorism, counter-subversion, community cohesion or crime prevention? And the primacy of ideology in de-radicalisation has made the boundaries between legitimate and illegitimate thinking and behaviour murky. Taken altogether, the data demonstrates the fact that de-radicalisation rests on a weak conceptual framework. It shows the disjuncture between the idea and practice of de-radicalisation and between preventive notions of counter-terrorism and the reality of counter-terrorism. When we consider the additional lacuna in the literature with regards to the absence of robust research on de-radicalisation, the non-existent empirical basis for de-radicalisation and the unavailability of data on intervention programmes, then the picture of what we know and can confidently pronounce on de-radicalisation is grim. To that effect, the data reveals how little we continue to know about de-radicalisation. However, this oblique state of affairs with respect to understanding de-radicalisation compels us to search for an alternative way of conceptualising it. A sketch of the contours such a concept will take will be outlined in Chapter 3.

References

Abuza, Z. (2009). 'The disengagement and rehabilitation of Jemaah Islamiyah detainees in Southeast Asia: a preliminary assessment', in *Leaving Terrorism Behind: Individual and Collective Disengagement*, edited by J. Horgan and T. Bjørgo. New York: Routledge.

Ashour, O. (2009). *The De-radicalization of Jihadists: Transforming Armed Islamist Movements*. New York and London: Routledge.

Ashour, O. (2012). 'Post-Jihadism and the ideological revisions of armed Islamists', in *Contextualizing Jihadi Ideologies*, edited by Z. Kazimi and J. Deol. New York and London: Columbia University Press.

Barrett, R. and Bokhari, L. (2009). 'Deradicalization and rehabilitation programmes targeting religious terrorists and extremists in the Muslim world: an overview', in *Leaving Terrorism Behind: Individual and Collective Disengagement*, edited by J. Horgan and T. Bjørgo. New York: Routledge

Bjorgo, T. (2009). 'Processes of disengagement from violent groups of the extreme right', in *Leaving Terrorism Behind: Disengagement from Political Violence*, edited by T. Bjorgo and J. Horgan. New York: Routledge.

Bjorgo, T. and Horgan, J. (eds) (2009). *Leaving Terrorism Behind: Disengagement from Political Violence*. New York: Routledge.

Chowdhury, N. and Hearne, E.B. (2008). *Beyond Terrorism: Deradicalization and Disengagement from Violent Extremism*. International Peace Institute, New York, http://ipacademy.org/media/pdf/publications/beter.pdf.

Analysis of research data 75

Change Institute (2008). *The Beliefs, Ideologies and Narratives of Violent Radicalisation.* Report for the European Commission. London: The Change Institute, www.change institute.co.uk.

Cobain, I., Ross, A., Evans, R. and Mahmood, M. (2016). 'Revealed: UK's covert propaganda bid to stop Muslims joining Isis', *Guardian*, 2 May 2016, www. theguardian.com/uk-news/2016/may/02/uk-government-covert-propaganda-stop-muslims-joining-isis.

Demant, F., Slootman, M. and Buijs, F. (2008). 'Decline and disengagement: an analysis of processes of deradicalisation', *International Migration and Ethnic Studies*, Amsterdam, http://dare.uva.nl/document/2/64714.

Disley, E., Weed, K., Reding, A., Clutterbuck, L. and Warnes, R. (2011). '*Individual Disengagement from Al Qa'ida-Influenced Terrorist Groups', Rapid Evidence Assessment (Rea) to Inform Policy and Practice in Preventing Terrorism*, RAND Europe, Home Office, UK, www.gov.uk/government/uploads/system/uploads/attachment_data/file/116722/occ99.pdf.

Home Office (HO) (2011). *Prevent, CONTEST 2011*, www.homeoffice.gov.uk/publications/counter-terrorism/prevent/prevent-strategy.

Horgan, J. (2008). 'Deradicalization or disengagement? A Process in need of clarity and a counterterrorism initiative in need of evaluation', *Perspectives on Terrorism*, 2 (4): 3–8.

Horgan, J. (2009). 'Individual disengagement: a psychological analysis', in *Leaving Terrorism Behind: Disengagement from Political Violence*, edited by T. Bjorgo and J. Horgan. New York: Routledge.

Johnson, S. (2009). 'Is the deradicalisation of Islamist extremists possible in a secular society such as Britain?', *PLOIS Journal* 2, University of Leeds, www.polis.leeds. ac.uk/assets/files/students/student-journal/ma-winter-09/sarah-johnson-winter-09.pdf.

Rabasa, A., Pettyjohn, S.L., Ghez, J.J. and Boucek, C. (2010). *Deradicalizing Islamist Extremists*, RAND Corporation, National Security Research Division, www.rand.org/content/dam/rand/pubs/monographs/2010/RAND_MG1053.pdf.

Schmid, A. (2013). *Radicalisation, De-Radicalisation, Counter-Radicalisation: A Conceptual Discussion and Literature Review*, International Centre for Counter Terrorism, Hague, www.icct.nl/download/file/ICCT-Schmid-Radicalisation-De-Radicalisation-Counter-Radicalisation-March-2013_2.pdf.

Taylor, C. (1995). *Philosophical Arguments*. Cambridge: Harvard University Press.

Wittgenstein, L. (1958). *Philosophical Investigations*: Basil Blackwell. Oxford

Yin, R. (2009). *Case Study Research: Design and Methods (Applied Social Research Methods)* (4th edn). London: Sage Publishing.

3 An alternative concept

De-radicalisation as the 'technologies of the self'

This chapter presents the case for conceptualising de-radicalisation as the technologies of the self. The concept of the technologies of the self was formulated by Michael Foucault in a series of seminars at the University of Vermont in 1982. As a context for the summary of his own work on the subject, Foucault proposes four major types of technologies, 'each a matrix of practical reason', that 'human beings use to understand themselves': (1) technologies of production, (2) technologies of sign systems, (3) technologies of power and (4) technologies of the self (Foucault 1988a: 17). Reflecting on his work, Foucault admits that he concentrated perhaps too much on the technology of domination and power in his earlier work and that he was more and more turning towards the study of the technologies of self, 'the interaction between oneself and others ... the history of how an individual acts upon himself...' (Foucault 1988a, 18). The technologies of the self are defined as that:

> ...which permit individuals to effect by their own means or with the help of others a certain number of operations on their bodies and souls, thoughts, conduct, and the way of being, so as to transform themselves in order to attain a certain state of happiness, purity, wisdom, perfection, or immortality.
>
> (Foucault 1988a, 18)

As a self-steering mechanism, the technologies of the self, developed in later works, comprise four critical dimensions (Foucault 1998b, 26–28; 1997, 263–266; Dean 2010, 26–27):

1. Ontology: what is the part of oneself that is the object of thought and work? Foucault's answer to this question is the 'ethical substance'. In other words is one working on thoughts, body, desire or identity, etc.? For example, in Christian ethics one works on the flesh, whereas in sports, the body.
2. Ascetics: how does the self achieve the ethical goal? How is the ethical substance worked upon? This takes the form of exercises and techniques and other practices (confession, diary writing, group discussions, etc.).
3. Deontology: this relates to the question of 'who' we are when we are governed in such a way (e.g. active jobseekers in social programmes). 'Is it as a

The 'technologies of the self' 77

member of a kin group or nation or religious tradition that one should observe them, or as an occupant of a particular social status?' (Laidlaw 2014, 103).

4 Teleology: this is concerned with 'why' we are governed and the ends sought. What is the mode of being the subject aims to achieve? What codes of knowledge support these ideals, and to what ethical valorisation are they tied (salvation, money, beauty, etc.)? (Rose 1996, 133).

These four dimensions notably constitute the ontological conditions and techniques involved in the formation of the self. The fourfold is deployed to interpret de-radicalisation as the technologies of the self as part of UK governmentality (more in the next section). For example, the conventional view of de-radicalisation is that it is an attempt to tackle the ideology (Islamism) and cognitive dimension of 'radicals' (ontology), through the practice of interventions, programmes and pastoral techniques (ascetics), targeting general Muslim citizens and radicalised Muslim subjects in particular (de-ontology), for the purposes of behaviour change, which means the abandonment of violence (telos).

However, this book offers a modification of Foucault's concept of the technologies of the self. Although the four step breakdown accurately describes what the technologies of the self entails, in the context of de-radicalisation, the real difference concerns 'teleology', because the real goal is less about abandoning violence and more the reconfiguration of citizenship and the production of politically approved subjectivity. Although his conception situated self fashioning as a form of freedom undertaken by individuals, I will use it more explicitly to conceptualise the focus of governmentality with the conduct of individual citizens. As I will elaborate further on, while it is true that governmentality also explains the governing of collective populations, I will demonstrate that the concept of the technologies of the self is suitable in capturing the focus of de-radicalisation in the UK with individuals and not groups and networks. I also want to deploy it in an expansive sense to include the way that *all individuals* and not just radicalised individuals fall under the preview of de-radicalisation. There is a sense that all citizens and subjects should scrutinise and hold their ideas in check in relation to Islamist thinking and practices.

Borrowing therefore the ethical fourfold that constitutes the process of self fashioning, I will present my fieldwork data through the domains of discursive technology (Chapter 4), disciplinary technology (5) and confessional technology (6). Organising the chapters this way enables me to incorporate Foucault's oeuvre over 25 years into my work: discursive technology, which corresponds to early Foucault, disciplinary technology with middle Foucault and confessional with middle-to-late Foucault. It also aligns the interconnected framework that shapes governmental relations that characterise political rationality in the modern age with the ethical constitution of subjects. For example, this form of government power entails the relationship between truth, power and identity or its 'episteme, techne, and its ethos' (Dean 2010, 27). This tripartite formulation corresponds to the ethical components outlined above: ontology (discourse),

78 *The 'technologies of the self'*

ascetics (discipline) and de-ontology (confessional). Chapters 4, 5 and 6 deal with the three technologies involved in producing a particular Muslim subject in the UK. To elaborate further, these are:

1   Discursive technology (truth): At the heart of discursive production is the coupling of knowledge/power. Power deploys knowledge with the help of the human sciences and a plethora of experts to represent objects through the claims of scientific methods and its language. It incorporates both the production of discourse and knowledge, which is about the objectification of objects, events and people in order to manipulate and transform, as well as the construction of representation, which frames things through discourse. This technology codifies and produces the 'problem' and makes it intelligible within structures of governance. As will be argued in Chapter 4, the production of radicalisation constitutes the 'Truth' of de-radicalisation, which formulates the ontological dimension of self-government. Its findings are rendered malleable for concrete action in non-discursive domains (Foucault 1991; Miller, Peter and Rose 1990).

2   Disciplinary technology (power): the punishment of crime evolved from retribution in the pre-modern world to reform and rehabilitation of the criminal in the modern world (Foucault 1991). This rehabilitative model is premised on the logic that transforming the soul leads to changes in behaviour (Foucault 1991, 104–134). The focus is therefore on discipline and control of subjects rather than physical retribution and punishment. Disciplinary technology refers to the way that institutions (Education, Health, Criminal Justice, etc.) interventions (rehabilitative, preventative), programmes, and rationalities of government (civil society) work and operate together to create 'docile subjects'. The discipline and control of populations is achieved through surveillance, judgement and different forms of the 'examination'. This is accomplished through the materialisation of systems of knowledge and normative frameworks known as 'regimes of truth', which subjects internalise. In the context of de-radicalisation, the Channel programme and the Prevent strategy are used to inscribe 'regimes of truth' into the bodies of the population. This is analysed in Chapter 5 and corresponds to the notion of 'ascetics' formulated above.

3   Confessional technology (identity): refers to pastoralist practices in the governance of the population, which focus on the body and soul of the individual, traced to Christian confessional practices, based on the relationship between expert and citizen, in order to acquire knowledge that feeds into discourses, as well as transform the subjectivity of individuals. Although the confessional can also be seen as a form of 'ascetics', this book conceives of the confessional as the deontological dimension of self formation because of the need to highlight the fact that Muslim radicalised subjects have to see themselves as deviant/problematic, that an imposed identity has been constructed through the production of radicalisation, which has to be rejected in favour of a more sanitised identity. Notions of 'sin', 'speaking truth to

The 'technologies of the self' 79

power' and 'redemption', which are characteristic of the confession, do well to capture the fact that radicalised subjects are compelled to view themselves as bad citizens, deviants with pathologies who are need of reform. This will be examined in Chapter 6.

An important addendum to the aforementioned theoretical lens that will be used to analyse the data in Chapters 4–6 must be made. The first concerns how I intend to use the fieldwork data. Chapter 2 discussed some critical reflections regarding fieldwork data, much of which was critical of the data. In subsequent chapters, I am not using the data in a critical way. That is to say, I will not be examining the data or scrutinising the claims and assertions made by interviewees. This is not because I take what interviewees say at face value, nor is it due to a lack of awareness with respect to research reflexivity. On the contrary, I am fully aware of the multiple influences involved in knowledge production, which include: the wider political, social, economic and historical context interviewees are speaking within, the organisational/institutional influences on what they say, complex and diverse personal motivations, the importance of where interviews take place and the level of trust between the interview and interviewee. Knowledge production is thus unequivocally a deeply embedded, multifaceted and complex process. Instead, I deploy the fieldwork data in order to paint what I claim is a coherent picture of de-radicalisation.

Second, the way the data has been organised into sections and chapters follows a particular logic, no matter how arbitrary it may seem upon first glance. Admittedly, some of the data could be organised differently. Some sections in Chapters 5 and 6 can easily sit coherently in alternate chapters. For example, the section on 'supporting vulnerable people' (a second pillar of Prevent) in Chapter 6 could also have been placed in Chapter 5, which examines Prevent more directly. However, I opted to have that section under Confessional technology because it reinforces the pastoral logic underpinning de-radicalisation. It therefore dovetails with the more powerful narrative about the underlying principle of 'redemption' and 'salvation' governing confessional practices we have in our societies today. This is acutely reflected in how 'radical' and 'extremist' young individuals are perceived as 'vulnerable' and how de-radicalisation can, similar to medical treatment, restore the patient back to 'normalcy', i.e. eliminating signs of 'extremism'. A similar rigorous thought process has been applied to the arrangement of the rest of the data in Chapters 4–6.

I want to return to the point regarding the interconnectivity of these technologies and how they shape modern subjects. This is because these technologies form the anonymous structures, networks of knowledge, social and cultural institutions that embody, as well as produce, the structural environment of the subject. All those structures shape people's lives and set the rules or procedures to be followed; they 'determine conduct of individuals' (Foucault 1988a, 17). It is useful to draw analogies here with the way the way the modern subject was created through the discourses on sexuality in nineteenth century England in order to see how the technologies operate in tandem. In the *History of Sexuality*

80 *The 'technologies of the self'*

(1990), Foucault charts a narrative about the two techniques that intersected to create the modern subject: scientific discourse and the confession. The modern subject, according to Foucault, was constituted as the source of deep inner 'truth' about itself.

However, instead of the subject as a sexual being, we now have the subject as a 'radical'/'extreme' being. If the modern subject for Freud was the locus of private desires and intentions over against public action, then the Prevent subject is the location of 'risk' festering in the minds of the Muslim subject. It is incumbent on the modern subject, as envisaged in Prevent, to discover the law of radicalisation, to identify its causes, and work on mitigating, if not entirely eradicating, its effects. What we have, in effect, is the fictitious unity of non-violent ideology, extremism and vulnerability as a causal principle of radicalisation. Like the sexualised being that is an artefact of Freudian discursivity, the radicalised Muslim subject is the artefact of discursive, disciplinary and confessional technologies of the past few decades.

It is also important at this juncture to clarify what is meant by 'technology' in the mechanistic formulation of the 'technologies of the self'. Nikolas Rose provides a comprehensive definition of Foucauldian understanding of technology as:

> ...any assembly structure by a practical rationality governed by a more or less conscious goal. Human technologies are hybrid assemblages of knowledge, instruments, persons, systems of judgment, building and spaces, underpinned at the programmatic level by certain presuppositions about, and objectives for, human beings.
>
> (Rose 1996, 131–132)

In other words, 'technologies' encompasses all those things that go into shaping the self in our contemporary society. Technologies are always local and multiple and enable the implementation of corrective interventions in order to accomplish particular ends:

> ...our very experience of ourselves as certain persons – creatures of freedom, of liberty, of personal power, of self-realisation – is the outcome of a range of human technologies, technologies that takes modes of being human as their object.
>
> (Rose 1996, 131–132)

Now, it must be said that the technologies of the self are compatible with the post-modern take on identity that conceives the self as emerging as a result of discourse and regular self-fashioning practices. Indeed, the post-modern concept of the self posits the self as emerging in response to linguistic practices and culturally available narrative forms (Hall and Du Gay 1996). It is a conception critical of the Enlightenment conception of an autonomous, rational and disengaged self. This is why, despite Foucault's constant interest in the theme of the

The 'technologies of the self' 81

subject, he did not develop a theory of the subject. He refused to set up a theory of the subject for the reason that

> ...beginning from the theory of the subject, you come to pose the question of knowing, for example, how such and such a form of knowledge was possible.
>
> (Foucault 1987, 121)

According to Foucault, setting an a priori theory of the subject implies an idea of a universal and timeless subject which attaches people to specific identities, a position he rejected. There is no autonomous transcendent subject which exists outside its context, but rather the subject should been seen as embedded within historical and social context. Stressing the point that the subject is not a substance but a form, Foucault noted that this form is not always identical to itself (Foucault 1987, 121). The subject and the notion of identity is therefore not fixed, but is instead constantly modified.

Notwithstanding the fluidity of identity or the fact that it is negotiable and no longer a given today, paradoxically one of the major drawbacks of the postmodern concept of the subject is the notion of a floating subject that can easily be made and re-made. After all, these accounts present the self as unfixed and 'decentred' (Hall 1996). However, the lack of permanence inherent in conceptions of the 'decentred' subject does not explain adequately the investment individuals make in taking up more secure identity positions. The attempt to soften the term, to acquit it of the charge of 'essentialism' by stipulating that identities are constructed, fluid and multiple – leaves us without a rationale for talking about 'identities' at all and ill equipped to examine the essentialist claims of contemporary identity politics. This is why theorists like Stuart Hall moved away from the notion of identity and preferred to speak about 'identification' (Hall 1996, 16) or Judith Butler in terms of 'performativity' (1990). As Hall asserts, for Foucault the 'decentring of the subject is not the destruction of the subject' (Hall 1996, 27). It is in this way that we should see Foucault's account of the practices of subject self constitution in later seminars, 'The Uses of Pleasure' (1998) and the 'Care of the Self' (1990) as providing a more measured and nuanced position to talk about the 'subject'.

It is important to consider the question of agency here. The biggest criticism levelled at Foucault is that he denies the notion of interiority for the human subject and, more importantly, denies the role of human agency (Laidlaw 2014, 93; McNay 1994; Connolly 1985). In particular, his account in *Discipline and Punishment* depicts the political subjugation of 'docile bodies' in the grip of disciplinary powers and the way the self is produced by processes of objectification, classification and normalisation in the human sciences (Foucault 1991; Connolly 1985). The passive subject is the outcome of power effects, where 'power produces the subject that becomes not a mere fiction of theory and law, but a real artefact' (Connolly 1985, 371). Paradoxically the very analytical theory that situates the subject at the heart of its concerns is also the theory that does away with

82   The 'technologies of the self'

subjectivity. After all, one reading of Foucault's work is that there is no subjectivity outside of discourse practices (McNay 1994, 104).

Foucault himself regarded his 'ethical turn' as a continuation of his earlier
work on the subject but approached from a different angle (Foucault 1998b, 5–6).
In these works, he performs an act of retrieval by immersing himself in the practices of self-fashioning of the Ancient Greeks and Romans, all the way through to
Christian Europe, in order to salvage a way of being that acts as a focal point of
resistance to modern forms of power. This 'ethical turn', therefore, entailed
rethinking the concept of how power worked as well as how the subject was constituted. In his 1982 essay the 'power and the subject' Foucault affirms that power
is only power when it addresses individuals who are free. The word 'power' used
alone is always a short cut to the expression 'the relationship of power' (Foucault
1987, 122). 'Technologies of power and domination' correspond to the relationship between social and economic structures and the relationships between individuals and groups. Those relationships only exist when they are exercised.
Power, according to Foucault, is defined as: 'action on others' actions': that is it
presupposes rather than annuls their capacity as agents' (Foucault 1982, 790).
'Power', he said, 'exists only over free subjects and only insofar as they are free'
(Dreyfus and Rainbow 1983, 221). It is important to note, that the relationships of
power are productive, i.e. they generate particular types of knowledge and cultural order, which is a positive and necessary conception of power, something to
which I'll return in the next section. Linked to this re-conceptualisation of power,
he also proposed two meanings of the word 'subject':

> ...subject to someone else by control and dependence; and tied to his own
> identity by a conscience or self-knowledge. Both meanings suggest a form
> of power which subjugates and makes subject to.
>
> (Foucault 1982, 781)

Foucault also makes the distinction between *the subject* and *the individual*. The
individual is transformed into the subject and the transformations take place as a
result of outside events and actions undertaken by the individual. Indeed,
Foucault's work on the technologies of the self includes analyses on the techniques of self-formation, 'specific techniques that human beings use to understand themselves' (Foucault 1988a, 18). By this point Foucault saw individuals
'as self-determining agents capable of challenging and resisting the structures of
domination in modern society' (McNay 1994, 4). I thus read Foucault's later
works as an attempt to revise some of the overtly limiting space for the subject
within the broad continuity of his oeuvre and not as an abrogation of his previous
positions on power and the subject. Notwithstanding the possibility for agency,
Foucault does not however set the subject free to do just anything. Foucault
explained the change in his thinking on subjectivity:

> I would say that if now I am interested, in fact, in the way in which the
> subject constitutes himself in an active fashion, by the practices of self,

The 'technologies of the self' 83

these practices are nevertheless not something that the individual invents by himself. They are patterns that he finds in his culture and which are proposed, suggested and imposed on him by his culture, his society and his social group.

(Foucault 1997, 291)

Subjects therefore take on different characteristics according to the range of cultural constraints that exist in a particular socio-historical context. Hence while Foucault does endow the subject with the possibility to actively constitute themselves or 'act upon themselves' (Foucault 1988a, 18), they are constrained by the resources available to them and not entirely free to act as they wish. Rose suggests that we understand the material concept of the self through Deleuze's concept of the 'fold' (Rose 1996). The fold is a critique of typical accounts of subjectivity – those that presume a simple interiority and exteriority (appearance and essence, or surface and depth) – for the fold announces that the inside is nothing more than a fold of the outside. Another way of framing the position of the subject and the process of self-formation is through the concepts of structure and agency. It is this small room for choice within wider relations of power that permits Foucault to employ 'technologies of the self' rather than 'technology of the subject'.

In summation, the technologies of the self are thus a third-person material conception of self formation and not a first-person perspective centring on how the 'I' is shaped psychologically or through interiority. Instead, it examines subject formation through the three technologies outlined above – discursive (truth), disciplinary (power) and confessional (identity). It also situates self formation within institutions of government, intervention programmes and governmental policy. In this way it incorporates the way that schools, universities, prisons and governmental agencies play a role in the socialisation of individuals, as well as the relationship between discursive domains and state structures. Another benefit of the technologies of the self is the recognition that knowledge and expertise play a critical role in guiding the lives of individuals, highlighting the ubiquitous mechanism of pastoral power in everyday life. Finally, the technologies of the self accommodate the agency of the self within structures of power and thus offers a sensible take on the relationship between structure and agency. Ultimately, these relations are constructed and historical and are to be addressed from the perspective of government relations, which is addressed in the next section.

Governmentality and bio-politics: 'Omnes et singulatim'

I have mapped out how de-radicalisation should be seen through the concept of the technologies of the self. De-radicalisation, like the technologies of the self, operates on the bodies, souls, thoughts and conduct of individuals in order for those diagnosed as 'radical'/'extremist' to transform themselves. As previously mentioned, the technologies of the self are deployed in this book as a form of

84   *The 'technologies of the self'*

individuating power belonging to governmentality. Before fleshing out how the technologies of the self should be seen as technique of governmentality, I want to bring to light other works on de-radicalisation that also use the theory of governmentality in order to emphasises the novelty of my argument.

There are only two works employing Foucauldian theory, one of which sees prison de-radicalisation as a state's disciplinary technique whereas the other views it within the lens of neo-liberal governmentality. Technically speaking, only the latter account uses governmentality to explain de-radicalisation. However, with the first account, Neil Aggarwal's (2013) journal article tries to establish convergence between Foucault's model of disciplinary power in 'Discipline and Punish' and prison de-radicalisation programmes in the ME and SEA. Aggarwal express reservations about the effectiveness of religious rehabilitative models divorced from political and economic context. As well as identifying the emphasis on a 'religious reform model' in de-radicalisation interventions as the cause of high rates of recidivism (Aggarwal 2013, 274), he concludes that de-radicalisation programmes suggest an attempt of the state to create docile subjects: 'This technical transformation of individuals is an attempt to instil discipline and self-governance to render subjects obedient to the state' (Aggarwal 2013, 272). Aggarwal's contribution to the conceptualisation of de-radicalisation lies in making a link between the discursive production of knowledge on de-radicalisation and programmes of interventions, as well as critically questioning the religious-ideological focus of de-radicalisation programmes. Aggarwal's analysis however, like the bulk of the literature on de-radicalisation, largely depends on the works of Horgan and Ashour and his analysis remains restricted to prison environments. In other words, Aggarwal's analysis is divorced from the realities of de-radicalisation in the UK context.

The second account, a book chapter on de-radicalisation interventions in Denmark by Lasse Lindekilde (2015), is the most relevant reading of de-radicalisation for the UK context. His study presents two crucial additions to other accounts of de-radicalisation in the literature; the first relates to the pastoral dimension of mentoring in de-radicalisation and the second to the fact that de-radicalisation is situated within governmentality. The pastoral dimensions of mentoring of de-radicalisation in the UK context bring to the fore the fact that de-radicalisation interventions are built upon existing crime-prevention infrastructures (Lindekilde 2015, 225). By examining the mentoring aspects of de-radicalisation, Lindekilde elucidates the flexible and pragmatic nature involved in de-radicalisation interventions. For example, he notes the diversity of opinions on what it means to achieve de-radicalisation as the end goal of mentoring interventions and that often the goal of interventions fell short of comprehensive de-radicalisation, which is the formal policy goal of de-radicalisation in counter-radicalisation policies (Lindekilde 2015, 233–4). With regards to the second point, it is through the multifunctional role of the mentor, e.g. mentor as role model, supervisor, coach and 'significant other' (Lindekilde 2015, 232), that he situates the pastoral logic within the workings of neo-liberal governmentality. He also challenges the 'post-political nature' of targeted de-radicalisation

The 'technologies of the self' 85

interventions, which distinguishes it from ordinary crime prevention because it essentially entails protecting individuals against political and religious views (2015, 236).

Lindekilde's analysis echoes a number of key features present in UK de-radicalisation interventions. This includes the fact that de-radicalisation was built on pre-existing crime prevention infrastructure, the multifaceted use of mentors in intervention programmes, the political nature inherent in such programmes, and situating de-radicalisation within neo-liberal governmentality. However, whilst Lindekilde does situate de-radicalisation within policy objectives to re-calibrate counter-radicalisation efforts to narrow the focus of Prevent's activities, it does not directly trace the relationship between discourses on radicalisation and de-radicalisation intervention, nor does it allude to the interplay between discursive domains and their concretisation in institutions and programmes. Yet it has been the discursive production of 'radicalisation' that has distinctively characterised the British experience in relation to fighting terrorism and which much of the literature on de-radicalisation has evaded and overlooked. And whilst he does use the concept of neo-liberal governmentality, he merely suggests that it is enacted through mentors without developing what is meant by governmentality and setting out in detail how it is that the mentors act as a vehicle for the transmission of neo-liberal views and practices. In short, his account provides an incomplete analysis of the relationship between de-radicalisation and governmentality.

I want to rectify the aforementioned theoretical shortcoming here, starting with a definition of the strange word 'governmentality'. As a neologism, 'governmentality' brings together two words: 'government' and 'mentality', resulting in a concept that transforms our understanding of what government is and does. A short definition of the term governmentality is captured by the phrase the 'conduct of conduct' (Burchell *et al.* 1991, 2; Dean 2010, 17). 'Conduct' here refers to the attempt by government to shape with some degree of deliberation aspects of our behaviour according to particular sets of norms and for a variety of ends (Burchell *et al.* 1991, 2; Dean 2010, 18). A more expansive definition of government as the 'conduct of conduct' is:

> any more or less calculate[d] and rational activity, undertaken by a multiplicity of authorities and agencies, employing a variety of techniques and forms of knowledge, that seek to shape conduct by working through desires, aspirations, interests and beliefs of various actors, for definite but shifting ends and with a diverse set of relatively unpredictable consequences, effects and outcomes.
>
> (Dean 2010, 18)

Governmentality therefore refers to political rationalities, or mentalities of rule, where rule becomes a matter of the calculated management of the affairs of each and of all in order to achieve certain desirable objectives (Rose 1996, 134). In his historical examination of governmental practice – the Greek City, Christian

86   The 'technologies of the self'

pastoral power, the early modern European state, the classical liberal state and finally neo-liberalism post World War Two – Foucault found that all concerns of governmental power were linked by a single theme – 'Omnes et singulatim' (all and each). In other words, Foucault saw in Western societies the tendency towards a form of political sovereignty which would be the government of all and each and whose concern would be at once to 'totalise' and to 'individualise' (Burchell *et al.* 1991, 3). Foucault found that the practice of government was characterised by the way it took freedom itself and the 'soul of its citizens' as a correlative objective of its own capacity (Burchell *et al.* 1991, 5) and 'to develop those elements constitutive of individuals' lives in such a way that their development also fosters that of the strength of the state' (McNay 1994, 121).

Significantly, this understanding of governmental power shows the relationship between government and ethics. For example, government takes an interest in promoting lifestyles, knowledges and mentalities that encourage the promotion of health and longevity for its citizens, such as stressing the importance of regulating diet and exercise. In similar fashion, in the context of de-radicalisation, individuals are expected to regulate and refashion their views and behaviours which are deemed 'radical' and 'extremism'. It is important when discussing the relationship between practices of government and ethics to distinguish the practices of the self from the practices of others by government. Whilst governmentality encompasses the notion of the government of self and others, the concept of the technologies of the self refers to the practice of the self. As explained in the previous section, this practice of the self within the sphere of governmental relations presupposes a freedom, which it is critical to single out, given that it provides a means for the resistance to norms of domination. Overall governmentality allows us to place the concern expressed by policymakers through the discursive production of radicalisation and the formulation of de-radicalisation as belonging to the sphere of governmental activities, which is concerned with regulating the behaviour of individuals, and not merely as a policy designed to counter-terrorism.

Another useful concept for us in trying to understand the role of government in shaping the ethics and behaviour of its citizens is the concept is 'bio-politics/power'. The concept 'bio-politics' elucidates historically how governmental practices became concerned with the lives of individuals and whole populations within its territory. Bio-politics signified the way that political rationality became concerned with the 'power over life' above the 'right over death'. In the pre-modern world, for example, power was more appropriately characterised as 'deduction' and 'subtraction', or in terms of seizure: 'in things, time, bodies, and ultimately life itself' (Foucault 1998a, 136). Foucault demonstrates that, with time, the rise of industrialisation, capitalism and the growth of the 'police', this type of deductive power was superseded by a mechanism of power working to 'incite, reinforce, control, monitor, optimize and organize forced under it' (1998a, 136). It led to the development of two poles of power in the beginning of the seventeenth century, both of which come together by the nineteenth century: one of the poles centred on the body, the other the species body. The first relates to the power of the body as machine:

The 'technologies of the self' 87

...its disciplining, the optimization of its capacities, the extortion of its forces, the parallel increase of its usefulness and its docility, its integration into systems of efficient and economic controls, all this was ensured by the procedures of power that characterised the disciplines: an anatimo-politics of the human body.

(Foucault 1998a, 139)

The second pole, concerned with the population, is

...imbued with the mechanics of life and serving as the basis of the biological process: propagation, births and mortality, the level of health, life expectancy and longevity...

(Ibid.)

Both these poles were no longer characterised by the right to kill but by the power to 'invest life through and through' (Foucault 1998a, 139). In short, bio-power was thus concerned with the welfare of individuals as well as collective populations. It is in this sense that government rationality was characterised by the power of individuating, as well as its tendency for totalising rationality. This transformation has considerable consequences: whereas, before the classical period, political rationality and power was exercised in defence of a sovereign over a territory, was couched in the language of juridical law, and belonged to the higher order of the heavens or the ethical/political community, bio-politics

...brought life and its mechanisms into the realm of explicit calculations and made knowledge/power an agent of transformation of human life ... Modem man is an animal whose politics places his existence in question.

(Foucault 1998a, 143)

In essence, bio-politics encapsulated the modern form of power and how it was directed towards humans as living beings. Moreover, following Foucault, Julien Reid (2009) illustrates powerfully how the process of bio-power is intertwined with the emergence of disciplinary societies, which became concerned with the transformation of human bodies. Reid calls this process 'logistical life' which he defined as:

...life lived under the duress of the command to be efficient, to communicate one's purposes transparently in relation to others, to be positioned where one is required, to use time economically, to be able to move when and where one is told, and to be able to extol these capacities as the values for which one would willingly, if called up, kill and die for.

(2009, 20)

We see how 'logistical life' operates through the example of sexuality, in which 'individuals are supposed to discern their own fundamental nature as sexual

88   *The 'technologies of the self'*

beings and, on the basis of this self-knowledge, transform their lives' (Gutting 2005, 96). In this example, sexuality operates as a tool for the infusion of bio-power into the social body.

> Through the deployment of sexuality bio power spread its net down to the smallest twitches of the body and the most minute stirrings of the soul ... the body, knowledge, discourse and power – were brought into a common localization.
>
> (Dreyfus and Rainbow 1983, 169)

The way that sex was used to intervene and shape the conduct of the population is analogous to the way that radicalisation in the UK context was deployed. With respect to de-radicalisation in the UK therefore, bio-power situates radicalisation within the two ordering poles of disciplinary bodies (the individual) and the population (the collective), and explains how power works to shape the subjectivity of individuals and wider population, through the technique of de-radicalisation. Ultimately, bio-power is a useful concept because it reconceptualises power as a positive and not merely a negative force, whilst also emphasising the way that government activity takes the life of humans as its main purpose, on the principle that enhancing human life strengthens the state.

However, there are critical differences between bio-power and governmentality. One such difference is the re-conceptualisation of power from objectivising power – a process that involves the transformation of individuals into objects or docile bodies – to viewing power as a subjectivising force (McNay 1994, 122). It is governmentality that affords space for the critical process of subjectification. Governmentality is the indirect manipulation of the mind and soul of individuals:

> ...this form of power cannot be exercised without knowing the inside of people's minds, without exploring their souls, without making them reveal their innermost secrets; it implies knowledge of the conscience and an ability to direct it.
>
> (Dreyfus and Rainbow 1983, 214)

Viewing de-radicalisation as a technique of governmentality concerned with shaping the conduct of individuals allows us to understand why policymakers in the UK are preoccupied with what Muslims are thinking. Second, despite the negative conception of power as subjection, this power should not be understood as domination, as articulated in *Discipline and Punish* (1991) and *History of Sexuality* (1998). This is the second difference: 'the process of subjectification through which individuals are regulated also provides the basis from which resistance to such government can be articulated' (McNay 1994, 123). Overall it is governmentality rather than bio-politics, despite its analytical use, which provides the subject with some autonomy to resist. This is important for our conception of the technologies of the self in both the broad sense, encompassing

The 'technologies of the self' 89

individuals in everyday life and how they act upon themselves and occupy certain subject positions, and also simultaneously in the narrow sense, which strictly pertains to individuals undergoing different forms of interventions, particularly de-radicalisation.

In sum, governmentality accommodates the variety of techniques, strategies and the development of certain practices characterising the evolution of governmental power. It also enables power to be conceptualised as positive and not merely negative, and bottom up and multi-directional, instead of top-down and linear. It also embedded the relationship between knowledge, power, institutions and interventions, and the conduct of subjects in its conceptualisation of power. This is important because it moves us beyond analysing de-radicalisation merely as a response to terrorism, or viewing discourses on radicalisation as an isolated knowledge domain disconnected from policy, or even supposing that change in conduct is merely brought about by elites. By conceptualising de-radicalisation as the technologies of the self within governmental relations we understand the role that the multifaceted dimensions of power played in executing de-radicalisation and in shaping the minds and souls of its citizens.

Regulatory norms: the political and neo-liberalism as paradigmatic ideals

This section explains in greater detail the significance of the 'background' or normative ideals that regulate the behaviour of citizens and individuals in the UK. If governmentality is about the 'conduct of conduct' and the technologies of the self is concerned with normalising individuals into a prescribed norm, it begs the question: what are these norms that citizens and subjects are encouraged to adopt? And how does this work? In order to explain this normative ideal, or what I later refer to as the 'central sphere', I will draw on a number of concepts, which include Foucault's notion of 'normalisation' and 'neo-liberalism', Thomas Kuhn's 'paradigm', and Schmitt's concepts of the 'central sphere' and 'the political'.

In order to explain the 'background' and begin situating the technologies of the self as an individuating power of governmentality, it is useful to begin with the metaphor of the 'paradigm'. In 'The Structure of Scientific Revolutions' (1970), Kuhn shows that scientific research operates by setting up a *total* interpretation of some region of reality. The ideal of 'normal' science is to show how the anomalies that emerge can be fitted into this total account. Kuhn calls such total interpretations and agreed upon science, 'paradigms' (1970, 43–63). Kuhn notes how 'results gained in normal research are significant because they add to the scope and precision with which the paradigm can be applied' (1970, 35–36). The paradigm therefore works in a way to reinforce its own structure by perpetuating 'normal science' whilst simultaneously bringing anomalies within its scope. In short, all the research conducted is codified, ordered, shaped and transformed in order to fit the paradigm, for the good of both the anomaly and the paradigm itself. It is the paradigm which demarcates and defines what is considered 'normal' and differentiates what constitutes 'anomaly'.

90 *The 'technologies of the self'*

This metaphor of the 'paradigm' is also explained in terms of the 'central spheres' by Carl Schmitt (1929) in his paper 'The Age of Neutralizations and Depoliticizations'. Schmitt identifies four stages over four centuries in which the 'European mind has moved' and the 'intellectual spheres' which formed the centre of human existence − from the theological to the metaphysical sphere, and from there to the humanitarian-moral and finally to the economic sphere (1929, 131). According to Schmitt, Europeans sought a 'neutral sphere' at each of the four stages in which there would be no more conflict and where disputes can be settled (1929, 137). Notably, a sphere becomes central when

> ...the problems of other spheres are solved in terms of the central sphere − they are considered secondary problems, whose solution follows as a matter of course only if the problems of the central sphere are solved.
>
> (Schmitt 1929, 135)

Schmitt illustrates how the 'central sphere' functions in his example of European technical progress during the nineteenth century and how 'technicity' (the religious belief in technology) was the central sphere that affected all 'moral, political, social and economic problems' in the nineteenth century (1929, 134). All these aspects were defined in relation to technical progress. Thus all concepts including:

> God, freedom, progress, anthropological conceptions of human nature, the public domain, rationality and rationalization, and finally the concept of nature and culture itself derive their concrete historical content from the situation of the central sphere and can only be grasped therefrom.
>
> (Schmitt 1929, 136)

Similarly, in the age of theology, when religion was the central domain in Europe, the driving force of thinking and behaviour was moral education and the ethical life and thus all domains were defined in relation to this paradigmatic morality. Progress in that context would be measured in reference to the Christian theological and moral ideal. The central sphere should thus be seen as providing the distinctive locus of purposive action and thought for subjects in a given place and time. What then, is the 'central sphere' defining the activities of government and society today? There are of course a number of different perspectives on what actually constitutes the 'central sphere' of our day. The social science literature for example, has identified 'post-modernity', 'late modernity', 'globalisation', 'technology', 'secularism', 'global capitalism' and the 'nation-state', amongst others, as central domains. In reality there are many ways of defining and understanding the structure or paradigm shaping the locus of our thoughts and actions today.

I will argue that the 'central sphere' that constitutes the regulatory ideal today is the nation-state. However, it is a take on the nation-state that comes with two caveats. The previous section conveys that I have opted to use the concept of

The 'technologies of the self' 91

governmentality instead of the nation-state, albeit that I sometimes employ each interchangeably. The concept of governmentality offers a distinct analysis of power from the various theories of the nation-state. In fact, Foucault deliberately defined his concepts of governmentality in opposition to prevalent notions of the state in both Liberal and Marxist thinking. Foucault avoided the state 'in the sense that one abstains from an indigestible meal' (Burchell *et al.* 1991, 4). Liberals viewed the state as a problematic repository of power, in which the freedom and autonomy of the individual was embodied in civil society and pitted against it (McNay 1994, 118). This theory presented the state as unitary and, as a result, modern activities in government are derived from the essential properties of being a state. Foucault was more concerned with practice and transformation of state practice than with structures of institutions (Burchell *et al.* 1991, 4). Meanwhile, Marxists viewed the state as playing a functional role in the service of capitalism, with power relations located in certain sections of the population. Such constructions of the state led to calls to denounce power as repressive and to espouse notions about occupying the state in order to ameliorate excess. Instead of Liberal and Marxist notions, Foucault spoke of the 'governmentalisation of the state' (McNay 1994, 18).

Analytically therefore I employ the category of governmentality. However, the term 'nation-state' will continue to be used in a more loose sense, perhaps tentatively and with reservations, to denote the constructed historical entity in which the state is the highest order in a territory able to make claims on a population. As explained in Chapter 1, every 'state' needs to have 'nation' and it is useful to maintain the concept of the 'nation' because it not only underscores the fluidity and the historical and constructed nature of 'nations', but analytically continues to help us make sense of the issues at hand. The three themes I have identified in Chapter 1 – the changing logic of security, questions of identity and belonging, and the relationship between the secular and religious in the European context – can only be understood within the category of the 'nation-state'. In other words governmentality has more explanatory power, whereas the category 'nation-state' has greater purchase on the imagination.

Second, the nation-state is one of those social science terms that has become reified and taken for granted in terms of its complexity and historicity. An example of the complexity inherent in conceptualising the nation-state is provided by Wael Hallaq (2013, 23–36). He identifies five form-properties possessed by the modern state: (1) its constitution as a historical experience that is fairly specific; (2) its sovereignty and the metaphysics which has given rise to it; (3) its legislative monopoly and the related feature of monopoly over so-called legitimate violence; (4) its bureaucratic machinery; and (5) its cultural-hegemonic engagement in the social order, including the production of the national subject. Another take on the state is offered by Francis Fukuyama (2012, 469), who presents successful state development under contemporary conditions as comprised of (1) state building; (2) rule of law; (3) democracy; (4) economic growth; (5) social mobilisation; and (6) ideas/legitimacy. Together, these dimensions represent everything needed to be a modern successful state,

92 *The 'technologies of the self'*

which is different from the prerequisite features required to form a functioning state, not to mention the fact that very few states today are able to achieve a healthy balance between all dimensions.

There is also a tendency to view the state as single unified entity that is ahistorical and fixed. Instead of delineating further what I mean by the nation-state I want to elaborate further on two particular features of several constitutive dimensions of the nation-state – (1) sovereignty, but focusing on the ontological conditions that make sovereignty possible, which I identify as the Schmittian 'Political'; and (2) the cultural-social feature of the nation-state ambit, which is being managed by neo-liberalism of governmental practice (not to be confused with neo-liberalism as theory). The focus on the two different features of the ontological state is not contradictory because both dimensions should be seen as complementary and as two sides of the same coin. The difference between these two distinct theories should be seen mostly in terms of the function of perspective. I have chosen to focus on these two features because of the different features of the nation-state. They help explain the background context shaping the discourse on radicalisation, Prevent policy and de-radicalisation initiatives.

My understanding of 'the political' derives from the work of Carl Schmitt (2007). Schmitt argued that whilst key domains can be defined by the relations of antithesis, such that in the realm of 'morality the distinction is between good and evil, in aesthetics between beautiful and ugly, in economic profitable and unprofitable', the political was consequently defined as the friend-enemy distinction (2007, 26). The enemy is a stranger, the other, something different and alien (Schmitt 2007, 27). This self-other distinction does not apply to individuals or the private sphere but to collectivities and the public sphere. And the enmity that comes as a result of the friend-enemy distinction does not have to be real – it just has to be perceived as real. Driven by the bio-political logic of administrating life, the political is about political identity, what constitutes the 'nation' and what is considered the focal point for activities within the state and externally with other states. The intense antagonism defining the political is what makes the political meaningful, whereby men could 'be required to sacrifice life, authorised to shed blood, and kill other human beings' (Schmitt 2007, 35). It is only though the construction of an other, therefore, that the self is formed and the 'political' exercised.

In this sense, the political precedes politics because it creates the conditions for politics. Mouffe distinguishes between the political and politics in terms of the ontological, which is concerned with the way society is instituted and the ontic, which has to do with manifold practice of conventional politics (Mouffe 2005, 8–9). As a result of this distinction the political cannot be restricted to certain types of institutions or confused with or reduced to the state but must be 'conceived as a dimension that is inherent to every human society and that determines our very ontological condition' (Mouffe 2005, 3). Seen in this light, there can be no juridical concepts of law, citizenship or even the notion of the 'social contract' without the foundational grouping to which an entity belongs. The political community, held together by political identity, must therefore exclude

The 'technologies of the self' 93

in order to exist, must base its politics on the spirit of antagonism and not the elimination of conflict and strife through rational debate.

The 'political' reaffirms the role of antagonism, conflict and war as features of how societies are managed and how government operates. In fact, Foucault also shares with Schmitt the notion that political rationality is built on the politics of antagonism. For example, Foucault inverts Clausewitz's assertion that 'war is the extension of politics by other means' so that 'politics is the extension of war' by other means. By this Foucault meant that the logic of war is inscribed in 'social institutions, in economic inequalities, in language, in the bodies themselves of each and every one of us' (Foucault 1988b, 90; 2004, 15–16).

The political creates the condition for the nation-state. The nation state exists for its own end following the development of what Foucault called the 'reason of state' – a political rationality that emerged in the sixteenth century and is embodied in the 'Polizeiwissenschaft', which is the rational concern for populations, the efficient management of resources and how the power of the state is safeguarded (Foucault 1997, 74). However, for Schmitt, 'reason of state' was analogous with metaphysics, the modern secular state constituting a temporalised God. Schmitt argued that, as a sovereign being, the state's 'decision has the quality of being something like a religious miracle: it has no reference except the fact that it is' (Schmitt 1985, xiv). This was because 'all significant concepts of the modern theory of the state are secularised theological concepts', whereby 'the omnipotent God became the omnipotent lawgiver' (Schmitt 1985, 36). The state for Schmitt was the new God that makes claims on its citizens. The citizen is an extension of the sovereign will and the ultimate manifestation of citizenship is sacrificing one's life for the state (Hallaq 2013, 28). Since the 'decision' was analogous to a miraculous act, it is the 'decision', outside the constraints of rational deliberation, parliamentary systems and juridical law, that actualises sovereignty. The real sovereign of a state is the one who rules by 'exception', who is able to make the decisions that matter.

As mentioned in Chapter 1, it is in the non-juridical space of the 'exception' that politics post 9/11 must be situated. 9/11 effectively ushered in a securitised pre-emptive order; one which is future orientated, geared towards tackling potential risks, dangers and threats, and which is characterised by mitigations in the present, through the execution of wars abroad, risk-management strategies domestically, 'resilience' in infrastructure, extensive architecture of surveillance and use of new technologies. The political provides the pretext that legitimises the securitisation of many domains unrelated to security, like education and health. It is also in the name of the 'omnipotent Law giver' (Schmitt 1985, 36) that the 'exception' has been normalised and extended, not to mention that it is under the ordering principle of the political that the redrawing of the political frontier between friend and enemy in the UK and the West developed. In the aftermath of the Cold War, the political situates Islam broadly as the radical and oriental enemy of the West, and Muslims, as embodied subjects of the enemy, as problematic citizens. The political also expedites the formation of collective identity around liberal values, which is posited as being the antithesis of Islam,

94 *The 'technologies of the self'*

the source of values for the enemy. In this sense, the political creates the conditions conducive for the production and adoption of neo-liberal values (more below). Given that citizenship is contingent on the Omnipotent Lawgiver, Muslim subjectivity (not all, for then the political would cease to exist) has to be refashioned in the image of the new God – the nation-state.

Meanwhile, neo-liberalism must be analysed and understood in terms of an art of government and less as a political and philosophical idea. Foucault (1997, 73–79) saw Liberalism less as a coherent doctrine or a politics pursuing clear goals, but as a critique of governmental practice. Liberalism breaks with the 'reason of state' in nineteenth century England, a dominant logic at the time which had sought to expand and strengthen the state with respect to the greater regulation and control of resources and people. In short, reason of state referred to the principle that 'one is governing too little' (Foucault 1997, 74). In contrast, Liberalism framed the problem of government in terms of 'too much'. Whilst there is no doubt that market reality and political economy as a theory played a role in Liberal critique, in reality the market sphere proved to be a 'testing ground' where the excess of government could be established. In reality it was the question of regulation of government, through law rather than relying on the actions of governors that ushered in the birth of liberalism and not theory and doctrine.

The idea of liberalism begins with society as its end point, and not the state (Foucault 1997, 75). Foucault stated that it was the existence of society that allowed the principle of 'too much' to be posited in relation to the rational justification for government. Thus, in his readings of liberalism, Foucault found that 'liberalism forms an auto-critique of governmental reason: a governmentality which develops and corrects itself through its own critique' (Donzelot and Gordon 2008, 57). It is in the modern Anglo-Saxon variant of liberalism, belonging to the Chicago school of the 1970s that Foucault finds the principle of market rationality being extended to non-economic domains like the family and penal policy (Foucault 1997, 79).

Neoliberalism is a striking form of governmental practice because it not only blurs the lines between private and public, market and society, but also deploys market rationality as a criterion to judge and shape other spheres of life. David Harvey (2005, 2) posits that neoliberalism is a theory drawn from political economy that proposes the idea that human well-being is best advanced through 'private property rights, free markets ... and free trade'. In this respect neoliberalism refers to governmental practice associated with late-Capitalism, which prizes capital accumulation, efficient markets and state interventions to ensure that markets are 'free'; not least to privatise and reconfigure social relations and subjectivities along market lines; and to a set of political doctrines championing the autonomy and freedom of individuals with the principles of equality and Human Rights.

Furthermore, neo-liberal governance is identified with 'a political rationality which seeks to develop a congruence between the economic subject – the rational, utility maximising individual – and the responsible, self-sufficient,

The 'technologies of the self' 95

moral individual' (Miller and Rose 1990; Rose 1999, 230–232). In essence liberal democratic societies seek to cultivate a citizenship able regulate itself, thereby enabling political government to relinquish its responsibilities for providing security, health care, education and so on for its citizens. Hence comes the fact that the neo-liberalism framework drives the individual/citizen towards imbibing values like autonomy, freedom and self-realisation (Rose 1996, 145). Neo-liberalism as a practice of government that is concerned with imposing limits on itself consequently 'acts at a distance' upon the choices and values presented to citizens and tries to forge symmetry between the political values (consumption, profitability, efficiency etc.) and citizens' lives. Contemporary government, according to Rose, thus operates through the 'delicate and minute infiltration of the ambitions of regulation into the very interior of our existence and experience as subjects' (Rose 1999, 10–11).

Furthermore, for Mitchell Dean, neo-liberalism has a certain affinity to technologies of risk (Dean 2010, 194). We see today the re-emergence of a 'prudentialism' that emphasises the monitoring of risks by 'active citizens', which include risks of

> physical and mental ill health, of sexually acquired disease, of dependency (on drugs, alcohol, nicotine, welfare or in personal relationships), of being a victim of crime, of a lack of adequate resources in retirement, of their own and their children's education, of low self–esteem and so on.
>
> (Dean 2010, 194–195)

Ultimately neo-liberalism seeks to create self-regulating, autonomous and responsible citizens, who are governed by market and consumerist logic, who are de-politicised and whose identity is alterable.

A few words must be said about the link between neo-liberalism and de-politicisation. Wendy Brown (2006) identities two different dimensions assumed by de-politicisation in Western Liberal democracies: de-politicisation involves 'construing inequality, subordination, marginalization and social conflict, which all require political analysis and political solutions, as personal and individual' (15). Second, de-politicisation presents such domains as problems that are natural, religious or cultural (ibid.). In short, significant issues that demand political solutions are replaced with therapeutic or behavioural solutions, as well as making religious, ethnic and cultural difference an inherent site of conflict (ibid.). Brown highlights several causes for de-politicisation: long-standing tendencies in liberalism itself, individualism and the diffusion of market rationality across the political and social spheres precipitated by the ascendency of neo-liberalism (2006, 17). The idea and practice of de-radicalisation is a by-product of this neo-liberal framework.

After all, de-radicalisation is seen as a therapeutic solution, framed at the individual level and explained in terms of 'cognitive' and 'behavioural' variables, implemented to eradicate 'radicalisation' – itself said to be caused by 'culture'. In addition, the narrative of radicalisation depicts Muslims as a security

96   *The 'technologies of the self'*

threat because of the problems with their identity and the misinterpretation of religious doctrine, which are also the reasons that they pose a social threat. It also attributes blame to political multiculturalism for rendering Britain conducive to the incubation of radicalisation. It is little wonder that political analysis evades radicalisation discourses, or that there is a glaring absence of politics in discussions surrounding de-radicalisation. De-radicalisation is a neo-liberal response par excellence.

It is important to consider the fact that neo-liberalism and the political do not have a monopoly on values, ideals, and normative models that exist in society or which operate within the nation-state. Whilst these form the background against which strategies, programmes, and techniques work, other domains like the family, religion, philosophies, alternative lifestyles, social movements, political ideologies, different cultural practices, education, etc. also play a part in forming and constituting the subject. Indeed, it is crucial to stress the heterogeneity of the ideals or models of personhood deployed in different practices. There are so many understandings, life style choices, and different teleologies of how the existence of human beings should be defined, promoted, and worked towards: ... manliness, femininity, honour, modesty, propriety, civility, discipline, distinction, efficiency. Harmony, fulfilment, virtue, pleasure – the list is as diverse and heterogeneous as it is interminable'...

(Rose 1996, 130)

The regulatory ideals differ too across places and time. And it is also important to reiterate that whilst the political and neo-liberalism may form the central domain that defines other domains and presents the regulative ideal that citizens are expected to adopt, internalise and then embody, the paradigm nevertheless generates counter ideas and practices and accommodates inconsistencies and contradictions. And many still fail to realise these mainstream ideals.

Consequently, it is the job of the technologies of the self in our society to bring the diverse assemblages of knowledge, techniques, persons, experts, and practices to bear on individuals in order to reconcile the subjectivities of individuals with the paradigmatic value of the state and society. Another way to understand this process is through the power of 'normalisation'. Notably, normalisation was Foucault's way of explaining how power works outside the conventional 'monarchical' view of power in which there is the unified symbol of power in the form of the King, institutions like the army, and the effects of juridical power. Instead of top-down and singular, power in modern societies for Foucault was circular, multiple, and operated through new invisible and continuous practices of control. Normalisation is a technique of power which:

imposes homogeneity; but it individualizes by making it possible to measure gaps, to determine levels, to fix specialties and to render the differences useful by fitting them one to another.

(Foucault 1991, 184)

The 'technologies of the self'   97

This concept refers to the standardisation of the human population, followed by differentiation. Human bodies are ranked and ordered in relation to each other and specialities fixed to each body. Based on this grid, individuals are not judged by the right and wrong of their actions (e.g. the law) but by where their actions place them on a ranked scale that compares them to everyone else. It does this by making a totalising grid of 'normality', in which clinical assessment of all anomalies is made by the social institutions of the state; individuals are then either normalised or pathologised with respect to their behaviour according to this grid of normality. Corrective technologies are applied to those who deviate from the norm. Normalisation techniques, such as the technologies of discipline and confession, are supposed to be an impartial way for 'dealing with dangerous deviations', but ultimately, according to Paul Rainbow, the 'end of government is the correct disposition of things – even when these things have to be invented so as to be well governed' (Rainbow 1984, 21). What matters in the end in modern forms of government, is the ontological reality of power: the totalising all-encompassing *ordering* of things. It is in this sense that normalisation can be distinguished from concepts of socialisation, which Hubert Dreyfus explains eloquently:

> Normalization is, of course, more than socialization into norms. Socialization into norms is the universal way the understanding of being or power governs the actions of the members of any society. In the new arrangement which has emerged more and more clearly since the Classical Age, however, norms are progressively brought to bear on '*all aspects of life*'. What makes normalization different (and dangerous) is that it seeks to cover *all* practices.
>
> (Dreyfus 1996, 13)

It is in this way that de-radicalisation must be seen as a corrective technique of normalisation operating to bring deviant individuals that fall outside the values and ideals of the central sphere/paradigm into line and closer to these ideals. Notably, the underlying principle of de-radicalisation applies not only to individuals on intervention programmes but also to individuals in everyday life, in civil society, at home, within the family. Seen in this light, de-radicalisation as the technologies of self targets all citizens and consequently blurs the lines between the 'public-private' dichotomies. The private is subject to the control of the public; all spheres of activity in essence belong to the public; governmental practice is in the business of 'governing the soul' (Rose 1999). It is fruitful in fact to see the technologies of the self, and therefore de-radicalisation, as an inclusive mechanism as opposed to viewing it as a mechanism of exclusion and marginalisation. It is nevertheless true that before this drive too inclusivity can begin, power has to exclude and divide subjects from others and within themselves. After the anomaly or deviant has been identified, objectified, represented as divergent and different, then the process of inclusion begins.

98   *The 'technologies of the self'*

References

Aggarwal, N. (2013). 'Mental discipline, punishment and recidivism: reading Foucault against de-radicalisation programmes in the War on Terror', *Critical Studies on Terrorism*, 6 (2): 262–278.

Brown, W. (2006). *Regulating Aversion: Tolerance in the Age of Identity and Empire*. Princeton: Princeton University Press.

Burchell, G., Gordon, C. and Miller, P. (1991). *The Foucault Effect, Studies in Governmentality*. Chicago: The University of Chicago Press.

Butler, J. (1990). *Gender Trouble, Feminism and the Subversion of Identity*. London: Routledge.

Connolly, W. (1985). 'Taylor, Foucault, and otherness', *Political Theory*, 13 August: 365–376.

Dean, M. (2010). *Governmentality: Power and Rule in Modern Society*. London: Sage Publishing.

Donzelot, J. and Gordon, C. (2008). 'Governing liberal societies – the Foucault effect in the English-speaking world', *Foucault Studies*, 548–562, Interview, file:///C:/Users/dell/Downloads/1409–5250–1-PB.pdf.

Dreyfus, H.L. (1996). 'Being and power: Heidegger and Foucault', *International Journal of Philosophical Studies*, 4 (1): 1–16.

Dreyfus, H. and Rainbow, P. (1983). *Michel Foucault: Beyond Structuralism and Hermeneutics*. Chicago: University of Chicago Press.

Foucault, M. (1982). 'The subject and power'. *Critical Inquiry*, 8 (4): 777–795.

Foucault, M. (1987). ' "The ethic of care for the self as a practice of freedom": an interview with Michel Foucault on January 20, 1984', Raúl Fornet-Batancourt, Helmut Becker, Alfredo Gomez-Müller and J.D. Gauthier, *Philosophy & Social Criticism* 12: 112–131.

Foucault, M. (1988a). *Technologies of the Self: A Seminar with Michel Foucault*, edited by L. Martin, H. Gutman and P. Hutton. Amherst: The University of Massachusetts Press.

Foucault, M. (1988b). *Power/Knowledge: Selected Interviews and Other Writings, 1972–1977*, http://uwf.edu/dearle/foucault.pdf.

Foucault, M. (1990). *The History of Sexuality: The Care of the Self: The Care of the Self* V. 3. London: Penguin.

Foucault, M. (1991). *Discipline and Punish: The Birth of the Prison*. London: Penguin.

Foucault, M. (1997). *Ethics: Essential Works of Foucault 1954–1984*, V.1, edited by P. Rainbow. London: Penguin.

Foucault, M. (1998a). *The History of Sexuality: The Will to Knowledge*, V. 1. London: Penguin.

Foucault, M. (1998b). *The History of Sexuality: The Use of Pleasure*, V. 2. London: Penguin.

Foucault, M. (2004). *Society Must be Defended: Lectures at the Collège de France, 1975–76: Lectures at the College De France*. London: Penguin.

Fukuyama, F. (2012). *The Origins of Political Order: From Prehuman Times to the French Revolution*. Croydon: Profile Books.

Gutting, G. (2005). *Foucault: A Very Short Introduction*. Oxford: Oxford Publishing Press.

Hall, S. (1996). 'Who Needs Identity?', in *Questions of Cultural Identity*, edited by S. Hall and P. Du Gay. California: Sage Publications.

The 'technologies of the self' 99

Hall, S. and Du Gay, P. (1996). *Questions of Cultural Identity*. California: Sage Publications.

Hallaq, W. (2013). *The Impossible State, Islam, Politics, and Modernity's Moral Predicament*. New York: Columbia University Press.

Harvey, D. (2005). *A Brief History of Neoliberalism*. Oxford: Oxford University Press.

Kuhn, T. (1970). *The Structure of Scientific Revolutions*, (2nd edition). International Encyclopedia of United Science. Chicago: University of Chicago. http://projekt integracija.pravo.hr/_download/repository/Kuhn_Structure_of_Scientific_Revolutions. pdf.

Laidlaw, J. (2014). *The Subject of Virtue: An Anthropology of Ethics and Freedom*. Cambridge: Cambridge University Press.

Lindekilde, L. (2015). 'Refocusing Danish counter-radicalisation efforts: an analysis of the (problematic) logic and practice of individual de-radicalisation interventions', in *Counter-Radicalisation: Critical Perspectives*, edited by C. Baker-Beall, C. Heath-Kelly and L. Jarvis. Abingdon: Routledge.

McNay, L. (1994). *Foucault: A Critical Introduction*. Cambridge: Polity Press.

Miller, P. and Rose, N. (1990). 'Governing economic life', *Economy and Society*, 19:1: 1–31.

Mouffe, C. (2005). *On the Political*. Abingdon: Routledge.

Rainbow, P. (1984). *The Foucault Reader*. New York: Pantheon Books.

Reid, J. (2009). *The Biopolitics of the War on Terror: Life Struggles, Liberal Modernity and the Defence of Logistical Societies*. Manchester: Manchester University Press.

Rose, N. (1996). 'Identity, genealogy, history', in *Questions of Cultural Identity*, edited by S. Hall and P. Du Gay. California: Sage Publishing.

Rose, N. (1999). *Governing the Soul: The Shaping of the Private Self, Free Association*. London: Free Association Books.

Schmitt, C. (1929). *The Age of Neutralizations and Depoliticizations*. New York: Telos Press.

Schmitt, C. (1985). *Political Theology, Four Chapters on the Concept of Sovereignty*. Cambridge, MA: MIT Press.

Schmitt, C. (2007). *The Concept of the Political*. Chicago: University of Chicago Press.

4 Discursive technology (truth)
The production of radicalisation

> Truth is not outside of power or itself lacking in power ... Truth is of this world; it is the product of multiple constraints ... Each society has its own regime of truth, its general politics of the truth...
>
> (Foucault in Rainbow 1984, 73)

This particular notion of 'truth', conveyed by Foucault above, is getting at something different. Rather than seeing truth as being grounded in something metaphysical and eternal like Plato's forms/ideas, or as something universally binding, 'truth' is placed in the context of place and time, not to mention as something produced by power in a particular society for a particular purpose. Truth is not outside of power but a construction of it. And, as discussed in Chapter 3, this is normally done for the sake of greater mobilisation, control, ordering and optimisation by governmental rationality in modern societies. The role of discursive technology, then, in the technologies of the self is to construct 'regimes of truth' which subjects are disciplined in reference to, and then subjected according to. This chapter reveals how this was done in relation to the production of radicalisation as a discourse.

The construction of threat narratives

The data indicates the existence of several narratives on the threat posed by Muslims living in Britain which can be simplified into two main narratives: the security threat posed by individuals in the British Muslim communities on the one hand and the inability of British Muslims to 'integrate' on the other. Both narratives are accompanied by sub-narratives: there are at least three narratives in the security context (Al-Qaeda, new terrorism and home grown bomber) and two with respect to the integration agenda (Muslims' inability to integrate because of their religion and political multiculturalism as the problem). These narratives frame the Muslim population as problematic and constituted the bedrock of the development of radicalisation as a concept.

What do narratives actually do? According to Roselle *et al.* (2014) narratives 'explain the world and set constraints on the imaginable and actionable, and shape perceived interests' ... Narratives can be a power resource setting out what

The production of radicalisation   101

characterizes any state in the world, or how the world works' (76). They also identify three levels in order to understand how narratives operates as a 'soft power' (ibid.): (1) international system narratives, which describe how the world is structured, who the players are and how it works; (2) national narratives, that set out the story of the nation state and what values and goals it has; and (3) issue narratives which set out why a policy is needed and desirable, and how it will be successfully implemented or accomplished. All three levels are at play in the radicalisation discourse. The narratives in this section set the context for the Prevent policy.

The 'War on Terror' problematised the threat of violence and terrorism posed by Al-Qaeda inspired groups, stressing the religious dimensions and 'exceptional' nature of religiously inspired terrorism. One interviewee frames it in the following way:

> ...9/11 makes us feel incredibly threatened, nuclear weapons, and all the rest of it − we are going to be destroyed. And then the next level comes, which is of course the 'home grown' threat; because for a period of time post 9/11 it's about foreigners coming to do something, to do things to us. In the period up to and not just from the London bombings there's the increasing concern about the 'home-grown' ... So what does it mean to say there's a home grown threat if you want to use this kind of language? It means people must go from being us to them. The foreigners were never us but they're gone. You've got to describe this road from being mainstream to radical and that is the label given to radicalisation.
> (Interview 6, Academic/Director of a research programme on radicalisation)

The 'home-grown bomber' narrative emerged after the attacks on 7/7 and moved the focus away from international terrorism to the threat of violence posed by domestic militancy (ESRC 2007; Croft and Cerwyn 2010, Githens-Mazer and Lambert 2010). A former Secretary General of a prominent organisation explains:

> Well 9/11 was done, although there are no absolute proofs, by Muslims; 7/7 was done by Muslims and there were the Madrid bombings in 2004, which was done by Muslims. That meant that here is a community that is producing terrorists, then what is it doing that it is producing these sorts of people? Then there must a problem in this community. Then if there's a problem with the community there must be a problem with Islam, although none of this was evidence based.
> (Interview 14, former Secretary General of representative organisation)

Both statements below, the first by a former Chair of a community organisation and the second by the President of a Prevent funded think-tank, mention the impact of the new-terrorism thinking in practical terms.

> We've always said to the police and the government we want to stop the crime. The police said the problem with this kind of terrorism is with the

102 *The production of radicalisation*

Irish it was okay to stop them at the last act but with this kind of terrorism – the police call it international terrorism – with international terrorism it's not the same thing, we have to stop them a few stages before the last act and the reason is because they would do suicide bombing whereas the Irish never did suicide bombing.

(Interview 18, former Chair of community organisation)

The term terrorism in its modern mode I argued in my thesis was maybe first cemented by Netanyahu in 1996 in which he first brought to light the danger of Islamic based terrorism as a new threat to Western way of life. That was adopted after 9/11 as a result of the attacks and it became a part of the language.

(Interview 27, President of a Prevent funded think-tank)

The second major threat narrative pertains to the problem of integration and identity posed by the Muslim population in the UK. Interviewee data suggests that this major narrative about integration and identity is characterised by two sub-narratives: the first places the problems of integration on Islamic beliefs and practices, whilst the second locates the problem with political multiculturalism. The overall narrative encompassing these two sub-narratives however frames the UK Muslim population as an obstacle to the wider political project of a cohesive single British identity. The following respondent summarises the underlying message of this narrative.

This notion that we are of a particular identity and this identity is how we succeed and solve our problems and that any other element is alien to our main structure, is a cost, a burden, and possibly a threat – that is what is emerging from the narrative and is being perpetuated by policy. The remit is to find this harmonious society that looks at one.

(Interview 27, President of a Prevent funded think-tank)

This focus on identity became not only a feature of the conceptual framework of radicalisation, but was also incorporated into the 'integration' agenda, which was one of the Home Office's policy responses to the London bombings (Blair 2005). This interviewee situates the problem of Muslim communities within the integration narrative.

It's related to extremism and integration because what was clear was that there was a lack of integration by certain Muslim groups in Britain. The Salafis, some of the Brotherhood groups, Hizb-el-Tahrir, basically preached in this country for many years that a good Muslim cannot integrate and be a loyal citizen of this country; cannot serve in the military or the police because that's allegiance to a Kufr system or man-made laws. So a lot of these Islamist ideas are holding back Muslims in this country and also it kinds of builds up rage with an over emphasis on foreign policy.

(Interview 25, Quilliam analyst)

The production of radicalisation   103

This interviewee highlights the first sub-narratives – the inability of Muslims to integrate and adopt British values. According to this sub-narrative, the problem resides in the incompatibility of the ideas, values and practices of the Muslim population with mainstream political, cultural and social spaces. Similar to the security threat narratives in which there is a marked absence of a consensus on the nature of the threat, there are several narratives depicting Muslims as the foreign and problematic 'Other'. Another academic describes the absence of socio-economic factors in discussions about the challenges facing Muslims. Instead the discourse on Muslims is characterised by reductionist accounts that employ an essentialised reading of Islam. This tendency to speak about Islam in a monolithic way is highlighted by interviewees below.

> If you look at deprivation it's about socio-economic status and not about your religion, identity, or ethnicity. We use all of this to problematise the Muslim communities and in all those spaces we use Islam as the explanation for that. Muslim communities that are isolated, well, it's because they are Muslims and their Islam tells them that … It's this constant problematisation of Muslims and Islam that has been accepted in all the different arenas of the British spaces that reinforces this problem…
>
> (Interview 11, Academic)

> If a Muslim does a bad thing it becomes racialised or Islamised – if I'm allowed to use this word. But if a similar kind of crime is done by other communities, then it remains an issue of individuals. The Eurabia and Londonistan theories are becoming more mainstream in European countries.
>
> (Interview 14, former Secretary General of representative organisation)

However, the second sub-narrative is defined by the 'death of multiculturalism' debate. This narrative situates discussions about radicalisation, extremism and problems posed by Muslims within wider attempts of policymakers to renegotiate Britain's political policy of managing diversity and immigration. An academic specialising on community approaches to counter-terrorism elucidates below.

> I think it's about structural issues with how minorities are viewed in the UK and again it goes back to the colonial mentality of there are problematic subjects and you have to treat them in silos as problematic communities and you deal with them like that and it's always about integrating minorities into a majority or people who are abnormal into an normative thing – that's a broad framework for operating … That was the immediate go to problem, it's all about integration and immigration, which is a constant theme since post-war migration and that lazy thinking has made it into CT arena.
>
> (Interview 12, Academic/freelance consultant on Prevent community engagement)

104   *The production of radicalisation*

The growing call by media commentators and think-tanks, and in official statements by politicians, to move away from political multiculturalism was exacerbated with the London attacks in 2005. An academic working on Islamophobia explains 'death of multiculturalism' discourse and its link to British values.

> So what you saw for a year or two years after 7/7 the discourse of radicalisation emerged and with it went hand in hand the death of multiculturalism. Because the politicians have allowed the community, and this is the mindset – 'allowed' – to be themselves, to develop, grow, and have their own identities, because multiculturalism requires us to respect difference without making a difference the argument went that because we allowed them to do that, we've also created this problem where within those communities they can 'hate us' and want to destroy us ... The argument was multiculturalism needs to die; it needs to come to an end so it gets to a stage when everybody can buy into Britishness, British values, and so on.
>
> (Interview 11, Academic)

More importantly, a return to a singular mainstream identity highlights the way the logic of counter-terrorism became intertwined with the notion of identity. This was reflected in David Cameron's Speech in 2011 at a security conference in Munich in which he made a link between integration, multiculturalism and security.

> You saw that with David Cameron's speech in Munich, where he started talking about that if you got a lack of integrated young men then you've got a terrorism problem. They're conflating two separate things and drawing the wrong conclusions; you can look at Aunty down the road who doesn't speak a word of English, she's not blowing things up. Well I mean, my sister, a Muslim convert with generations of forefathers in Scotland – you couldn't really describe her as not integrated?
>
> (Interview 12, Academic/freelance consultant on Prevent community engagement)

Despite the powerful effect of these various narratives about the Muslim threat, these narratives are not objective but are constructed. In other words these narratives are not based on objective facts. The Director of a research programme on radicalisation explains:

> So basically what I've argued is that it's a set of constructed narratives; there isn't an objective way of rooting these sorts of things and because they are a set of narratives, it's always emotional, it's always moving, and there are a set of political projects that are trying to shape it in particular ways.
>
> (Interview 6, Academic/Director of research programme on radicalisation)

Connected to the construction of the threat, some interviewees believed that the threat of Islam and Muslims was over-exaggerated. The interviewee below

The production of radicalisation   105

highlights a critical point. He points to the disproportionate 'funding, attention, and discourse' invested in radicalisation by policymakers for political expediency in a way that does not reflect the reality of the threat. The very small likelihood of attacks against the UK indicates the huge disjuncture between the reality of the threat and the social perceptions of this threat. This was reflected in the comments of the following academic:

> The point I want to make is that the proportions dedicated to extremism and radicalisation is much higher than the reality is. I have spoken to hundreds of Muslims all over the UK and I can tell you they are more bothered about football, relationships, and X-Factor, like other citizens are, and what we need to accept that if a Muslim is against foreign policy, which many Muslims are, it doesn't make them an extremist or likely to commit terrorism. Those people that are likely to commit a terrorist act are a small number of people but the amount of funding, attention, and discourse, is much higher than it needs to be and I think it's a fundamental political tactic, which anyone who studies politics knows, that if you want to generate support from the mainstream population the best way to do that is to create the problem and to show that you are tackling it effectively.
>
> (Interview 20, Academic)

This section has shown the significant role that threat narratives played in the construction of the Muslim problem for interviewees. Overall, there were two major narratives produced – the security threat and the problem of integration – with a number of other concurrent sub-narratives also peddled. These narratives produced the problematisation of the Muslim presence in the UK, which became embedded in policy documents, and also became a feature in the construction of radicalisation, which will become evident in this chapter.

The contested boundaries of expertise and knowledge

Chapter 3 highlighted the fact that 13 interviewees, roughly 48 per cent of the sample, referred to the importance of experts in the formulation of deradicalisation. Similarly, the data indicates that the formulation of radicalisation as a body of knowledge was not the result of organic academic enquiry but was instead constructed and developed by a diversity of 'experts' – academics, media 'experts' and think-tanks. Moreover, the data shows that the expertise in the policy domain of counter-terrorism is contentious, with many interviewees critical of the notion of the 'expert'. It also indicates the importance conferred on particular modes of knowledge and the competition amongst experts. This section attempts to elucidate the significance of expertise and knowledge in the explosion of discursive production.

The data points to the existence of a multitude of 'experts' involved in the production of radicalisation, drawn from diverse and seemingly disassociated fields: probation officers, managers, public servants, academics, and social

106   *The production of radicalisation*

workers, mentors, therapists, and Prevent Police Officers amongst others. However, many respondents were critical of the notion of the 'expert' in counter-terrorism.

> I think the expert circuit is very much a politicised circuit because experts that talk to government are selected because they say to government what they would like them to hear or think they like what they are going to say.
>
> (Interview 10, Investigative journalist)

According to the interview above the expert circuit is 'politicised'; it is characterised by the selection of certain experts, a media presence and the absence of critique of state power. In other words, experts in this policy domain are seen as individuals who legitimise the government's narrative and policy. This presents a pejorative view of experts which questions the objectivity and the knowledge produced by some experts. Indeed, some of the data thus suggests that 'expertise' in the field of terrorism studies and policy domain is constructed in the interstitial spaces between the state, media and academia. The interviewee below brings to light the business demands of the media for 'explanations' and how this compels them to find 'experts'. Also intrinsic in his response is the notion that discourse emanates from 'elites' and that it flows down to institutions in order to convert into action, one of the institutions being the media.

> When 'that' elite had a shared discourse that there was this big new radical threat to the United Kingdom, it created the consequences that flowed through each of those institutions. When it flowed through the media it created the demand; the demand for expertise – who are the people who can come and create some explanations and understanding? Actually it's normally some commentary to fill a bit of a newspaper or fill a few seconds on radio. And you know, it's a capitalist society, when you create demands you get supply.
>
> (Interview 6, Academic/Director of research programme on radicalisation)

This respondent raises important points regarding the fact that a shared discourse comes from elites and the business needs to fill media headlines, couched in terms of the language of economics – 'supply and demand'. This view of the relationship between experts and the media is supported by the interview below.

> But I would say on the whole terror experts are on the right and the press are naturally attracted to them for that reason. They usually say a lot of crap and the press rely on that crap in order to run their own stories and that their papers have stories on terrorism on them so that they can sell papers, creates hysteria, gets people clicking onto websites and a bit of panic doesn't harm either.
>
> (Interview 19, Academic)

The production of radicalisation   107

The implication of such a close relationship between experts, government and the media undermines the notion of genuine knowledge on terrorism and radicalisation. Indeed this notion regarding the intermeshing of the media and the notion of the expert in the production of radicalisation has been raised by the likes of Awan *et al.*, for whom 'radicalisation' has been 'incubated in the cracks' of the 'new media ecology' (2012, 6). The new media ecology is characterised by a set of somewhat paradoxical conditions of 'effects without causes' and profound connectivity through which places, events, people and their actions and inactions, seem increasingly connected (Awan *et al.* 2012, 5). Linked to this symbiotic relationship, is the fact that the media logic creates the demand for expertise. A former Vice-Chair of a community organisation explains how Prevent work created a space for 'expertise' and created work for people who did not necessarily have the knowledge and expertise.

> I don't know what I'm talking about but I still want money. I've seen quite a few so-called experts who don't know a thing about a thing … Okay, you can be called an expert only because you've been in the area longer than anybody else and there's a niche, there's nobody here, there's a gap for the Muslim community, certainly. If you then put so called experts and people around Prevent, Prevent officers and all that, it's only because there's nobody else. Put them next to an expert in another field, they will fall down quite drastically.
> (Interview 13, former Vice-Chair of community organisation)

This respondent highlights the poor knowledge base of some experts and the real motive for many experts: money. Other interviewees mentioned the low level entry requirement for experts in this policy domain and the financial imperatives underpinning the work of many experts. Indeed. There are clear instances of academics, organisations and individuals with no prior experience in this field moving into the policy domain in order to contribute to it. The ability of some experts to capitalise on the opportunities generated from funding and work in this area is discussed below.

> [X] is a great example of someone whose entire career was completely in a different area of expertise and was able to move into this field. People are pulled in because they are the talking heads. So I think it's about the setting of a discursive frame amongst 'that' London elite and the consequences of that flowing down those various institutional channels and when it is the media the editors want to have coverage on these topics and as I said demand creates supply. And some people made a lot of money out of it.
> (Interview 6, Academic/Director of research programme on radicalisation)

This respondent frames some experts as 'talking heads' and explains the role of supply and demand. As a result, the data shows that the boundary of legitimate

108 *The production of radicalisation*

expertise and illegitimate expertise is fluid. This has hitherto been attributed to the fact that the state anoints experts, the role of the media, and the competition for money, jobs and prestige in a capitalist system. However, a few interviewees have expressed the view that research on radicalisation and the Prevent strategy as a policy has morphed into an industry.

> You know there are many people out there looking for money and a job. I know think-tanks who have sought money from government sources and what is interesting is how they've tailored their approach and outputs to suit what government will like ... There's a lot of insincerity in the expert industry; they are not talking based on research, evidence, and passionate belief but instead for money and status. If you go on the news or are mentioned in a policy paper, then that's something to be proud off and it's also an opportunity for you to get funding for your organisation to conduct research and keep yourself alive.
>
> (Interview 20, Academic)

This interviewee doesn't just highlight the influence of money and the role of government in selecting experts. There are structural, organisational and personal reasons for the emergence of the expert industry. The notion that the experts in the policy domain of counter-terrorism have become an 'industry' was acknowledged by an analyst at DEMOS.

> Yes, I would call it a cottage industry that's popped up out of nowhere and has probably been detrimental, and I include myself in all of that; there is suddenly a million of Prevent experts and terrorism experts who knew nothing about the subject three years ago and are now parading themselves as the world's leading experts on the subject but they're all bringing a lot of baggage with them. I'm just as guilty and I'm open about that.
>
> (Interview 1, DEMOS analyst)

However, despite the overall critical response by many to the role of experts in radicalisation discourse, the data does reveal a more nuanced categorisation of expertise. For example, the data shows the different types and levels of expertise and knowledge. This includes experts belonging to different epistemic domains such as the intelligence services, government, academia, communities, think-tanks, the religious sphere and politics. An analyst at IPPR explained to me that despite the diversity of actors conceiving, implementing, executing and adapting the principles of counter-terrorism, the overall hard-hitters were 'white guys in suits'.

> David Omond is important; he was head of GCHQ and was the government's intelligence and security coordinator; he was on our IPPR security commission; he was a primary architect of CONTEST ... But who's making the decisions? I think on this stuff the answer has to be senior civil

servants and a handful of tomatoes; the Foreign Office, the Home Office, the Treasury, no. 10, and they are probably doing it within a framework laid down by senior ministers that say muscular liberalism or go here and don't go there; they lay out the parameters and civil servants fill in the details. The spooks would be pretty influential so MI5 and MI6 people; but I think it's one of those areas that isn't about public debates and think-tanks, it's about a few experts – white guys in suits – deciding, because when it comes to national security there's a sense of leave it to the experts, which I think is misguided.

(Interview 4, IPPR analyst)

Notably, the categorisation of expertise in this field does not necessarily correspond directly to a vertical hierarchy. In fact all forms of capital – personal relationships, flows of knowledge, competition for space, dissemination of knowledge, competition for influence – leveraged by experts are actually in constant interaction. Knowledge became extremely significant in the production of radicalisation discourses. Knowledge was important not only to codify the reality of radicalisation; from the perspective of many experts it was crucial in enhancing their status. This explains the democratisation of the enterprise of collating knowledge on radicalisation, as well as the horizontal structure of expertise given the premium that was placed on particular forms of knowledge. In terms of radicalisation, knowledge was required on a very niche area – Islam (encompassing many areas of specialisation) and political Islam and other related knowledge domains. This was attributed to the fact that the source of the problem was said to be Islamist ideology. The comment below illustrates the highly specialised nature of expertise.

Also, through our research we found out that there were generally five topics that Muslims who were classed as radicals or extremist, had misunderstandings in. Those five were: Takfir – Calling Muslim's non-Muslims and the understanding of that. Another one would be Jihad and their understanding of that – what is Jihad and what is allowed and not allowed in Jihad? Another understanding would be what would you class as a place of war? Another would be what are the responsibilities of Muslims in places with no Islamic rule? … What was the last one? And the last one is where did they take the knowledge from? And what is something that you can say that you took knowledge in the correct manner?

(Interview 23, Director of prison intervention provider)

This passage shows the type of knowledge valorised by policy-makers in this field; especially the technical nature of this knowledge, and the way in which experts employed this knowledge to stamp their authority and augment their claims to expertise. Based on the data above, critical to the attributes of authority were proficient knowledge of Islam, theology, politics, history and Arabic. Indeed, an understanding of this niche knowledge legitimised the credibility of

110   *The production of radicalisation*

many experts, many of whom capitalised on this discourse to great effect, not least because it was lucrative in career terms.

In fact, the classical tradition, which holds a special status within Islam, was referred to in various ways by a diverse range of experts for different ends and strategies. For example, whilst the interviewee above refers to tradition, he nevertheless does so from a particular school of thought within the tradition (one that stresses the right of the individual to interpret the tradition without the aid of scholars); whereas the interviewee below, an analyst at Quilliam, provides an example of how the classical tradition can be understood, accessed and then deployed from the perspective of another school of thought within Islam, that is even more liberal with respect to interpretation of texts:[1]

> As someone with a background in Islamic Studies I could only talk from an Islamic point of view, which is losing the balance of life. So religion is supposed to be balanced, this was the Sunnah of the Prophet (PBUH) ... From the teachings of the prophet and the classical tradition of Islam it's always been understood that if you get too extreme in your Islam or your thinking then you're basically wrong...
>
> (Interview 25, Quilliam Foundation analyst)

The analyst at Quilliam, like the Director of a prison provider above, invokes the 'classical tradition' and reminds me of his credentials as someone with a 'background in Islamic Studies'. Despite working for different organisations, with their divergent approaches to tackling radicalisation and their different understanding of the Islamic faith, these experts nevertheless both refer to Islamic Jurisprudence and the classical tradition. They are effectively making a claim to possess knowledge and expertise. A crucial dimension to consider here is the existence of a vast diversity of schools, interpretations, etc. making competing claims of what the 'real' and 'correct' interpretation of Islam as a religion and discursive tradition actually is.

However, it is clear from that data that knowledge and expertise on Islam and the classical tradition are not the only prerequisite criteria that give a person a licence to be an 'expert' on radicalisation. Other knowledge domains unrelated to religion are a feature of expertise in the Prevent strategy. These include knowledge on diverse subjects such as youth empowerment, mentoring, psychology, Middle Eastern politics and history and the local community, to name but a few. For example, the importance of 'local' knowledge being based in communities is further explained below.

> I think it works when people actually give a damn and that can only work locally. So someone from London coming down to tell me how to do de-radicalisation is never going to work because you cannot explain why, what we talked about earlier, why something always feels right. Because you look at multiple factors in what is actually happening and know why that person came to that mosque and stuff like that. Local knowledge is with local

The production of radicalisation 111

people. They are able to know what's happening and know what's best for their community.

(Interview 8, Prevent practitioner)

Interestingly however a Senior Prevent Officer does stress the importance of expertise in tackling radicalisation but distinguishes instead between the kinds of expertise in her department that specialises in 'preventative' approaches vis-à-vis the kind of expertise in traditional counter-terrorism.

It's a skills and expertise thing. The traditional skills of CT were in investigative skills rather than understanding communities and what vulnerabilities look like ... The CT world is not going to do that and so it's really important if you're looking at a preventive strategy that you haven't got an investigative arm leading that preventative strategy because they're not going to know where to start; they will not theoretically understand it and in practical terms they have no idea.

(Interview 23, Director of prison intervention provider)

This section has tried to present the production and development of radicalisation as a discourse that was formulated by policymakers, popularised by the media and legitimised by a plethora of experts. It also highlighted the sheer diversity of 'experts' involved in the production of discourses on radicalisation and the various ways that experts make claims to expertise. In fact, one of the distinguishing characteristics of expertise in the production of radicalisation is the competitive dynamic between distinct epistemic knowledge domains. It has suggested that through competing analysis and solutions advanced by experts, those who are given credibility and are allowed to speak are those legitimising governmental policies, evidenced with the dominance of the idea-action formulation underpinning the conceptualisation of radicalisation. The ontological makeup of radicalisation that became legitimised and substantiated by expertise will be explored in the next section.

The 'conventional wisdom': the question of root-causes and process

With the emergence of radicalisation as a concept and discourse, the enterprise of developing and codifying the science of radicalisation focused on the 'root-causes' and 'process' of radicalisation. Indeed, the preoccupation of identifying 'root-causes' and 'process' in explanations of radicalisation mirrors the methodology of the hard sciences, where the methods of building knowledge depend on establishing universal fixed 'laws' for all places and time. However, 'root-causes' and 'process' are distinct ways of conceptualising radicalisation. Understanding radicalisation in terms of 'root causes' tries to ask questions about the objective of radicalisation, e.g. restoring a caliphate or reversing Western foreign policy, whereas the 'process' definitions of radicalisation view the phenomenon

112 *The production of radicalisation*

as a linear narrative and do not ask questions of 'why' but are more concerned with questions of 'how' (Githens-Mazer 2012, 5). The Prevent conception of radicalisation represents the process view of radicalisation. This section analyses the ontological framework of radicalisation governing Prevent.

The majority of respondents did not dismiss the findings articulated in the literature on the process of radicalisation. Many believed that factors like ideology and social groups' dynamics were important to the radicalisation process. The objections by some however to the focus on ideology in Prevent conceptions is two-fold: (1) the degree of influence accorded to ideology in radicalisation and how it actually functions and (2) the policy ramifications of valorising ideology in explanations of radicalisation. The notion underpinning the process conception of radicalisation is that ideology directly leads to violence. The two statements below by the Director of a prison provider and a researcher at Quilliam explain this logic.

> So what tafkir does, takfir is legitimate in Islam, but the wrong understanding means I can label a Muslim a non-Muslim and then allows me to put them in a category which makes it easier for me to justify killing them.
>
> (Interview 23, Director of prison intervention provider)

> When we are looking at Islamist extremism it's very clear that it's notions of Jihad and the misuse of the notions of Jihad which drive people towards violence. They convince themselves, or delude themselves, that they are carrying a sacred duty and that they will be martyrs or Shahid.
>
> (Interview 25, Quilliam analyst)

The role of ideology presents radicalisation in terms of the direct causal relationship between ideas and actions. For example, the interviewees believe that a misunderstanding of the ideas about 'Takfir' and 'Jihad' leads to terrorism. A few others express the belief that ideology plays a role at the end of a long process. In his view, ideology does not necessarily lead directly to violence but is actually one factor amongst many which allows the radicalised subject to interpret the world in a certain way.

> Ideology is the kind of final factor, it's not the driving force that radicalises someone. It's the final factor where someone has gone through this whole process and they've looked for something to do and the ideology comes and the ideology plays off the fact that you're probably isolated, you probably don't connect with your family, you don't have a safe space at home, you don't have a safe space externally, so this network provides you with that space, that belonging, provides you with a sense of worth and purpose.
>
> (Interview 10, Investigative journalist)

However, for many respondents, having ideology as the primary cause of radicalisation and enshrining it as the first objective of Prevent in counter-terrorism

The production of radicalisation   113

policy had a number of consequences. Given the influence afforded to ideas as a prime mover in the radicalisation process (since ideas lead directly to action), the Prevent strategy valorised counter-ideology as a strategy and has led to an inordinate focus on what individuals are *thinking* rather than *doing*. This was strikingly articulated by the Director of a research programme on radicalisation.

> However, the principles, the idea for example that there is a conveyor belt from 'X' through radical to terrorist which can or can't be interdicted at various points is commonly shared. And that phrase 'radicalisation' is like a black box in the middle of someone's mainstream life on one end and some-one's terrorist life on the other. So anybody's views we don't like, 'we' the mainstream don't like, can be black boxed in that way and by definition imagined to be on the road towards terrorist acts.
> (Interview 6, Academic/Director of research programme on radicalisation)

The interviewee below, who has been arrested for trying to download material online, also explains how the focus on ideology leads to a criminalisation of ideas.

> So what they are saying is that violence comes after the ideology and this is what the centre right were saying, like Quilliam. And then what you do is counter the ideas and by default people won't want to commit the violence. What you'll find is that if you start countering ideas and don't allow them to engage with ideas that challenge their own understandings and views then how will they ever develop an understanding about how to take action? That leads to frustration when you start to criminalise people for trying to under-stand things.
> (Interview 19, Academic)

A second implication of having ideology as the prime catalyst of the radicalisation process is that radicalisation becomes synonymous with violence. In the Prevent conception of radicalisation, it almost always means or implies violence.

> There are three priority areas and ideology is the first and most important priority in the new Prevent strategy. So they say that actually ideology matters; there are certain ideologies that are compatible with the potential drift towards violence and we won't work with anybody with that ideology because it's a slippery slope towards who knows what.
> (Interview 9, ISD analyst)

This lead to models of radicalisation in which the distinction made is between political activism and violence, rather than between apathy and political mobil-isation (McCauley and Moskalenko 2008, 2009; Baker 2011). The salient fea-tures in these models are (a) the causal link between ideas and action and

114 *The production of radicalisation*

between ideology and violence and (b) placing political participation by Muslims along the same spectrum as violent radicals. The conceptualisation of radicalisation in these models thus has the effect of making ideas the central concern and preoccupation of policy-makers, as well situating the political participation of Muslim individuals and organisations in the UK, not as a positive form of democratic practice, but rather as representing the beginning of a radicalisation process that might potentially lead to violence. This consequently means that political mobilisation is viewed within a security lens, therefore potentially criminalising legitimate democratic activism. This model stressed, in short, the causal relationship of Islamism as the first step towards terrorism.

> I think it's the idea you don't end up being a terrorist without being an Islamist first and therefore Islamism is the first step towards terrorism; Islamism is your marijuana – terrorism is your cocaine. That's the basic idea. I think there are Islamists who never thought a violent thought and there are terrorists who were never Islamists and certainly weren't members of HT.
>
> (Interview 4, IPPR analyst)

Doing this has effectively justified criminalising certain ideas, because it is believed to be leading to violence. The focus on ideas also justifies intervention in the theological lives of Muslims, legitimising the surveillance approach of Prevent which seeks to monitor public spaces in the name of purging them of early signs of radicalisation. Second, as explicated above, it is deployed to delegitimise the involvement of certain individuals and organisations in Prevent, despite their effectiveness in countering radicalisation (more in Chapter 6).

Meanwhile, the second major factor identified in models of radicalisation is the role of identity. The problematisation of Muslim identity is constructed in various discourses. This is reflected in the data in different ways. One interviewee situated the identity problem abstractly within wider questions about modernity.

> So identity choices are just a way of life now and some of them are great, some of them empower people. People get empowered to do things they couldn't imagine they could do and it's great, whether it be in the commercial world, in religious life, whatever, it's fantastic. But there is that radicalised edge as well that people might shop in. They might go into that radical shop; they might stay there and buy lots; they might go in and come out. I don't know you can play with this metaphor in all sorts of ways.
>
> (Interview 6, Academic/Director of research programme on radicalisation)

This interviewee employs the metaphor of the 'shop' to frame the issue of identity as a reflexive process intrinsic to modern life. This is linked to the narrative expounding the crisis of identity experienced by young British Muslims, articulated in Chapter 1. We saw there how the wider literature explains the move

The production of radicalisation   115

towards radicalisation in terms of British Muslims embracing the transnational 'ummah', made possible by globalisation, in which they adopt the more rigorous practices of Salafism. A former analyst at Forward Thinking challenges the narrative that a lack of integration leads to radicalisation.

> Yes the teacher from Leeds. If you look at whether he was integrated or not, some would argue that he was really integrated. He broke the norm within his family by marrying someone outside his kinship, which was a big issue in his family … If you talk about integration would you say that he wasn't well integrated as British values were concerned? … We all have our own understanding of what British values are and from Prevents perspective it was about the narrative that a lack of integration led certain people to become radicalised.
>
> (Interview 26, Forward Thinking analyst)

Hence the narrative propelled, seen in previous sections, is that a lack of integration leads to radicalisation. Whilst some interviewees were sceptical about the validity of this narrative, others saw the issue of identity as crucial in the radicalisation process.

> What I'm arguing and others are too is that we need to look at this as a structure where the individual goes through the process, because of the perception of being an outsider and due to foreign policy grievance as well as the sense that many Muslims, not all but many, feel like they are not being treated the same as mainstream society, then that creates the feeling of an outsider's identity.
>
> (Interview 10, Investigative journalist)

The notion expressed in the comments above – the importance of identity, the link between identity and radicalisation, and the experience of Muslims of being an 'outsider' – all point to the problematisation of Muslim identity. The respondent below, former Vice-Chair of a community organisation, eloquently describes the way in which categorical Muslim identity was pushed onto her by others.

> I think it's a good question, what is British? If you asked me a few years ago what I was, I don't think I chose to define myself as a Muslim British person – I thought I was just a normal person. About five or ten years ago or whatever I suddenly noticed and identified as a Muslim. So what am I, a Muslim what?
>
> (Interview 13, Vice-Chair of community organisation)

Another way that the problem of identity is articulated is through the concept of 'vulnerability'. Although this concept will be addressed properly in Chapter 6 because it is an essential feature of Prevent and de-radicalisation, it is nevertheless important to note that the question of identity, radicalisation and

116　*The production of radicalisation*

'vulnerability' are connected. The way in which the problem of identity and the concept of 'vulnerability' are linked is through the idea that a lack of identity is one of the 'vulnerability' factors that make some individuals susceptible to ideology and therefore radicalisation. This is explained by a Prevent Officer.

> Radicalisation is where the people who have extreme views find somebody who is vulnerable in order to make them believe they could change things. So if somebody is a vulnerable position, whether it is being in prison, criminality, drugs, or not having an identity or not understanding religion, it could be anything that gets that vulnerability.
>
> (Interview 21, Prevent Officer)

However, the problem of identity is not only seen as a symptom of vulnerability. It is also viewed as an indication of 'risk'. So an identity problem makes you vulnerable and puts you at risk of radicalisation. The dominant narrative posits that vulnerable individuals adopt alternative points of identification which, when activated amongst religious groups or online environments, ignites the radicalisation fuse. It is in this way that 'identity' is understood in policy terms as playing a causal role in the radicalisation process.

What was equally instructive, besides those factors that were deemed within the legitimate scope of the narrative on radicalisation, was what was excluded or marginalised within the formation of the discourse: the role of foreign policy in accounts of the 'root-causes' of radicalisation. In the following, a research analyst at ISD explains how the official narrative did not acknowledge the role of foreign policy in the radicalisation of Muslims.

> ...I've always got the sense when I've done interviews in communities, back at that time particularly, people were angry at foreign policy, but so was everybody frankly, but one of the things most people were angry about was they were not even allowed to talk about it. There was a complete lack of willingness to go there and that was while at the same time behind the scenes memos were being prepared for the Home Office and other departments that were saying that we know the war in Iraq and foreign policy is directly causing recruitment. When you have a situation when a government doesn't have legitimacy because it's refusing to acknowledge obvious truth because it doesn't suit its immediate ends, that can't be a good thing, right?
>
> (Interview 9, ISD analyst)

This 'official' line on the causes of radicalisation was contrasted with the statement and actions of prominent Muslim public figures. At the PET workgroups in 2005 Muslim representatives requested that the working groups look into the effects of UK foreign policy on Muslims and called for a Public Inquiry to help place 'facts as opposed to speculation – informed or otherwise – into the public domain about the process by which some British Muslims are being radicalised' (Brighton 2007). While this request was rejected, others like Shahid Malik,

The production of radicalisation 117

(ex-Labour MP) and Salma Yacqoob (former RESPECT Party member), as well as bodies like the MCB amongst many others, stressed the role British foreign policy plays in radicalising British Muslims. In addition, this 'official' position had been contradicted by the video statement of the ring-leader Mohammed Sidique Khan, who had invoked the Iraq War as a motivation to take 'revenge' for his 'brothers and sisters' (Brighton 2007; Rai 2006; Devji 2008). It was also discredited by numerous leaks from government documents linking foreign policy to the radicalisation of British Muslims (HO/FO 2004).

Moreover, the concern with the influence of foreign policy by some Muslims was reported by the security services to the British government a few weeks before the 7/7 bombing in 2005, acknowledging that events in Iraq were continuing to act as 'motivation and a focus of a range of terrorist related activities in the UK' (Rai 2006, 19). In fact, Eliza Manningham-Buller, Director General of MI5 between 2002 and 2007 told a parliamentary enquiry in 2010:

> Our involvement in Iraq radicalised, for want of a better word, a whole generation of young people – not a whole generation, a few among a generation – who saw our involvement in Iraq and Afghanistan as being an attack on Islam.
>
> (Awan *et al.* 2012, 1)

Notably, it became easier to discuss the impact of foreign policy as a source of radicalisation only once former Prime Minister Tony Blair left office in 2007, given that he had been associated with the War on Iraq (Briggs 2010). However, a legacy of this period was that the Prevent policy formulated, with the assistance of the radicalisation concept, a narrative that focused on micro factors affecting the individual, primarily ideology and identity, with macro factors like Western foreign policy being marginalised (Kundnani 2012; Baker-Beall *et al.* 2015, 1). The following interviewee aptly speaks of the 'psychologicalisation' of radicalisation accounts, identifying instead what he considers to be the real cause of radicalisation – Western foreign policy.

> I actually don't think human beings are as complicated as psychologists make them out to be. So there's a lot of psychologicalisation, if such as word exists, of the terrorist – what motivates them? Why? Was he traumatised? Was the father absent? No actually it's actually quite simple why people choose to commit political violence. It's because they feel disempowered at the might of the Western military superstructure that does do unjust things in the Middle East.
>
> (Interview 20, Academic)

This section attempted to understand what interviewees thought on the 'conventional wisdom' of radicalisation and the factors believed to lead some individual British Muslims to terrorism. Respondents did not dismiss the role that ideology and identity crisis played in radicalisation and some believed that they were

118   *The production of radicalisation*

indeed significant factors. However, the majority of interviewees were critical of the emphasis placed on these particular factors at the expense of others and frequently commented on the consequences of privileging ideology in accounts of radicalisation. The main issue is that the central role afforded to ideology enabled the activation of a type of counter-terrorism policy that becomes more preoccupied with policing thought crimes in public institutions than with actually fighting terrorism. Other interviewees identified foreign policy as a critical source of radicalisation but one which was deliberately marginalised in accounts of radicalisation. Focusing on micro factors like ideology and identity shifts the focus away from more macro and politically contentious issues like foreign policy and politics. Prospective chapters will address the impact the conceptualisation of radicalisation had on Prevent the Channel programme, and de-radicalisation.

Radicalisation as a body of knowledge: spurious social science

The explosive incitement to discourse on radicalisation made ostensible claims to the language and methods of the natural sciences. As addressed in the last section this could be seen in the language used in this discourse – 'root-causes', 'processes' and 'models'. This positivist framework employed by 'experts' is used with the goal of providing solutions to the problem of radicalisation. However, many interviewees were very critical of radicalisation as a research area. The major point raised by interviewees is the flimsy research foundations underpinning the codification of radicalisation enterprise. This section addresses radicalisation as a field of knowledge.

Despite claims to scientific rigour and the appropriation of scientific methods, many interviewees were explicitly clear that the concept and idea of radicalisation was not rooted in the sciences or backed up by 'empirical evidence'. This contradiction between the aspirations of many theories on radicalisation to acquire the legitimisation of being scientific and the actual reality of these theories and causal explanations is raised by a think-tank analyst whose reports were influential in the early days when the Prevent strategy was being formed.

> I think that, on the whole, particularly in the preventative area, it hasn't been evidence based as much as it should be. In many ways, it's because the evidence is really hard to get. As I was saying, there's great theories on all this stuff … let's imagine we were talking about, rather than violent extremism, talking about a particular health issue, what would we do? We would find a big enough sample size, we would create that sample and compare it to a control group, we would have longitudinal data, we would have large data sets, we would test, triangulate, we would apply all sorts of scientific rigour to the analysis of whatever data it was we were going to use. We simply haven't done that in this area. There are some areas where there's scientific rigour. You know, a lot of it is qualitative, a lot of it is based on views of

The production of radicalisation   119

frontline workers, a lot of it ends up being dominated by individuals who've got polemical views, are able to communicate them effectively and then they've got hold and then they become the dominant norms in terms of thinking.

(Interview 9, ISD analyst)

This respondent makes an important critique of Prevent – that in contradistinction to other policy areas, research on radicalisation was not evidence based and scientific enough. In terms of methodology for example, she notes the absence of substantial data, the lack of data analysis, the predominance of qualitative data and the tendency towards polemical approaches in counter-terrorism. The absence of robust methodologies characterising research on radicalisation, as well as the scant evidence base for policy development is also highlighted by the following think-tank analyst at DEMOS.

First, how difficult it would be to identify the root causes, and everyone has their personal philosophical view and there isn't any evidence to support any of it. So some people say it's the ideology because they hate the ideology. Some people say the ideology is a symptom of broader structural problems and inequality in society and discrimination against Muslims in Britain. Some people say what the spark here is, is the war in Iraq, so if we wanted to prevent anything we should stop the war in Iraq. But we are not going to do that so what can we deal with? I don't think there's anyone to blame for all of that. It just happened very quickly without being able to answer the root cause.

(Interview 1, DEMOS analyst)

An important point raised by this interviewee was the notion that discussions regarding 'root-causes' of radicalisation reflect 'personal philosophical views'. It reinforces the shaky empirical and methodological foundations of research on radicalisation. Equally important is the idea that the question of 'root causes' was not in the end answered because 'it happened very quickly'. Both previous observations suggest that the production of discourse on radicalisation was ultimately characterised by the absence of methodological rigour and empirical data, and was in the end undermined by policy imperatives. The same two interviewees questioned the overall objective of radicalisation as a body of knowledge.

Now I don't think we are ever going to answer root cause because it's different for each person. But even if we were able to perfectly identify root causes, which is a fool's errand for social scientists anyway, it wouldn't necessarily tell us anyway what our response would be.

(Interview 1, DEMOS analyst)

So I went through this really exhaustive process of all these dominant theories of radicalisation, whether they were grievances, segregation, divisions,

120 *The production of radicalisation*

criminal networks, ideologies, and so on. It all sounds great in theory. Then when you start to define, what are the things you would do to prevent each of those causal factors and how would you measure each of those to know you're moving in the right direction. It's actually like the emperor's new clothes, when you actually look at it, it actually looks really ridiculous because you think even if all indicators were moving in the right direction does that mean there would be less radicalisation?

(Interview 9, ISD analyst)

According to these interviewees the government does not have the resources to tackle radicalisation. There are too many factors involved in radicalisation for the government to be able to address it. There is thus a disjuncture between the discourse of radicalisation and the actual political capacity to resolve the problem of Muslim radicalisation. This observation is coupled with the fact that the development of radicalisation was not the result of organic academic enquiry but was formulated by policymakers and popularised by the media before it found its way into academia.

Consequently, the radicalisation discourse brings into question the relationship between the codification of knowledge by the social sciences and wider governmental objectives. In other words, was the discursive production of radicalisation actually supposed to accurately codify the radicalisation process in the real world or was it merely supposed to provide a retrospective blanket narrative for already agreed political objectives for policymakers? The implication there is that, given the relationship between government funding and the research community, the independence and objectivity of the research, knowledge and overall discourse produced is compromised.

The terrorism field is a big field and huge money has been poured at it. How much of it is real solid? It's not solid in the same way that other disciplines in social sciences are which have been around for over a hundred years and have evolved, you know, and terrorism is a very new field in that sense; it's very modern, it's very driven by government agendas. This is the other thing: who's funding terrorism research? Overwhelmingly its governments and even academic governing grant making bodies that are giving funding are doing it under the parameters established by states.

(Interview 10, Investigative journalist)

The issue at hand relates to the politicised nature characterising the production of knowledge on terrorism and political violence. The funding provided by governments to academia is one of the chief ways research grants and money is provided in research. In particular, topics like political violence and radicalisation require funding because the study of radicalisation and terrorism are not considered disciplines in their own right and primarily belong as sub-branches in international relations. Research contributions to the field have been made from numerous other disciplines – like psychology, medicine, criminology, sociology,

The production of radicalisation   121

economics, etc. Thus research has been overwhelmingly fragmented and multi-disciplinary and undertaken in the crevices and sub-disciplines of academia. For example, the interviewee below explains the popularity of psychology over sociology amongst politicians and media in explaining radicalisation.

> I think it's the easy option; it's the easy way out for politicians. The politicians and the media actually love psychologists and don't actually come to sociologists for solutions. Psychologists offer quick-fix solutions and formulas; follow these description and it's very black and white, it's like statistics. The politicians and the media love statistics because it's a quick fix. Psychological models suit the agenda and the speed at which politics needs to work. So if someone talks about a deradicalisation programme – it sounds nice, it's easy to sell, easy to fund and implement. But if a sociologist comes and talks about social policies and different structures, this isn't easy to manipulate and implement. There is also a myth around psychology that it is scientific, which seems to give them more credibility that they are dealing with the problem. But they don't want to address root causes about British foreign policy.
>
> (Interview 20, Academic)

In other words, the respondent believes that the time and scholarship required to produce quality research are not amenable to both the imperatives and objectives of the world of policy and 24-hour media, centres of power that demand simple, accessible and quick information and the spectacle of an event. Psychologists, 'experts' and many commentators that deploy information are therefore more suited to the logic of the media and policy machine. Again this reinforces the inbuilt politicised and sensationalised approach to knowledge building. Another academic underscores the policy driven nature of knowledge development in Prevent.

> These people do not have any background in social science and academic research. They haven't done any research they've just claimed first-hand experience and some politicians just buy it like this. They don't realise that actually the expertise of these people is pretty much secondary. I'm not saying we can't learn from them, of course we can, but only as one source amongst other sources, and distinguishing between what they actually experienced and their accounts of these experiences, which are obviously already processed and catered for certain people, politicians, and the Prevent programme, whatever. Look at the Quilliam papers; they're always policy driven.
>
> (Interview 15, Academic)

His gripe is with the so-called 'experts' making knowledge claims that are not rooted in the social sciences. According to this academic the problem is thus not the social sciences. Instead the problem is that the discourse is being led by the

122   *The production of radicalisation*

experiences of certain individuals. Again, the suggestion here is that personal experiences are not scientific enough. Given that the social sciences, as well as a diversity of actors outside the social sciences, played a significant role in the production of multiple discourses, knowledges and theories, it is striking that the conceptual framework of radicalisation, as posited by policy-makers, and supported by academic discourse and research, can be reduced to a few salient features. Despite such shortcomings, a whole raft of counter-radicalisation measures and the implementation of the Prevent strategy was delivered on the basis of this knowledge of radicalisation. This raises an important question: does the same laxity towards the veracity, integrity and credibility of research exist in other policy domains? In other words, would other policy areas like Education or Health build their strategies and polices on the basis of such weak research foundations?

This critique of the knowledge foundations of radicalisation was also corroborated in two reports commissioned by the Home Office in order to examine radicalisation. The first report, 'Understanding vulnerability and resilience in individuals to the influence of Al Qa'ida violent extremism' (HO 2011), was prepared for the OSCT. Having reviewed the 39 main studies that looked at Al-Qaeda influenced violent extremism, the report identified the key challenge characterising research in this area from an empirical perspective; the difficulty of interviewing or accessing actual terrorists, which means that, as a result, much of the current literature provides only anecdotal evidence (HO 2011, 1). Another challenge is that when factors leading to terrorism are evaluated and analysed it is done without referencing the fact that the vast majority of people who share the same background as terrorists do not become involved in terrorism (ibid.). Moreover, there is limited evidence that can provide suggestions on what causes individuals to become involved in violent extremism. With respect to methodology the report concluded that:

> The majority of studies are based on a small number of case interviews or secondary analysis of documents, such as trial transcripts, radical websites or other publications promoting violent extremism, where terrorists document their thoughts. Qualitative research involving interviews with participants is often limited to those who are more peripherally involved in terrorism than suicide bombers, such as bombers' family or friends, or other group members who have not taken that final step towards violence. There is also a large body of 'think-pieces', based largely on anecdotal evidence.
>
> (HO 2011, 2)

Meanwhile, the second report, 'Al-Qaeda influenced Radicalisation: a rapid evidence Assessment guided by Situation Action Theory' (2011), provides a useful summary on the problems of conducting research on radicalisation.

> The study of the causes of radicalisation in particular, and of course on terrorism in general, is in its infancy. A number of factors contribute to the

The production of radicalisation   123

scientific immaturity of the field, among them: the low volume of incidents and the relatively small number of individuals implicated, notably in the West; the security issues involved in accessing non-open data; the lack of integration between disciplines; and the imprecise boundaries of the problem area.

(Bouhana and Wikstrom 2011, 2)

In summation, the foundations of radicalisation research and its integrity as a research area were questioned by many interviewees. The rocky foundations of radicalisation as a body of knowledge were also corroborated by government commissioned reports. There was a salient contradiction between the claims made by the social sciences to the methods of the natural sciences and the reality of the research output. Despite the weak state of the field, the knowledge on radicalisation was incorporated into the Prevent Policy, as well as counter-radicalisation and de-radicalisation efforts.

Note

1 Ramadan (2004, 24–28) identifies six trends: (1) scholastic traditionalism; (2) Salafi literalism; (3) Salafi reformers; (4) political literalist Salafism; (5) 'liberal' or 'rationalist' reformism; and (6) Sufism. Although I do not know precisely the hermeneutical groupings the aforementioned interviewees subscribe to, based on their organisation affiliation and interviews, it can be said that the Quilliam Analyst interprets the classical tradition from the position of liberal reformism, whereas the Director of a prison provider argues from the standpoint of Salafi literalism.

References

Awan, A., Hoskins, A. and O'Loughlin, B. (2012). *Radicalisation and Media: Connectivity and Terrorism in the New Media Ecology.* Abingdon: Routledge.

Baker, A.H. (2011). *Extremists in Our Midst, Confronting Terror. New Security Challenges.* London: Palgrave Macmillan

Baker-Beall, C., Heath-Kelly, C. and Jarvis, L. (2015). *Counter-Radicalisation: Critical Perspectives.* Abingdon: Routledge

Blair, A. (2005). *Prime Minister's Press Conference*, 5 August 2005, http://webarchive.nationalarchives.gov.uk/20060715135117/number10.gov.uk/page8041.

Bouhana, N. and Wikstrom, P.H. (2011). *'Al Qa'ida-influenced Radicalisation: A Rapid Evidence Assessment Guided by Situational Action Theory.* London: UK Home Office, www.gov.uk/government/uploads/system/uploads/attachment_data/file/116724/occ97.pdf.

Briggs, R. (2010). 'Community engagement for counterterrorism: lessons from the United Kingdom', *International Affairs*, 86 (4): 971–981.

Brighton, S. (2007). 'British Muslims, multiculturalism and UK foreign policy: "integration" and "cohesion" in and beyond the state', *International Affairs*, 83 (1): 1–17.

Croft, S. and Cerwyn, M. (2010). 'The evolution of threat narratives in the age of terror: understanding terrorist threats in Britain', *International Affairs*, 86 (4): 821–835.

Devji, F. (2008). *The Terrorist in Search of Humanity: Militant Islam and Global Politics.* New York: Colombia University Press.

124 *The production of radicalisation*

ESRC (2007). *New Security Challenges: 'Radicalisation' and Violence – A Critical Reassessment Specification*, www.esrc.ac.uk/ESRCInfoCentre/Images/Specification_tcm6-18574.pdf.

Githens-Mazer, J. (2012). 'The rhetoric and reality: radicalization and political discourse', *International Political Science Review*, 33 (5): 556–567.

Githens-Mazer, J. and Lambert, R. (2010). 'Why conventional wisdom on radicalization fails: the persistence of a failed discourse', *International Affairs*, 86 (4): 889–890.

Home Office (HO) (2011). 'Understanding vulnerability and resilience in individuals to the influence of Al Qa'ida violent extremism', www.gov.uk/government/uploads/system/uploads/attachment_data/file/116723/occ98.pdf.

Home Office/Foreign Office (HO/FO) (2004). *Young Muslims and Extremism*, www.globalsecurity.org/security/library/report/2004/muslimext-uk.htm.

Kundnani, A. (2012). 'Radicalisation: the journey of a concept', *Institute of Race Relations*, 54 (2): 3–25.

McCauley, C. and Moskalenko, S. (2008). 'Mechanisms of political radicalization: pathways toward terrorism', *Terrorism and Political Violence*, 20 (3): 415–433.

McCauley, C. and Moskalenko, S (2009). 'Measuring political mobilisation: the distinction between activism and radicalism', *Terrorism and Political Violence*, 21: 239–260.

Rai, M. (2006). *7/7: The London Bombings, Islam and the Iraq War*. London: Pluto.

Rainbow, P. (1984). *The Foucault Reader*. New York: Pantheon Books.

Ramadan, T. (2004). *Western Muslims and the Future of Islam*. Oxford: Oxford University Press.

Roselle, L., Miskimmon, A. and O'Loughlin, B. (2014). 'Strategic narrative: a new means to understand soft power', *Media, War & Conflict*, 7 (1): 70–84.

5 Disciplinary technology (power)

Surveillance, detection, discipline

> It reinforced the idea of bad and good Muslims; it reinforced the idea of those who want to be a part of us and those who don't, and as the independent review of the Prevent programme stated, 'Prevent was a means for government to impose a British version of Islam on Muslim communities', and this was from an independent Prevent review; the perception was that this was a way of generating a form of Islam that was palatable and suitable to British social and political spaces.
>
> (Interview 11, Academic)

CONTEST was launched in 2003 and became public in late 2006 (HC 2010, 7). CONTEST comprises of four 'P's' (HO 2011): (1) 'Prevent': preventing people from being drawn into extremism; (2) 'Pursue': pursuing those who become involved in planning; (3) 'Protect': protecting critical national infrastructure to reduce vulnerabilities and populations; (4) 'Prepare': preparing to manage the consequences of attack. The aim of the Prevent strategy is to 'stop people becoming terrorists or supporting terrorism' (HO 2011, 61). The rationale underpinning Prevent was that government would work in partnership with Muslim communities to counter the long-term conditions that lead to violent radicalisation. This 'soft' turn in counter-terrorism was largely the by-product of the Preventing Extremism Together (PET) workforce and the Wilton Park Conference in 2006, which had predated the Prevent strategy and had brought Muslims leaders and the government together in order to address the issue of violent extremism.

The PET workforce published their recommendations in November 2005, some of which were incorporated in the Prevent strategy of 2006 (HO 2006, 82). PREVENT II also built and led to other initiatives, like the publication by the Department for Communities and Local Government (DCLG) in April 2007 of 'Preventing Violent Extremism: Winning Hearts and Minds', which set out a community-led approach to tackling violent extremism; the sponsoring of the 'Radical Middle Way' by the FCO and DCLG to challenge terrorist ideology; and a programme of work to improve the capacity of NOMS and other agencies to manage the risks posed by violent extremist offenders, amongst other initiatives (HO 2009, 82–83). A consensus emerged between 2005 and 2006 that the

126 *Surveillance, detection, discipline*

most effective and legitimate strategy for tackling violent extremism was through the support and mobilisation of the Muslim communities (Briggs *et al.* 2006; Briggs 2010; Lambert 2011).

The delivery of Prevent fell on the DCLG with funding available to organisations and charities in local municipalities seeking to counter radicalisation. Prevent allocated £6 million in 2007, which increased to £140 million by 2008–09 (HO 2009, 16; Briggs 2010, 971). Prevent funding was distributed according to the population size of Muslim communities in a particular locality (HO 2006, 2009; HC 2010, 50). In 2008, the Prevent strategy was rolled out nationally, along with National Indicator 35 (NI35) − building resilience to violent extremism − which incorporated a measure of a local authority's 'engagement with and understanding of Muslim communities' (Briggs 2010, 975). All local areas were therefore required to report to government whether they had engaged with the Muslim communities as part of their performance measures (Briggs 2010, 975). Police Prevent coordinators were also created in 2008, as well as the trialling of the Channel project (ibid.). Since its inception in 2006 Prevent has undergone two revisions and is currently in its third iteration (2006, 2009 and 2011).

The first and second Prevent strategies were designed to address the causes, or drivers, of radicalisation at a variety of stages. The strategic objectives were designed to:

1   Challenge the ideology behind violent extremism through targeted communications and work with credible religious authorities both in the UK and overseas to counter the extremist narrative.
2   Disrupt the activities of those who seek to recruit vulnerable people.
3   Provide interventions to support vulnerable people, largely concentrated in high priority, high risk geographical areas as well as within specific sectors, such as prisons and higher education.
4   Build community resilience primarily through work at a local level but also including initiatives to build community capacity, such as the support of national bodies and the establishing of best practice guidance for mosques.
5   Address wider grievances including work in the UK and overseas (HO 2009, 80; HC 2010; Briggs 2010).

However, the introduction of a second version of Prevent (2009) was characterised by two important features. First, Prevent II shifted the focus further away from violence and towards a new category called 'non-violent extremism' (HO 2009, 81). The most immediate challenge with this term was its meaning (Briggs 2010, 976). This new categorisation proved problematic given that some of leading partners of government in the delivery of counter-radicalisation initiatives, such as the MCB and STREET, in addition to several other organisations, were considered 'non-violent extremists'. The second critical dimension of Prevent II was the move towards a greater focus on 'Our Shared values' (HO 2009, 87), defined loosely as a commitment to rights, support for institutions and democracy, and respect for the rule of law and equality (HO 2009, 87). This

Surveillance, detection, discipline 127

categorisation was used by the former Labour government not only to restrict and marginalise 'non-violent extremists', which by then included the MCB, who had previously been championed by New Labour as representatives of Muslim communities, but also to delineate a set of national and cultural values.

Meanwhile, the publication of Arun Kundnani's 'SPOOKED!' in 2009 was a significant intervention in the discourse on Prevent because it presented the first empirical critique of it as a policy in the public domain. The overall conclusion of the report was that Prevent had little to do with preventing radicalisation and more to do with counter-subversion, particularly intelligence gathering by the secret services and the government (Kundnani 2009). His report also stated that Prevent was perceived by British Muslims as a way to police 'thought-crimes', restrict legitimate dissent and construct models of the 'good Muslim' (Kunadi 2009, 39–41). With the arrival of the Coalition government in 2010, Prevent was subjected to review by the House of Commons Select Committee. The Select Committee investigation highlighted a number of critical issues. These include, among others, the following issues (HC 2010):

- Prevent is situated within a counter-terrorism strategy and the Muslim community is therefore guilty by association (8, para 11).
- The focus on Muslims alienates them and legitimises the views of the Far Right and Islamophobes (8, para 13).
- Problems with terminology: the language of Prevent 'lends itself to the idea that there lies a dormant terrorist within Muslims' (9, para 14).
- Being labelled 'at risk from violent extremism' criminalises Muslims (9, para 17 and 18).
- Prevent was accused of being a vehicle for spying, surveillance and intelligence gathering (11–14). For example, in late 2007 the West Midlands Police created project 'champion'. The Police planned the installation of 218 CCTV Cameras in Muslim areas, particularly Alum Rock and Sparkhill in Birmingham. The installation of the cameras began in January 2010 and by April questions were being asked by the community (Thornton 2010, 8). By July 2010 the West Midlands Police agreed to halt the project.
- Prevent was using the Channel programme to delegitimise dissent, spy and pursue 'suspects' (14–17 and 52–55).
- It promoted envy amongst other faith groups who did not have access to the same amount of money and attention for community projects (18, para 41–43).
- South Asian Organisations were accessing Prevent through emphasising the 'Muslim aspect of their identity'. It had thus led to anti-cohesion projects. (19, para 43).
- It did not target other forms of extremism in other communities and ideologies (20, para 45).
- It did not appreciate the diversity of Muslim communities and the Muslim identity has been reduced to the faith persona. It has reified the Muslim identity and divided the Muslim communities even further (22, para 51).

128 *Surveillance, detection, discipline*

- It tried to socially engineer Muslim communities by promoting 'good Islam' against 'bad Islam' (34, para 85–87).
- It was accused of funding extremist individuals and groups (37–8, para 94–95).
- It conflated community cohesion work with the narrower objective of preventing violent extremism/radicalisation, which impeded the ability of policy-makers to effectively tackle the problem of violent radicalisation (37, para 92 and pp. 56–961).
- It was criticised for sitting within the DCLG. This meant that Local government had to deliver security work it was not familiar with (40, para 101 and 108)
- It could not be measured. Policymakers cannot gauge success (52, para 136–138).

Consequently, a revised version of Prevent was released in June 2011. Prevent III was different to previous strategies in that it widened the scope of its objectives to cover all forms of terrorism and extremism, like those of the Far-Right, and not just Al-Qaeda inspired types, whilst narrowing the focus of the strategy, e.g. not funding integration projects (HO 2011, 60). Furthermore, the objectives of Prevent, although similar in many respects, focused on *ideas, people and institutions* (HO 2011, 63) i.e.:

1 Respond to the ideological challenge of terrorism and the threat we face from those who promote it;
2 Prevent people from being drawn into terrorism and ensure that they are given appropriate advice and support; and
3 Work with a wide range of sectors where there are risks of radicalisation which we need to address.

According to the revised strategy, the biggest change was disentangling the integration strategy from the Prevent strategy (HO 2011, 62). With this streamlined strategy, Prevent officially introduced 'de-radicalisation' interventions under the second objective, 'supporting vulnerable people' (HO 2011, 65) and delivered them through the Channel Programme (59–71). Channel emerged under Prevent II in 2009, and yet the concept of de-radicalisation itself was not articulated until Prevent III in 2011. De-radicalisation was only mentioned in passing in Prevent II, without an attempt to define it (HO 2009, 90). Channel is a police run programme that is anchored institutionally in pre-existing crime prevention infrastructure and is administered through a multi-agency approach. It has 28 coordinators and a handful of support posts and covers about 75 local authorities and 12 police forces (57). The total funding for Channel for the period April 2007 to March 2011 was approximately £4.7 million (60). Notably, this second objective of Prevent is linked to the third – supporting sectors and institutions where there are risk of radicalisation (66). This includes schools and children, higher and further education, health, the criminal justice system, prison and probation, youth offenders and youth justice, Prevent Policing Officers, and the charitable sector (66–72). As part of the strategy, government will work with these sectors in order to raise an 'awareness of the risks of radicalisation and of how radicalisers work, and to develop an effective response' (ibid., 66). Where Prevent II previously encompassed various community projects, the current strategy, focuses on Channel and de-radicalisation interventions.

Prevent: counter-terrorism, counter-subversion, community cohesion or crime prevention?

This section highlights the assessment of Prevent by interviewees. Of the 27 interviews, the senior researcher at Quilliam was the only interviewee who spoke positively about Prevent. A couple of others distinguished between 'old' and 'new' Prevent and believed that 'old' Prevent was a more effective strategy. The notion of 'old' Prevent refers to Prevent I in 2006 in which organisations like Siraat and STREET were funded for counter-radicalisation. 'New' Prevent designates PREVENT III, which terminated such projects out of the principle of not funding 'non-violent extremist'.

> This government now for example have fallen into the trap and got rid of all the work and just left it to people who profess what they profess. You don't find Prevent anymore; you don't find any successful prevent. That was even mentioned by Mr (inaudible) who came from the FBI in New York who came and sat with the Home Affairs Select Committee. What was his statement? Old Prevent is better than New Prevent.
>
> (Interview 23, Director of prison intervention provider)

However, interviewees were overwhelmingly critical of Prevent. An example of a critical verdict of Prevent is articulated by a former Chief Inspector, someone who sat on the Prevent Delivery Board as well as being responsible for assessing the community impact of counter-terrorism.

> It was an ill thought out strategic approach in my view and that's been acknowledged by government now. The whole issue was poorly researched, not properly understood, and as a consequence of that we ended up with an ill-judged policy approach.
>
> (Interview 24, former Chief Inspector/Prevent Board member)

This interviewee provides an overview of Prevent from someone who was involved in it at a strategic level. A more detailed breakdown of Prevent from another prominent interviewee is explained by the former Secretary General (SG) of the representative organisation. The interviewee highlights a number of problems with Prevent, ranging from the way that the strategy was framed at the outset, to its delivery through local councils who were reluctant to implement security work, to the negative impact on Muslim communities in

130 *Surveillance, detection, discipline*

terms of 'spying' and dividing Muslims. Again, his comment is significant, given his former position as one of the main representatives of Muslim communities.

> From day one it was seen from the community in a very negative light in the sense that government was giving lots of money to councils and many of them weren't interested to do this sort of work because local Councils had done work in the Muslim communities – youth groups, mosques, and other bodies – but the way it was framed, as if the problem was with the Muslim community and we have to deradicalise them. Many local councils rejected it, and some Muslim organisations got some money and then realised it was Prevent money, which was seen as more or less spying on the community and then it divided the community.
>
> (Interview 14, former Secretary General of representative organisation)

However, contra Prevent, the data reveals a disconnect with the delivery of Prevent between different stages of the policymaking framework, starting with policymakers at the top, such as the OSCT and the Home Office, to Local Authorities and the Police below them, all the way down to community organisations. In other words the data shows that Prevent meant different things to different people. So while it was officially about the prevention of terrorism, beneath the surface it meant a plethora of things; to be publicly seen tackling a problem for politicians; career progression for civil servants; funding for organisations unable to get funds elsewhere; administrative tick-box initiatives for local government; and the building of relationships with communities for the police, amongst many other things.

Examples illustrating the myriad understandings of Prevent from the perspectives of the different individuals and organisations can be seen below. The first interviewee, explains his own career motives and those of civil servants for getting involved in Prevent.

> The problem with OSCT, despite having a good guy at the top, was basically a bunch of young ambitious civil servants who thought they were spooks ... they put their mobile phones in the lockers as they go in because what they do is an important secret. But actually, a lot of them worked there for six months, got the t-shirt and left. None of them stuck at it, it was a flash place to be in government. Part of the problem with this whole agenda for ten years was that it was sexy. If I'm honest it was partly why I got into it, front page stuff every day. It was sexy.
>
> (Interview 4, IPPR analyst)

This comment suggests that Prevent was an attractive prospect from the perspective of career progression; in the interviewee's words: 'it was sexy'. There are other examples in the data set that reinforce the notion that Prevent had in fact become an industry with money and jobs. The interviewee below, the

Surveillance, detection, discipline 131

Director of an organisation that received Prevent money for counter-radicalisation projects, explains his organisation's experience with Prevent.

> It's really interesting for us that the only significant resources we were able to access was through Prevent, the only significant press coverage we were able to get was press coverage that's going to inform Prevent about Prevent. The press were never interested in any of the stories around the work we did about us being the first professional Muslim theatre company in the UK, around being a theatre company that brought together artists of different faiths, around our delivering work in places like Shakespeare's Globe, the press was never interested. But the moment we started doing Prevent work, all of a sudden there was all sorts of interest.
>
> (Interview 5, Director of company receiving Prevent funding)

His account shows that Prevent money provided both crucial financial support and publicity for his company's work. He told me that he had struggled to obtain funding from the arts bodies before the advent of Prevent. It is an insight into the reasons behind the involvement of many organisations with Prevent. In other words, in many instances it was less about countering radicalisation and more about access to funds in order to ensure organisational survival. Again, the key idea here is that Prevent was understood and implemented differently at all levels according to the individual and organisational remit. This is exemplified below by a Prevent Officer who viewed Prevent in terms of building relationships between the police and the community.

> So with Prevent the idea was it's about taking some secret stuff and having a forward facing side in order to engage with the community. If something happened the public have a face to talk to and be able to build a relationship. So, if I'm at Preston I know we have a link worker working with the Mosques and Imams and police officers now visit Mosques once a week or a month just as a normal routine to see if there's any problems with crime or anti-social behaviour so that you build a relationship with your community and understand what their problems are.
>
> (Interview 21, Prevent Officer)

Ultimately, Prevent was understood and implemented differently by diverse actors for all sorts of reasons and motivations. It is unsurprising then that the majority of interviewees were critical of the notion that Prevent was supposed to tackle radicalisation or that it was in the end effective in directly preventing terrorism. There was a clear disjuncture between the objectives of Prevent and the projects it funded.

> There were lots of other samosa and pancake projects … It was basically asking Muslim women to tackle violent extremism without any research, prior experience, or any practical tools or trialling. I think it was, again,

132 *Surveillance, detection, discipline*

> doomed to failure because having people, or social workers, or at best do-gooders who felt they were proud to be British, and getting them to deal with something as heavy as this was ridiculous. They neither had the qualifications, nor the understanding of the problems, nor the time to bring on board academics or any other kind of strategy...

> (Interview 2, Director of an organisation countering extremism on campus)

The comment above by the Director of a company involved in counter-radicalisation work situates the failure of Prevent in the securitisation of community cohesion projects, or what he calls 'samosa and pancakes' projects. He raises the important issue that local authority and public sector workers had neither the expertise nor experience to perform counter-terrorism related tasks. In addition, the notion of the push towards community cohesion projects in a counter-terrorism strategy is seriously questioned by the former Chairman of the the main police-community relations body.

> But in real counter-terrorism terms it hasn't done an iota of good and that's something we and the police agree, that Prevent has not done anything tangible in the fight against terrorism. I remember in 2006 and 2007 the DCLG did this conference at the Queen Elizabeth Centre to showcase what Prevent has achieved, you know, what the funding has achieved; they had six or seven projects and one of these projects was we took these young girls to a camping trip, we took some boys to the cinema, we went to the seaside, fantastic...

> (Interview 18, former Chair of community organisation)

These comments highlight the disjointed nature of the implementation of Prevent, particularly between the stated threat (terrorism), the proposed solution (preventing radicalisation), the delivery of the strategy (local government, police) and the means (community projects). In short, interviewees frequently pointed at the irrelevance of the bulk of Prevent activities in relation to its objective, which is reflected above in the observation that Prevent has not done anything 'tangible in the fight against terrorism'. In addition, a number of interviewees mentioned a significant weakness of the strategy – the absence of a criterion to measure the successes and failures of Prevent. The inability to calculate the output of the strategy in relation to whether it has stopped or prevented terrorism is a remarkable drawback for such a high profile policy area. The following interviewee discusses the difficulty of measuring preventive work in this area.

> Well it's really difficult isn't it? It's really hard to prove the negative of something. It's difficult to prove something hasn't happened because it might not have happened anyway. How do we prove that it not happening was because of something we did? I mean you are always confronted by this question working in the area of security, or most areas of preventative policy

Surveillance, detection, discipline 133

making – that's the challenge. And particularly when you have really, really, small numbers. So for instance, in health policy there's all sort of preventative policy you can prove. You can prove you know introducing more hand sanitation units in hospital, you bring down MRSA or whatever it's called.

(Interview 9, ISD analyst)

She raises two crucial questions: how do you prove the negative of something? And conceding her point that proving preventive work in other policy domains is possible, why then is there a high tolerance by policymakers for the absence of measuring tools and techniques in Prevent? Why invest political and financial capital in a policy you do not know is working? While this section does not attempt to answer these questions directly, such questions nevertheless challenge the assumptions that the strategy is supposed to tackle terrorism or even prevent radicalisation. The fact that Prevent was not linked to terrorism and that policymakers were not preoccupied with establishing a direct connection between measuring Prevent work and terrorism, provokes a significant question: what was the purpose of Prevent?

Overall, Prevent was seen by interviewees to be a muddled policy exhibiting different policy logics. Instead of an effort to win the 'hearts and minds' of Muslim communities, the data reveals that the majority of interviewees believed that Prevent was about two main objectives: (1) intelligence gathering on Muslims and (2) social re-engineering of communities. With this in mind, Prevent was viewed more as a counter-subversion strategy than as a counter-terrorism strategy.

With regards to intelligence gathering, interviewees have pointed to a number of features: the fact that Prevent was delivered in local areas with Muslim populations; that community projects had to be documented; that signs of potential radicalism had to be reported to the authorities; that project Champion in Birmingham involved placement of cameras to spy on the community; the fact that Prevent was coordinated by the police, amongst others. The long quote below is by someone who was arrested for downloading material as a university student. His comment aptly encapsulates the notion of intelligence gathering in Prevent.

...this is why they rolled out the programme to areas with more than 2,000 Muslims, was because they were trying to understand all Muslims and where the problems were, and then eventually they found that Universities were a problem, schools and colleges were a problem, community centres and Mosques were a problem and so the new Prevent strategy decided to focus on these institutions ... The Prevent programme was rolled out in order to gather information on the community which then became intelligence and then was used to form new policy and new actions by the police towards the community...

(Interview 19, Academic)

134 *Surveillance, detection, discipline*

Crucially, he highlights the role of institutions marked out by policymakers as sites of potential radicalisation as well as focal points of surveillance networks in structures of governance, something this chapter address in subsequent sections. Meanwhile, the second dimension raised by many interviewees was the push by the government towards remaking Muslim communities. This view is expressed by the former Head of a counter-terrorism unit.

> But then CLG started up, first with Ruth Kelly and then with Hazel Blears, they made very clear they were looking to engage with a different set of communities rather than communities that are or happen to be. But to construct new ones with the help of created bodies like Quilliam and the Sufi Council of Britain and I remember witnessing that first hand and yes you could describe elements of that as post-colonial. You need to ask the question of whether Labour government ministers could ever dream of taking the same approach with other communities.
>
> (Interview 17, former Head of counter-terrorism unit)

The interviewee calls the approach of government to Muslim communities 'post-colonial' in reference to the fact that it was trying to recreate community leadership by promoting certain organisations and other religious denominations over existing ones. This view is also echoed in the comments below. Similar to the interviewee above, this interviewee identifies the Quilliam Foundation and the Sufi Muslim Council as key players in the efforts of government to construct new partners.

> They tried to create the Sufi Muslim Council – that failed. They tried to create the British Muslim Forum – that failed. They have somehow coerced an organisation called MINAB, which has for all intents and purposes fallen flat on its face; they heavily funded the Quilliam Foundation ... They've not changed anything and wherever they go they get kicked and shouted at. So all this money they spent on all this, all it's done is help to identify who the sell outs are in the eyes of the community and who aren't.
>
> (Interview 18, former Chair of community organisation)

The point in this section is to shed light on how Prevent was seen by many as a cover for other governmental objectives. Prevent was sold as an attempt to counter radicalisation and yet the data reveals a disconnection at every level of the policy chain, from policymakers at the top, all the way down to the layperson at the receiving end of Prevent. The availability of funding, delegating the delivery of the policy to DCLG, investing in community cohesion projects – all revealed the confusing logic at the heart of Prevent and how far removed the work of Prevent was from its stated objectives. However, a closer inspection of the data indicated that, instead of tackling radicalisation, Prevent was about intelligence gathering, surveillance and the reconstruction of Muslim communities. The next section examines the normative aim governing Prevent in relation to Muslims.

'British values' and 'extremism' in prevent: 'four legs good, two legs bad'

Fieldwork data conveys how Prevent created a dichotomy between the category 'British values' on the one hand, and 'extremism' on the other hand. Whereas 'British values' encompasses notions such as democracy, the rule of law and human rights and is associated with the mainstream and therefore the 'Good', 'extremism' connotes categories like Islamism, Salafism, Sharia, and violence, and embodies the abnormal and deviant, thus representing the 'Bad'. Whilst interviewees predominantly expressed a constructivist take on categories like 'British values' and 'extremism', they nevertheless argued that the aforementioned binaries had created a classification system which acts as a regulatory mechanism in policy terms so that activities, people and objectives are ordered according to 'Good' and 'Bad'. Classification systems apply 'a principle of difference to a population in such a way as to be able to divide them and all their characteristics into at least two opposing groups – us/them' (Woodward 1997, 29).

The concept of 'shared values' became prominent in the second iteration of the Prevent strategy in 2009. It is important to recognise that the notion of 'British values' (Albeit Prevent does not refer to it as British values, but as shared values) is not enshrined in law and that it sits merely within a policy document. It does not have any juridical effect. Many interviewees believed that 'British values' were constructed values. Below, for example, an academic expresses his understanding of British values.

> When you start to talk with people about what British values are, they will mention democracy, equality, and fairness, etc. and is that any different to the Swedish, or the Italians, or the Spanish, or the Canadians, or the Japanese? No ... At the cultural level you can go down the route of, you know, it's the monarchy; but if you look back, they are German and Greek, not exactly British so then you look at the food we eat; the favourite dish is the chicken tikka masala, well, tikka masala might have been invented in Glasgow but it was invented by Pakistanis and Bangladeshis for the British palate, you know, making a curry that reflected British sensibilities ... Where do we go?
>
> (Interview 11, Academic)

The underlying argument above is that the search for British values and a singular and 'mainstream' national identity is depicted as an elusive exercise. It is instead arbitrarily defined, shaped historically by various immigrant communities settling in Britain. Another example of the tenuousness of British values is expressed by the former Chair of the MSF who raises the contested nature of British values:

> So the idea of British values is a red herring. It fell flat on their face ... What did they come up with? Everything they came up with was airy fairy

136 *Surveillance, detection, discipline*

and universal. They were human rights things. I still can't figure a single British thing.

(Interview 18, former Chair of community organisation)

Alongside discourses on British values in Prevent is the notion of the 'good' Muslim or 'moderate' Muslim. Notably, some interviewees were not clear what the category 'moderate' Muslim meant. An academic aptly describes below the way that different groups and organisations compete to occupy the 'moderate' category and also the way in which such groups and organisations compete for the 'moderate' category in relation to each other. The 'moderate' category in short does not exist as an empirical fact and only makes sense in relation to other groups.

So the carrot's being dangled and what you have is one organisation saying 'we are moderate Muslims'. Then you have another organisation saying 'they are moderate, but we are moderate mainstream Muslims' and then you have another group say 'they are moderate Muslims but we are middle of the road mainstream Muslims' and then you end with a group that says 'well, we are not even Muslim but we'll deal with the problem'.

(Interview 11, Academic)

The term is even rendered meaningless, encapsulated by the parody – 'we are middle of the road mainstream Muslims'. In this case, terms like 'moderate' come attached to the 'carrot' of funding, as does the term 'extremism'. In many respects the use of these terms can be understood in relation to the strategic manoeuvring of actors for various ends, thus reinforcing the hollow nature of such categories. Another conception of moderate relates to foreign policy. The criterion for being 'moderate' Muslims below is then not religious but instead is political, especially with regards to acquiescence with Western foreign policy.

I think it was Tariq Ramadan who said that a real test of who is a moderate and extremist Muslim is who supports American foreign policy. So you can have people with extremist Islamic beliefs in Saudi Arabia but because they bump along okay with the US government, they are okay. But if you are Syrian or Iranian and you don't like the US government and even though your concept of Islam might be a lot more moderate, you are an extremist.

(Interview 24, former Chief Inspector/Prevent Board member)

Again, people have different conceptions of these terms. According to the Director of a think-tank that received Prevent funding, the distinction between the dichotomy of 'good' and 'bad' is the distinction between apolitical and political. The notion of a 'good' Muslim corresponds to the idea of someone who is spiritual and prays but is non-political, and a 'bad' Muslim is someone who is political. However, this binary is challenged by the interviewee. If he has political views, then it is the result of being a 'citizen'. Being a good citizen means he has the freedom to engage with society and politics. Again, this understanding of 'bad' Muslim inverts the prevalent understanding of 'bad' Muslims.

> Good and bad Muslims today in the government's eyes and mainstream establishment's eyes unfortunately is about if you are somebody who prays and is into spirituality and the such and you embody that and that alone and whether you have a political dimension. My argument is this: I have a political view because I am a citizen of this country and have a freedom to do so not because I'm obliged to have this view by my religion.
>
> (Interview 27, President of Prevent funded think-tank)

So the binary presents the 'moderate' Muslim according to interviewees as spiritual, non-political and someone who agrees with Western foreign Policy. The 'moderates' are of course those who subscribe to British values. What then about the 'other'? The 'other' in discourses of radicalisation is represented by 'Islamism', or 'political Islam'. The Director of a think-tank that received Prevent money explains the association the discourse has with Political Islam.

> Unfortunately, Political Islam when we talk about it today, say through the mainstream prism or talks to people in positions of governance and the like, the understanding is that the term pertains to the term Sharia, which pertains to subjugating women, amputating people and the penal code, which people take as whipping and stoning. So Political Islam is seen as something as enforced, which in my dictionary goes against the value system of Islam, which creates a schism in terms of rights for men and women, which again I see as contradictory to the value system of Islam. And that it seeks to eliminate the 'Other'; it cannot exist within the realm of any other idea or faith and hence in order to exist has to eliminate everything else.
>
> (Interview 27, President of Prevent funded think-tank)

So Political Islam, referred to often in the discourse as 'Islamism', is associated with: the Sharia, the subjugation of women, amputating people and stoning, and eliminates the 'other'. Political Islam also became associated with 'non-violent extremism' in 2009. The advent of 'non-violent extremism' in Prevent 2009 was not only a symbolic distinction but also a policy re-calibration of resources and effort towards tackling 'extremism'. The underlying principle of this approach was that Government would not support groups and individuals who did not subscribe to British values, despite the acknowledged experience and knowledge such groups and individuals have in tackling the threat of violent radicalisation. The category 'non-violent extremism' was superseded by the term 'extremism' in the Prevent strategy of 2011 and was defined as:

> ...the vocal or active opposition to fundamental British values, including democracy, the rule of law, individual liberty and mutual respect and

138 *Surveillance, detection, discipline*

tolerance of different faiths and beliefs. We also include in our definition of extremism calls for the death of members of our armed forces, whether in this country or overseas.

(HO 2011, 62, footnote 52; HM 2015, 3)

Hence 'extremism' is defined as the opposite of British values. Despite the definition offered in Prevent most interviewees believed that 'non-violent extremism' was synonymous with 'extremism' and that there were various understandings of what 'extremism' actually means. The interviewee below discusses the difficulty in defining 'non-violent extremist groups'.

> There's difficulty in defining who non-violent extremist groups are. Because it is a relative term everyone has their own definitions … Hypothetically, let's imagine we had a good definition: it's a belief in this or that view makes you extremist. How do you then determine whether a group is an extremist group or not? Will it have to be written in their governing articles? Will it be based on the fact they once invited a speaker who once shared that view? What if you have a chairman, who used to be an extremist, but is now renounced, but used to sit on another board? And this is the problem; it's not just about how you define but what is your criterion for making that decision?
>
> (Interview 1, DEMOS analyst)

However, as articulated above, the term is ill-defined and vague, a problem it shares with the word 'extremism'. One view of 'extremism', explained below by a prison de-radicalisation agency provider is that it leads to violence. His notion of 'radical' does not equate with that of radicalisation, which makes more of an explicit link between extremism and violence.

> We made a distinction between radical and extremist. An extremist is somebody who would allow the killing of innocent people based on those five areas [identified by this interviewee in Chapter 4]. A radical is somebody who misunderstands those five areas but wouldn't go so far as to call for other people to cause harm.
>
> (Interview 23, Director of prison intervention provider)

Thus, according to the interviewee below, an extremist is someone who legitimises violence whereas 'radical' merely has radical ideas but does not act upon those ideas. His understanding of 'extremism' emphasises the diversity of interpretations the word entails. Another view of 'extremists' is not necessarily linked to violence but associates it with Salafi Muslims, as explained by a Prevent practitioner.

> If you ask people what extremism is and what de-radicalisation means, you have too many different things to explain; so you hide behind words that

Surveillance, detection, discipline 139

you don't understand yourself. So 'Salafi' has become a buzzword of saying what is wrong rather than saying what is right.

> (Interview 8, Prevent practitioner)

According to the comment above, Salafi Muslims are associated with 'extremism' and with 'what is wrong rather than saying what is right'. Another perspective on 'extremism' is shared below by an academic posing the question through the hypothetical eyes of the EDL.

> You scratch the surface and you ask the EDL what does an extremist Muslim look like? ... So actually, when you start looking at that, well, actually an extremist is a Muslim who prays and goes to mosque and eats halal meat – they are all extremists. Actually, you'll find they are huge swathes of Muslim communities. So are we talking about extremist or are we talking about Muslim in culture terms only? Like cultural or secular Jews.
>
> (Interview 11, Academic)

This comment suggests that according to the EDL 'extreme' Muslim equates to practicing Muslim, 'someone who eats Halal meat, who prays, who wants a mosque to go to'. This conception of 'extremism' moves the lines of demarcation beyond the narrow fringe of individuals and small groups and situates the entire Muslim community within the purview of 'extremism'. The problem therefore resides with Muslim communities and the religion of Islam and not extremism of thought and action. The suggestion above is that when Muslims abandon religion and become 'cultural Muslims', then Muslims cease being seen as 'extremists'. Overall therefore, 'extremism' means different things to different people and yet it still occupies the position of 'bad', violent, alien and thus the opposite of British values.

In light of the above, how do we make sense of the role of contested categories like 'British values' and 'extremism', which remain undefined legally in Prevent? What in other words is the significance of British values in counterterrorism? The first is the creation of a criterion for distinguishing in policy terms between the legitimate (good) and the illegitimate (bad), whilst the second pertains to the discipline and control of individuals, organisations and structures in line with this criterion. Hence the classification system produced by Prevent created a regulatory norm. The first dimension is explained by an academic.

> We need them to see what is proper and improper and what is legitimate and illegitimate and so on. Policy-makers need a kind of criteria to know what is legitimate and what is not so they came up with the ideas of British values. And also, it's a good idea because it resonates with all sorts of public policy aspects and resonates with the general public.
>
> (Interview 15, Academic)

This comment elucidates that classification systems are about drawing boundaries in public life for policymakers and thus delimiting the spaces and ideas of what

140 *Surveillance, detection, discipline*

constitutes acceptability. Moreover, it generates a shared vocabulary – one that is moral, intellectual, scientific and institutionally and organisationally workable. It also allows for the formation of the vast and loose associations to come together in administrating governance: between various governmental departments internally, and externally with other sectors and partners; think-tanks, pressure groups, civil society organisations, the media and their apparatus, the security establishment, the various public institutions, the market, experts, managers and parents.

Second, the by-product of this new classification was that organisations that were previously considered 'moderate' and as partners in the delivery of counterterrorism, were branded as 'extremists' and eventually marginalised. This approach was explained by the former SG of a prominent representative organisation in the following way.

> The problem with the current Prevent is that there are categorisations of Muslims, probably from QF's paper, categorising Muslim organisations into violent and nonviolent extremist and advising government not formally to talk with non-violent extremism. So these are the very laughable positions the government has taken. Even organisations like the MCB and mainstream Muslim organisations like FOSIS, which has been around since 1963, organisations like these are seen, because they were defined by Quilliam Foundation and neo-Cons as non-violent extremist – we are somehow extremists – and so now government won't formally talk to them. So they will formally not talk to us but will talk informally.
>
> (Interview 14, former Secretary General of representative organisation)

The above respondent highlights how the categorisation of 'non-violent extremism' effectively precluded and debarred them from gaining access to government. Such classification systems should also be viewed as an instrument of producing certain behaviours and conducts. The following interviewee explains the intended meaning behind 'non-violent extremism', which ultimately aims at creating 'moderate' Muslims.

> The Tories are double-speaking … comes and says we are not interested in violent extremism but we're interested in non-violent extremism … they have certain problems with Muslim theology and aspects of Sharia and Muslim life. They want Muslims whole heartedly to accept homosexuality and ideally they want Muslim women to stop wearing niqab, they would like Muslim women to freely marry non-Muslims. We can't get away from the fact certain elements within Western societies have a problem with elements and practices within Islam.
>
> (Interview 5, Director of company receiving Prevent funding)

In summation, Prevent produced a classification system dichotomised between 'British values' and 'extremism'. Data analysis conveyed that for the majority of interviewees these terms and ideas were contested and yet the intended meaning

Surveillance, detection, discipline   141

– 'we are good, they are bad' – was still secured through a classification system. A notable feature in the data was that Muslim identity, particular associated with politics, foreign policy and religious commitment was synonymous with 'extremism'. The promotion of 'British values' outside juridical channels is consequently seen as the antidote to 'extremism', or Muslim surfeit. The classification system was deployed to discipline certain players and promote others, whilst also producing a particular conduct labelled 'moderate' Muslims.

Community approaches to countering radicalisation

The use of communities and civil society actors to counter-terrorism predated the Prevent strategy. Special Branch at the Metropolitan Police had set up the Muslim Contact Unit (MCU) in 2003 to support the Muslim communities in counter-terrorism (Lambert 2011). According to the former Head of a counter-terrorism unit, their work was successful in tackling the influence of Al-Qaeda at the Finsbury Park Mosque, the Brixton Mosque and other places before the advent of Prevent. In the two passages below he explains what community approaches to countering terrorism entailed.

> …yes 2006, there was still that MCU approach which as far as possible was trying to adopt the post-Laurence approach of engaging with communities as they are; the idea really that the police should not be concerned with engineering change; that you work with communities as they are…
>
> (Interview 17, former Head of counter-terrorism unit)

> So I think that the Muslim Contact Unit just went to places where particular problems existed and so particular solutions. I don't think there was any attempt to import some kind of solution that wasn't local.
>
> (Interview 17, former Head of counter-terrorism unit)

Community approaches to countering terrorism were primarily characterised by (1) engaging with the Muslim communities as they existed on the ground rather than having to engineer a change of social and community representation and (2) the solutions to the problem of radicalisation had to emanate from already existing communities, which required a type of expertise that was local rather than national. Moreover, the interviewee argues that the MCU's community-led strategy was based on deploying the Islamists at Finsbury Park and the Salafis in Brixton and was justified on the basis of legitimacy and effectiveness. Legitimacy was derived from the fact that the likes of STREET and MAB had both the religious and the political profile, as well as local experience working with their communities. Their effectiveness was based on the fact that they were legitimate to begin with and that they possessed the right skills and expertise. Their skills and expertise are based on both their religious and ideological similarity, and therefore their familiarity with religiously inspired Jihadi discourse, coupled with actual experience of countering radicalisation. This notion of expertise was

142 *Surveillance, detection, discipline*

certainly the case with the Salafis in Brixton, who had the experience of countering radicalisation in the 1990s, as explained below.

> I think the best examples of successful elements are engagements with groups that had a long track record that sort of pre-dates Prevent. The one example I mention in the book is the Salafi community around the Brixton Mosque. I mean this community had the advantage of being well established and later becomes known as STREET, so I will use that name. When the individuals in STREET meet the top-down approach of the Home Office they have the skills and the experience to negotiate; if they think the police got something wrong, I mean I know this from experience, they were never frightened to say to the Muslim Contact Unit, 'we want to do it this way'.
>
> (Interview 17, former Head of counter-terrorism unit)

Meanwhile, when Prevent first began in 2006, it embraced the notion of community approaches in counter-terrorism, empowering organisations and individuals drawn from local communities amongst the Muslim population. Alongside with preventative strategies post 7/7, a number of initiatives developed the notion of communities working in partnership with government to counter radicalisation. The positioning of the role of the Muslim community as a 'partner' with the then New Labour government was cemented at the Wilton Park Conference in 2006, which hosted a number of think-tanks, community organisations and representatives, and the Home Office and Foreign Office amongst others (Briggs *et al.* 2006). Hence the theme 'community approaches' characterised the approach of Prevent in the early years. A former research analyst at DEMOS at the time brings to light the overarching theme of community approaches to countering terrorism under the narrative 'Bringing it Home' (ibid.).

> So the 'Bringing it Home' report, it wasn't the only thing written on that theme, but at that point of time a few of us were working very carefully on, you know, trying to reshape the counter-terrorism policy to broaden it out and put more emphasis on the preventative side of things. To a certain extent we succeeded. Obviously with the change of governments there are certain think-tanks that are more in favour at the moment.
>
> (Interview 9, ISD analyst)

Community expertise was legitimised in the early days of Prevent and it was this model that was championed by the Home Office. It was the pioneering work of organisations such as STREET, Siraat and ACF, alongside community and political engagement by the likes of the MCB and Muslim Association of Britain (MAB) and others, in conjunction with academia, which laid the ground work in terms of knowledge building on radicalisation, not to mention the delivery of counter-radicalisation and de-radicalisation interventions. This is explained below.

Surveillance, detection, discipline 143

I don't want to trumpet us as the best thing since sliced bread but most of that was because of the work we did – [X], STREET, ACF – we were fore-runners of Prevent and de-radicalisation from 2005, at least us definitely, between 2005 and 2011. It's only when the new government came in that they decided to change the discourse ... the idea of how to do it and the best people to do it were generally looked at through our prisms because the police had done their research and they come and asked us and then the Home Office moved towards the way we were doing it.

(Interview 23, Director of prison intervention provider)

Whilst a few Islamist and Salafi groups had been identified as possessing the skill and knowledge to provide more bespoke interventions, it is worth mentioning that the number of individuals and groups involved in community approaches to tackling terrorism was in fact limited. The usual suspects mentioned are primarily three organisations – STREET, Siraat and ACF – all of whom operate with the same model. This limited number of best-practice examples of counter-radicalisation and de-radicalisation interventions could be attributed to the fact that work in this area demanded a type of specialised expertise that was scarce and in short supply, as well as the fact that it was a new strategy for the Home Office. The interviewee below made this point directly.

There's kind of a handful of celebrated people like Abdul Haqq Baker; actually, the list is too short which means the same people use the same examples all the time, which is a problem. Everything you read ... talks about Finsbury Park Mosque or Brixton Mosque, which is a limited set of examples to draw upon five years later.

(Interview 4, IPPR analyst)

However, the role of community approaches to countering radicalisation was challenged by think tanks like the Policy Exchange and the Quilliam Foundation. Instead of preventing 'violent extremism', these think-tanks stressed the importance of tackling 'non-violent extremism'. Their criticism was twofold: attacking community organisations for being unrepresentative of Muslim communities and establishing the ideological similarity between Islamists and Salafis with violent extremists.

Regarding the first critique, the MCB was criticised for representing a small constituency of the British Muslim communities who were Islamist in orientation (Bright 2006, 26). This argument was made by the Policy Exchange at a time when the MCB, which enjoyed a degree of influence with the New Labour government in the late 1990s, was sidelined and ostracised by government for failing to support the government's position on the Iraq War (Abbas 2005; Brighton 2007). The interviewee below explains the issue of representation and its link as an argument with other political factors.

144 *Surveillance, detection, discipline*

You know, when I write an article people come back to me and say 'who do you represent?' I've always said I represent myself and whoever agrees with me, I don't represent anyone. The common attack on the Muslim Council of Britain or the Muslim Association of Britain is that you don't represent anyone. Well okay it doesn't negate my views. The whole argument about the Muslim community itself needs to be revised. The MCB was once in the favour of the Labour government until they spoke against the War in Iraq and after that they marginalised them and government then went on the crazy track of trying to find a replacement of the MCB...

(Interview 27, President of a Prevent funded think-tank)

The second critique made against the community expertise by Quilliam and Policy Exchange, was that Prevent should not start with 'violent extremism' but with 'non-violent extremism'. This argument was based on the rationale that Islamist and Salafi groups shared a religious and ideological affiliation with 'violent extremists' and therefore these organisations were similar to 'violent extremists' in belief, their difference being merely one of tactics. It was an argument that was made forcibly by the Policy Exchange in a pamphlet titled 'Choosing our Friends Wisely':

PVE is thus underwriting the very Islamist ideology which spawns an illiberal, intolerant and anti-western world view. Political and theological extremists, acting with the authority conferred by official recognition, are indoctrinating young people with an ideology of hostility to western values.

(Maher and Frampton 2009, 5)

The logic of this thinking was encapsulated in Maajid Nawaz's catchphrase that 'not every extremist is a terrorist but every terrorist is an extremist' (Nawaz 2010). In effect, this argument situated STREET and the MCB on the trajectory towards violent extremism. Ascribing STREET and MCB to the category 'non-violent extremist' effectively rendered them part of the problem of radicalisation. In fact, Quilliam considered many mainstream organisations and groups in the Muslim communities to be 'extremists'.

In June 2010, Quilliam compiled a list of extremist sympathisers in a document entitled 'Preventing terrorism; where next for Britain?' which was sent to the Director General of the OSCT, Charles Farr. The document was leaked to the press. Quilliam accused several organisations and institutions operating in the UK, such as the MCB, MAB, MSF, FOSIS, the Cordoba Foundation, Islam Channel, the MCU, the East London Mosque and many others, who were sympathetic to Islamism of being part of the problem (Nawaz and Hussain 2010, 59–62). 'The ideology of non-violent Islamists is broadly the same as that of violent Islamists; they disagree only on tactics' (Nawaz and Hussain 2010, 7). The following interviewee explains how community experts became problematic 'gate-keepers'.

Surveillance, detection, discipline 145

...and yet a group like the MCB has been put into this category of problematic Islamists, all of a sudden they are spoken of as 'gate-keepers' in the pejorative sense, and government says we are no longer going to do anything because you are somehow preventing us from engaging with real communities. I think somehow this is disingenuous because government doesn't say that to other faith communities. I think this is one of the outcomes of all anti-Islamism hysteria, all this good and bad Muslim category and therefore you could also ask what the negative impact for Prevent when groups, whether it's a national body like MCB or a local project like STREET, when either of these groups are being excluded I don't think the funding is the key issue.

(Interview 17, former Head of counter-terrorism unit)

This two-pronged strategy by Quilliam and Policy Exchange to discredit the likes of STREET and the MCB as 'extremists' was integrated into the second iteration of Prevent in 2009, which was testament to the success and influence of the elite expert approaches. The category of 'shared values' and 'non-violent extremism' concretely impacted the role of community approaches to countering terrorism. It manifested in the way that government sidelined a number of previously key organisations, promoting other organisations like the Sufi Council of Britain; the severing of funding for Prevent projects (albeit this was an outcome of a combination of factors following the 2010 review on Prevent); and the centralisation of Prevent. Hence Quilliam and Policy Exchange were successful in changing the narratives surrounding the Prevent strategy, thereby affecting the way the rules of the games were executed. Indeed, the data largely supports the idea that think-tanks played a significant role in the Prevent strategy.

...the MCU approach, instead of that being adopted, the policy Exchange/ Quilliam approach was adopted. This was an approach that could be described as top-down, you know it was an approach that the ideology was going to be tackled.

(Interview 17, former Head of counter-terrorism unit)

Why was it easy to marginalise the likes of STREET and other Islamist organisations despite their early success in laying the groundwork for tackling radicalisation and developing de-radicalisation intervention programmes? One factor discerned from the data is the existence of a tension between the discursive domains of politics vis-à-vis the distinct domain of professional experts. This distinction between public and professional domains explains the political move by policymakers to support elite approaches over community expertise in delivering the Prevent strategy by 2010.

The disjuncture evident with the quality of expertise between community organisation and think-tanks like the Policy Exchange and the Henry Jackson Society (Quilliam is a little different) suggests that, behind closed doors, professional expertise operates according to a logic that is governed by a greater

146 *Surveillance, detection, discipline*

commitment to knowledge and expertise, whereas the same expertise is not as useful in the public sphere of policy, public opinion and political imperatives. The discursive dynamic in this domain has a different objective and strategy, which makes different use of the same expertise and knowledge. Indeed, knowledge and expertise are subjugated to the demands of politics and therefore have to go through the political production line for sanitation and repackaging. The additional political dynamic makes the policy domain of counter-terrorism more politicised and sensitive than other policy domains. This process is explained in the following way:

> But the discourse at the time was being led by organisations like Quilliam and the government looked like they were supporting that. Therefore, they couldn't come out openly and say they're supporting us and the way we do things. They could however publicly support Quilliam and so the discourse became Quilliam-esque. And that ended up being what was written in the last Prevent document. What is written in the document isn't exactly what people tried to do. Because if you ask anybody from the MET police, if you ask anybody from the Home Office prior to 2012, they will tell you who were the successful people and who weren't. The will tell you why they had the outward facing discourse and then the ones actually doing the work.
>
> (Interview 23, Director of prison intervention provider)

Another factor explaining the marginalisation of community expertise was the fact that their knowledge was integrated into a more centralised approach once a substantial amount of the knowledge has been extracted and codified. Despite the work, capital and resources invested by community expertise in delivering Prevent, they were not only branded as a part of the problem, but their approach to countering radicalisation was abandoned in favour of Quilliam and the Policy Exchange's counter-ideological approach. It is important to note that their marginalisation began in 2009 but it was not until the advent of the Coalition government in 2010 that they became excluded from Prevent. 2010 is significant because the Prevent strategy was suspended for re-evaluation under the new government. Debunking the position of community approaches in Prevent therefore coincided with the apogee of the codification of knowledge on radicalisation and the initial experimental years of an innovative instrument in counter-terrorism policies. A substantial amount of learning and experience had occurred in this period off of the back of community expertise, in addition to the information gathering on Muslim populations, for preventative strategies to become increasingly centralised. In short, community expertise had 'confessed' and passed over information and knowledge pertaining to Muslim populations in the UK into the structures of power. This made community expertise more disposable once government was able to lay down the foundations of a preventive infrastructure in counter-terrorism.

Hotspots of radicalisation: sectors and institutions

This section examines the third objective of Prevent, which is about supporting sectors and institutions where there are risks of radicalisation (HO 2011, 66). Identifying 'vulnerable' individuals requires institutions and sectors to have the knowledge and capacity to identify individuals 'at risk' of radicalisation and report them to Channel. Channel then examines the individual, makes a risk assessment and if the individual satisfies the risk triggers he or she is assigned to an intervention provider. It is the job of sectors and institutions to identify and report potential radicals for de-radicalisation interventions and for Channel to act as the hub which receives these reports as well as placing individuals with agencies providing de-radicalisation interventions. The Director of an intervention provider explains the actual role of Channel in relation to wider work on sectors and institutions.

> Channel was basically ... the Met Police, what they did, was try to set up in certain boroughs across community support where they can find individuals to sit on a board and tell the Met Police that we are concerned XYZ people. And then the Channel board would invite known deradicalisers to come and work with those individuals. So Channel was just a conduit to get information on people they thought were radical and try to signpost a community de-radicalisation programme.
>
> (Interview 23, Director of prison intervention provider)

Channel thus acts as a 'conduit' between the community and intervention providers. According to the data set there are seven or eight intervention providers, whilst others have also mentioned the existence of local community mentors who work on a contractual basis but who do not belong to an agency or organisation as such. The Prevent strategy does not list the agency providers and this information is generally difficult to access online. The most commonly cited examples of de-radicalisation intervention providers in most if not all papers and reports are STREET and the ACF. One respondent working on Prevent discusses the different intervention providers.

> There are I think seven or eight intervention providers nationally, funded by the Home Office who operate differently – this is about accreditation and a pool of mentors, that's what's unique about this bit and they've all undertaken a six day training course. I think in London you got ACF, Active Change Foundation, don't know if you've met them; you used to have STREET and Siraat for example but they've now been curtailed because they are too Salafi for the government – so they used to be intervention providers; you got Inner City Guidance in Birmingham. There's an organisation in London called FAST, which do kind of family sort of therapy but they all concentrated on the hard range interventions.
>
> (Interview 8, Prevent practitioner)

148   *Surveillance, detection, discipline*

This was the closest I could get to a general overview of intervention providers operating in Prevent. More will be said on de-radicalisation intervention providers in the next chapter. To recapitulate, the radicalisation 'hotspots' incorporate primary and secondary schools, universities, hospitals, local government, probation services and other institutions and bodies. One of the main aims is the building of networks and relationships between the various parts of society and government with the community. This is embodied in the role of Channel, which works with a board where various community and public representatives assess potential radicals. Channel relies on the active assessment of many stakeholders in the risk identification process and as a result there are two important features: first, a criterion of risk or what constitutes 'at risk' (albeit until recently this was not specified). These 'risks' refer to indicators which correspond to certain behavioural types and patterns, as well as the articulation of particular views and beliefs by individuals.

A second feature of the identification process is the ability and capacity for employees, managers and experts in civil society and public institutions to understand radicalisation and associated risk triggers. This idea is based on giving ordinary citizens in society the knowledge and education to identify and report 'risks' and threats in the community. Hence we see the investment of Prevent in the teaching and training of individuals in professional positions across the various sectors and institutions on radicalisation and risk indicators. For example, training is available to frontline staff that are integral to the identification process. This includes the Home Office developed 'Workshop to Raise Awareness of Prevent' (WRAP) training. WRAP is an hour long DVD-led interactive workshop. Prevent III claims that 15,000 frontline staff have received WRAP training (HO 2011, 58). Also, the National Counter-Terrorism Policing Headquarters (NCTPHQ), in conjunction with the College of Policing, has developed an e-learning package for Channel. There is training also available in local authorities arranged by local Police Prevent Co-ordinators (HMG 2015, 19–20).

Regarding a criterion of risk in order to identity 'vulnerable' and radical individuals, interviewees overwhelmingly believed that this was formulated around the religious and political views and behaviour of Muslims. The respondent below, an analyst at DEMOS, explains the way that young adults were referred to Channel based on political views expressed in class.

> In the beginning they didn't know on what basis to refer someone. So they were hearing about some kid in class mouthing off about Palestinian bombings being justified by religion, which isn't controversial amongst many Muslims, and if you end up referring every Muslim that said that, you end up having hundreds of thousands. It's a difficult case, especially young kids they are going to say that of course they are being segregated and got no other ways to express their freedoms, what do you want them to do? So initially they were referring people that were expressing that type of view and realised quite quickly it was stupid, not the right people to go through the programme.
>
> (Interview 1, DEMOS analyst)

Surveillance, detection, discipline 149

This comment implies that identifying people according to views was something that Channel has revised and improved on with time. There is the implicit suggestion that it is either not done anymore or that Channel has got better at identifying 'at risk' youngsters. Whilst some others have similarly acknowledged the learning process involved in identifying 'real risk' from 'non-threat risk' by Channel, the majority still believe that the identification process is linked with indicators pertaining to political and religious views. However, interviewees were roughly divided into a group that questioned the existence of a coherent identification criterion and another group that spoke in terms of the criterion being nuanced, complex and multifaceted, and said that assessments were undertaken according to each individual. Despite this, none of the interviewees dismissed the notion that the risk triggers corresponded to religious and political views. Examples of both views on the criterion of risk held by interviewees can be read below. They come from a Police Officer and a Prevent Officer.

> I don't think it works. First of all, what are the indicators of being radicalised? I haven't seen any written indicators. If you go by the line of questioning at Heathrow airport by counter-terrorism officers: Do you pray five times a day? Do you read the Quran? What are your views on the Iraq war? If you say yes to the first two and I don't agree with the third, does that mean you are at risk of being radicalised? So I think there are questions to do with indicators and a question of awareness and understanding about people who refer people to Channel.
>
> (Interview 16, Representative of NAMP)

> ...when you're talking about where's the line for intervention, the line is so variable sometimes. On top of that, what's your level of intervention? ... Not everyone we get notified about gets referred to Channel, you know, all it is, is a way of doing things, and only if there's evidence they are going down a certain road. It's like a young lad starts ordering chemicals from the internet to do experiments with in his shed. Do you think we should do something about that? And it's about intervening before something happens.
>
> (Interview 21, Prevent Officer)

The first interviewee states that he has not seen any written indicators but only infers from the questioning at airports that such indicators related to religious and political views. The second point he raises relates to the relationship between 'at risk' and radicalisation. What is the link between being 'at risk' and radicalisation? Channel, for example, emphasises the importance of 'risk', to quote the Prevent document:

> Risk is a theme that runs through the entire Channel process, i.e. risk to the individual; risk to the public; and risk to partners or organisations providing support to the individual, including any intervention providers. The panel is responsible for managing the risk in relation to the vulnerable individual.
>
> (HMG 2015, 16, para 74)

150 *Surveillance, detection, discipline*

Meanwhile, the second respondent talks of 'variables', 'levels', 'evidence' and non-ideological factors, like 'ordering chemicals'. Being a practitioner, this respondent articulated a complex view of the risk identification criterion. Both views thus emphasise the centrality of religious and political indicators as highlighting whether an individual is 'at risk', whilst simultaneously remaining officially elusive.

> What that's left us with is this wishy-washy thing without a clear criterion of how to actually identify how someone might be at risk. I think that's why you have had this wide net approach because if you don't know what the pathways are, and you know, anybody can become an extremist whether you are religious or not, then it's kind of an open playing field, how do we identify people? We don't know. Your criterion becomes diluted and as a consequence it vindicates this surveillance approach, well in that case we need to have endeavours like the Channel project.
>
> (Interview 10, Investigative journalist)

This comment alludes to the consequences of an ambiguous criterion. The respondent believes that it justifies the surveillance approach. It is important to examine however what interviewees said about the role of institutions in reporting radicals to Channel. An insight is given by the former President of a prominent student society.

> ... student unions have reported back to the NUS how they have been approached for data on Muslim students. This all kicked off with Christmas bomber Umar Farouk so UCL union were pressured into providing the contact details of Muslim students to the police without a warrant and they weren't just details of Muslim students at the time of Umar but also of Muslim students who weren't around at the time of Umar. Those contact details were handed over ... We know this is happening it's coming from Prevent.
>
> (Interview 3, former President of a student society)

This passage describes the experience of Muslim students at University College London (UCL) following the revelation that the Christmas day bomber, Umar Farouk, had been ex-President of the Islamic Society at UCL. He tried to blow up a transatlantic flight on Christmas Day 2009. In January 2010 the Council, the governing body of UCL, set up an independent inquiry to investigate the case of Umar Farouk and whether he had become radicalised on campus. The panel concluded that 'there is no evidence to suggest either that Umar Farouk Abdulmutallab was radicalised while a student at UCL or that conditions at UCL during that time or subsequently are conducive to the radicalisation of students' (Caldicott 2010, 3).

Despite the fact that the investigation revealed that Umar had not been radicalised at University, there was subsequently growing scrutiny of ISOCs at

Surveillance, detection, discipline   151

Universities by think-tanks like the Centre for Social Cohesion (CSC – now known as the Henry Jackson Society) and Quilliam (QF 2010). For example, the CSC produced a report titled 'Radical Islam on UK Campuses' in 2010, which made the case that 'British university campuses are breeding grounds of Islamic extremism' (2010, v). The Quilliam Foundation also published, 'The Threat of Radicalisation on British University Campuses'; using the Islamic Society at City University as a case study, the paper argued that Islamic Societies at Universities potentially represent a vehicle for radicalisation.

The above interviewee highlights how this incident was used by the police to obtain the names of Muslim students held by the NUS. It reveals the extent to which sites like the university became places of surveillance. Notably the focus on institutions or sites of potential radicalisation in Prevent has evolved over the three iterations. Initially the concern was with Mosques in Prevent I, and then with universities in Prevent II and more recently with Prevent III the focus has turned towards the internet (HO 2011; Neumann and Rogers 2007). This shift on hotspots of radicalisation represents the incorporation of knowledge into the strategy over time. The rationale underpinning supporting institutions is the notion that radicalisation and particularly ideology becomes incubated in certain places and so the strategy attempts to buffer institutions against such threats. Another example of the pressures on institutions to report 'radicals' is shared by one respondent, who was arrested for downloading material online and on campus whilst a student at University.

> In a way, I don't blame the management for picking up the phone and calling the police; ten years of constant Islamophobic news reporting and pejorative words used to describe Muslims and negative headlines, create a moral panic about Islamic terrorists so when they did find me in possession of a book you could buy from WH Smith they reported that and that's what they're told to do.
>
> (Interview 19, Academic)

He explains lucidly the impact that the wider securitised environment had on the University management committee in making their decision to report him to the police. In addition, he situates this decision taken by the University, which substantially affected his life in many ways, with the fact that 'that's what they're told to do'. Other interviewees have made remarks regarding the culture of suspicion accompanying Prevent's message on reporting signs of radicalism. The academic below alludes to the exhortation by a government Minister for Muslims to report other Muslims when they see the 'tell-tale' signs of radicalisation.

> I remember John Reid and that amazing speech he did in East London to Muslim parents where he told them to look out for the 'tell-tale' signs in the children. So what are the 'tell-tale' signs? John Reid never told us. But

152 *Surveillance, detection, discipline*

I was like we don't know, by 'we' I mean the white British majority, we don't know what the 'tell-tale' signs are but you know what, as Muslims, what the 'tell-tale' signs are. It's again about putting the problem elsewhere.

(Interview 11, Academic)

There is the hint in this comment that the onus was put on the Muslim community to self-regulate radicalism in their communities. However, it points to something more substantial than the instruction for parents to spy on their children. Instead it brings to the fore the notion of building institutional resilience as protection against potential radicalism. It suggests that the Channel programme and Prevent more widely should be seen through the lens of risk management strategies. Indeed, some of the interviewees have spoken about the impact this risk management logic underpinning Prevent has had both at an individual level and at a collective level. For example, the Senior Prevent Officer uses the language and logic of risk management to explain the work of Channel.

What we are trying to do is build Lancashire into safeguarded hubs. So our referrals when they come in, there would be a risk assessment of whether it's violence, sexual, extremism, or whatever, and then the case is referred to a panel of expertise that exists to help that person. So we are trying ... some people may get referred to us thinking they're being radicalised when actually what people are seeing is child exploitation going on. Partner agencies don't have the skill to recognise what's actually going on. That's the approach we have here in Lancashire.

(Interview 22, Prevent Officer)

The following respondent also analyses the work of Channel through the lens of risk management and the securitisation of spheres previously unrelated to security, like education.

Otherwise they would be flagged up by teachers who are becoming increasingly concerned that little Johnny said something in class and later become a terrorist – are they going to be held responsible for not flagging this up? Again, it's about risk management and people getting a little bit scared because this mainstreaming of the security consciousness has gone into all sorts of different areas, into housing, into education.

(Interview 12, Academic/freelance consultant on Prevent community engagement)

The risk management logic therefore explains the relationship between being 'at risk' and radicalisation. It was believed, according to one respondent, that the 7/7 bombers had written things about Osama Bin Laden in their exercise books at school and so the link between youngsters, certain behavioural indicators and radicalisation was established.

Surveillance, detection, discipline 153

I get the idea, the idea is you want to make sure that people like Mohammed Sadique Khan and some of the 7/7 bombers ... there were identifiers, they were writing things about Osama Bin Laden from a young age at school. This came out apparently with one of the bombers. So there is this idea if we pick up on these things early we can actually talk to the kids.

(Interview 10, Investigative journalist)

Despite being designed to address all forms of terrorism, research data, as well as limited data available on Channel, suggest that the identification process is preoccupied with individuals from a Muslim background. The limited data available on Channel suggests that the identification process is preoccupied with the youth. For example, of the 1,120 individuals identified by Channel between 2007 and 2010, 290 were under 16 and 55 were under 12 (HO 2011, 59). When the Security and Counter-Terrorism Act came into law in July 2015, it was reported that there were 349 referrals that month (Tran 2015). Of the 796 individuals referred to Channel between June and August 2015, 312 were under 18 (ibid.). Therefore, according to these figures a high proportion of individuals identified by Channel were under the age of 16, with some being under 12. The interviewee below believed that anyone under the age of 18 was too young to be put on an intervention programme.

With the work we did we tried not to work with anybody below eighteen years of age because their ideas were not formed. We were asked to work with some fifteen to sixteen years old but we find that their ideas were not formed and more importantly the last issue – who they were hanging around with. They are just taking ideas off people they're hanging around with.

(Interview 23, Director of prison intervention provider)

Notably, on this matter, Channel states that:

Participation in Channel remains voluntary and consent for the individual must be given by the individual or by a parent/guardian in the case of a child (a child being defined as anyone under the age of 18). If consent is refused by a parent but there is sufficient evidence that the child is at risk of particular harm, then social services become involved in the decision making process.

(HMG 2015, 16)

So Channel has established that de-radicalisation for those under 18 requires consent. It is interesting nevertheless to see the negative reaction elicited by the notion of re-educating youngsters without consent. Even the biggest advocates of countering extremism and counter-ideology found the prospect of primary school children being subjected to an intervention ethically questionable:

154 *Surveillance, detection, discipline*

Nine is too young, primary school kids, yes it's a concern. I'm not convinced they should be in Channel; they could just grow up to be racist but not violent. They could become an offender or grow out of it, depends on friends and company. They could be normal with no issues.

(Interview 25, Quilliam analyst)

The young targets of intervention and the 'vulnerability' (more in Chapter 6) label employed by Channel seem to suggest that the programme is administered according to the conventional mechanisms associated with the youth and probation services in its implementation of de-radicalisation. This, after all, is no surprise given that Prevent 2011 stated that de-radicalisation programmes are akin to crime prevention programmes. Questions arise regarding the purpose of observing and looking out for 'early sings' in children in a counter-terrorism strategy. Prevent is supposed to mitigate the likelihood of support and engagement with terrorism. The fact the Channel appears to be preoccupied with youngsters who have not committed a crime but exhibit signs of 'extremism' suggests that the pre-emptive framing of Channel effectively makes particular subjects problematic (Islam, politics, religion, etc.) through future potential, thus permitting mediation in the present.

Consequently, this section has argued that many interviewees understood the third objective of Prevent through the lens of risk management. It aims to build institutional resilience and mitigate future risks of radicalisation through the surveillance of public space and the identification of bodies deemed radical for the purposes of rectification.

References

Abbas, T. (2005). *Muslim Britain: Communities Under Pressure*. London: Zed Books Ltd.

Briggs, R. (2010). 'Community engagement for counterterrorism: lessons from the United Kingdom', *International Affairs*, 86 (4): 971–981.

Briggs, R., Fieschi, C. and Lownsbrough. H. (2006). *Bringing it Home, Community-based Approaches to Counter-Terrorism*, DEMOS, www.demos.co.uk/files/Bringing%20 it%20Home%20-%20web.pdf.

Bright, M. (2006). *When Progressives Treat with Reactionaries, the British State's flirtation with radical Islamism*, Policy Exchange, www.policyexchange.org.uk/images/ publications/when%20progressives%20treat%20with%20reactionaries%20-%20 jul%2006.pdf.

Brighton, S. (2007). 'British Muslims, multiculturalism and UK foreign policy: "integration" and "cohesion" in and beyond the state', *International Affairs*, 83 (1): 1–17.

Caldicott, F. (2010). *Umar Farouk Abdulmutallab: Report to UCL Council of independent inquiry panel*, www.ucl.ac.uk/caldicott-enquiry/caldicottreport.pdf.

Centre for Social Cohesion (CSC) (2010). *Radical Islam on Campus, A Comprehensive List of Extremist Speakers at UK Universities*, http://henryjacksonsociety.org/wp-content/uploads/2013/01/RADICAL-ISLAM-ON-CMAPUS.pdf.

HC House of Commons, Communities and Local Government Committee (2010). *Preventing Violent Extremism, Sixth Report of Session 2009–2010*, www.publications. parliament.uk/pa/cm200910/cmselect/cmcomloc/65/65.pdf.

HMG (2015). *Channel Duty Guidance, Protecting Vulnerable People from Being Drawn into Terrorism, Statutory Guidance from Channel Panels Members and Partners of Local Panels*, www.gov.uk/government/uploads/system/uploads/attachment_data/file/425189/Channel_Duty_Guidance_April_2015.pdf.

Home Office (HO) (2006). *Countering International Terrorism: The United Kingdom's Strategy*, www.gov.uk/government/uploads/system/uploads/attachment_data/file/272320/6888.pdf.

Home Office (HO) (2009). *The United Kingdom's Strategy for Countering International Terrorism*, www.gov.uk/government/uploads/system/uploads/attachment_data/file/228644/7547.pdf.

Home Office (HO) (2011). *Prevent, CONTEST 2011*, www.homeoffice.gov.uk/publications/counter-terrorism/prevent/prevent-strategy.

Kundnani, A. (2009). *Spooked! How Not to Prevent Violent Extremism*. London: Institute of Race Relations, www.irr.org.uk/pdf2/spooked.pdf.

Lambert, R. (2011). *Countering Al-Qaeda in London, Police and Muslims in Partnerships*. London: C. Hurst & Co.

Maher, S. and Frampton, M. (2009). *Choosing Our Friends Wisely, Criteria For Engagement With Muslim Groups*, Policy Exchange, www.policyexchange.org.uk/images/publications/choosing%20our%20friends%20wisely%20-%20mar%2009.pdf.

Nawaz, M. and Hussain, E. (2010). *Preventing Terrorism: Where Next for Britain? The Quilliam Foundation, Leaked Memo to Government*, www.scribd.com/doc/34834977/Secret-Quilliam-Memo-to-government.

Neumann, P.R. and Rogers, B. (2007). *Recruitment and Mobilisation for the Islamist Militant Movement in Europe. International Centre for Studies of Radicalisation*, Kings College London, http://ec.europa.eu/home-affairs/doc_centre/terrorism/docs/ec_radicalisation_study_on_mobilisation_tactics_en.pdf.

Quilliam Foundation (QF) (2010). *The Threat of Radicalisation on British University Campuses: A Case Study*, www.quilliamfoundation.org/wp/wp-content/uploads/publications/free/the-threat-of-radicalisation-on-british-university-campuses.pdf.

The Express Tribune (2010). 'Not all extremists are terrorists, says ex-jihadist', 26 June 2010, http://tribune.com.pk/story/23819/not-all-extremists-are-terrorists-says-ex-jihadist/.

Thornton, S. (2010). *Project Champion Review*, Thames Valley Police, www.statewatch.org/news/2010/oct/uk-project-champion-police-report.pdf.

Tran, M (2015). 'Large proportion of those referred to UK deradicalisation scheme are under 18', *Guardian*, 8 October 2015, www.theguardian.com/uk-news/2015/oct/08/large-proportion-of-those-referred-to-uk-deradicalisation-scheme-are-under-18.

Woodward, K. (1997). *Identity and Difference*. California: Sage Publications.

6 Confession technologies (identity)
'Salvation in this life'

> This form of power applies itself to everyday life which categorises the individual, marks him by his own individuality, attaches him to his own identity, imposes a law of truth on him which he must recognise and which others have to recognise in him.
>
> (Foucault 1982, 781)

Pastoral power has its origins in the Christian practice of Confession. According to Foucault, the Church had in fact adopted many of the techniques of self-examination derived from pre-Christian practices, from the Stoics and even the Pythagoreans of the fifth and fourth centuries BC (Foucault 1987, 1988a). These techniques included:

> mortification of the flesh, contemplation to rid oneself of earthly desires, absolute obedience to one's spiritual director, and the examination of conscience as a prelude to public confession at the end of the period of penance, knowledge of the self...
>
> (Foucault 1988, 133)

Following the Lateran Council in 1215, in which the sacrament of penance was codified, the confessional became a central feature in religious and civil power (Foucault 1998a, 58). The confessional was centred on the relationship between the Church and its flock, the priests and the congregants, between a party that speaks and confesses and an authority 'who requires the confession, prescribes and appreciates it, and intervenes in order to judge, punish, forgive, console, and reconcile' (Foucault 1998a, 62).

Notably, pastoral power encompasses several important themes. The first dimension is that pastorship hinges on the notion that the leader is a shepherd in charge of a flock. What matters in pastoral power is the relationship between the shepherd and the flock, his ability to unite the flock, without which the individuals would be dispersed. Also, the shepherd's role is to ensure the salvation of his flock through 'constant, individualised and final kindness' (McNay 1994, 120), not to mention watch over his flock with scrupulousness. Hence pastoral power is a form of power that looks after both the community and the individual,

'Salvation in this life'   157

which cannot be exercised without knowing the 'inside of people's minds, without exploring their souls, without making them reveal their innermost secrets' (Foucault 1982, 783). This type of power therefore, unlike royal or legal power, is salvation orientated and individuating (ibid., 783).

Whilst the influence of the Church has waned, the pastoral function has nevertheless evolved and moved beyond its previous localisation, even multiplying in the modern world, impacting a number of other domains. In a long passage Foucault describes the extent to which 'Western man has become a confessing animal':

> It plays a part in justice, medicine, education, family relationships, and love relations, in the most ordinary affairs of everyday life, and in the most solemn rites; one confesses one's crimes, one's sins, one's thoughts and desires, one's illnesses and troubles; one goes about telling, with great precision, whatever is most difficult to tell. One confesses in public and in private, to one's parents, one's educators, one's doctors, to those one loves; one admits to oneself, in pleasure and pain, things it would be impossible to tell to anybody else, the things people write books about. One confesses – or is forced to confess ... Western man has become a confessing animal.
>
> (Foucault 1998a, 59)

The Christian Confessional is governed by a religious logic that seeks salvation in the next life, whereas the confessional logic of contemporary society is concerned with 'salvation in this life' (Foucault 1982, 784). 'Salvation in this life' assumes different forms, such as the promotion and safeguarding of individual and collective well-being, health and longevity, security, etc. (Foucault 1982, 783). Thus, pastoral power has been employed in a whole series of relationships: 'children and parents, students and educators, patients and psychiatrists, delinquents and experts' Foucault 1998a, 63). Where the language used by pastoral power was once religious and then legal, in the modern world it became medical and psychological.

Moreover, the techniques employed in confessional practices have been adopted in pedagogy, medicine, psychiatry, literature and popular culture. They have taken on various forms, such as 'interrogations, consultations, autobiographical narratives, letters; they have been recorded, transcribed, assembled into dossiers, published, and commented on' (ibid.). With these new techniques of self-inspection, self-examination, self-evaluation and self-regulation, citizens are persuaded and encouraged to be 'free', 'true to oneself' and to 'realise oneself' (Rose 1999, 114).

Similar to the role of priests in the Christian confessional, today's 'experts' – therapists, psychologists, doctors, counsellors, mentors, academics, managers, etc. – are the new priesthood of our secularised societies. They perform the old pastoral functions in terms of guiding and directing the individual in this life, selling their expertise and their knowledge, techniques, language and models of self formation to everyone. Governing at 'a distance', expertise achieves its

158 'Salvation in this life'

effects 'not through the threat of violence or constraint, but by way of the persuasion inherent in its truths, the anxieties stimulated by its norms, and the attraction exercised by the images of life and self it offers to us' (Rose 1999, 10). More significant however for Rose is the fact that experts (psychologists, psychiatrists and psychotherapists) are considered 'engineers of the soul' that operate in conjunction with neo-liberal government in the subjectification of citizens.

However, implicit in the notion of 'salvation in this life', is the 'repressive hypotheses' (Foucault 1998a, 17–35). This hypothesis, which has become a valorised maxim in the West, states that power represses individuals and that the truth can be unleashed by opposing power. It posits that power and truth are diametrically opposed and also independent of each other. The belief in 'salvation' of the subject in popular discourse has therefore been deliberately depicted as hinging on the act of 'speaking truth to power'. Foucault criticised the notion that somehow the suppression of sexuality was caused by power and questioned popular conceptions that 'speaking truth' to power and 'coming out' was a method of liberating individuals from repression (1998a, 34). Instead, it is this underlying pressure to speak, to confess all, to lay bare, that must be seen as an instrument of power. In the confession, the agency of domination does not reside in the person that speaks, but in the one who questions and listens. *Confessing does not set you free, but makes you a subject of power.* 'Truth' therefore, according to Foucault, exists through power, is shaped by it, and not outside of it (Rainbow 1984, 72–47).

Consequently, expressed in the quote at the beginning of this chapter, pastoral power imposes a 'law of truth' on individuals in two main ways: incitement to discourse in order to improve the knowledge and codification of a phenomenon and, second through the transformation of individual subjectivity. Incitement to discourse relates to producing discourse on 'truth', which encourages the production of discourse. Knowledge gained from the confession is then re-codified into discourses of medicine, psychiatry, etc. which establishes a normalising field – a regime of truth – in which individuals are categorised as deviant or normal (McNay 1994, 122). The second function of the confession is to direct and shape the subjectivity of the individual. Indeed, confessing and telling the truth, having one's guilt absolved, repenting and performing religious rituals has the effect of reconstituting the thoughts, soul and behaviour of the individual repenting. Foucault aptly explicates the ritualising effect of the confessional on subjectivity:

> The confession is a ritual of discourse in which the speaking subject is also the subject of the statement ... a ritual in which the expression alone, independently of its external consequences, produces intrinsic modification in the person who articulates it: it exonerates redeems, and purifies him; it unburdens him of his wrongs, liberates him, and promises him salvation.
>
> (Foucault 1998a, 62)

'Salvation in this life' 159

It is thus the act of verbalisation, alongside the act of proclamation, that turns the individual into a subject. In other words, it is the performative function of language that turns the individual into a subject (Besley 2005, 85). This occurs because the confession is both a communicative and an expressive act, 'a narrative in which we (re)create ourselves by creating our own narrative, reworking the past, in public, or at least in dialogue with another' (Rose 1999, 222). The critical role language plays in the modification of subjectivity consequently reinforces the significant effect that the pastoral techniques in the de-radicalisation process (counselling, dialogue, debate) have on the radicalised subject. Alongside the guidance offered by experts, who are responsible for re-interpreting and re-constructing the knowledge professed by the radicalised individual, the act of recantation results in the individual acquiring self-knowledge, which paves the way for a recalibration of the self to occur.

This chapter deploys the conceptual framework of the confessional to understand the pastoral dimensions inherent in de-radicalisation interventions in the UK. As an ordering power of government, pastoral power not only preoccupies itself with the welfare of individuals within its territory, but more importantly, with their subjectivity. De-radicalisation must be viewed through the lens of the confessional; the existence of countless experts involved in the identification process, as well as the implementation of intervention; the shepherd/flock relationship assumed by the imam/mentor/experts on one side and the radical/vulnerable/extremist individual on the other; and the stated objectives of experts to have the radical/vulnerable/extremist individual transformed and to ultimately have the individual re-integrated back with the whole flock, or mainstream society.

Elite approaches to countering radicalisation: the Quilliam Foundation

Many interviewees emphasised the significant role that think-tanks such as Quilliam and the Policy Exchange had in shaping the Prevent strategy. As analysed in Chapter 2, many respondents associated de-radicalisation with Quilliam. In fact, there is no evidence linking the emergence of de-radicalisation in the UK as interventions on the ground and its incorporation into the wider national strategy with Quilliam. Instead it was community experts such as STREET and ACF that developed local de-radicalisation interventions before it became centralised by Channel. The link between de-radicalisation and Quilliam in the minds of a number of respondents underscores the influence think-tanks had in this policy domain. Whilst several think-tanks played a role in contributing to the discursive production surrounding the Prevent policy, and I even interviewed a number of analysts from those key think-tanks, this section primarily focuses on Quilliam because they are perceived by interviewees to be the most influential players in Prevent.

Quilliam was set up in November 2007 by Maajid Nawaz and Ed Hussain as Britain's first 'counter-extremism' think-tank. Both were former members of

160 *'Salvation in this life'*

Hizb-ut-Tahrir (the Liberation Party – HT), an organisation which was founded in 1953 in Jerusalem. Ideologically, HT had its roots in the anti-colonial ideas of Palestinian Taqiuddin al-Nabhani. Islam, through the prism of HT, is viewed as anti-nationalist, transnational and pan-Islamic. HT is ideologically committed to establishing a political Islamic polity, with Sharia law and the Caliphate as its core aims. The Hizb has an estimated membership of 8,500 and is particularly popular amongst university students and professionals. In the 1990s both Ed and Maajid had become active members, with Maajid occupying a senior role within the organisation, a position which saw him travel abroad, trying to establish organisational roots in other countries. Whilst Ed naturally transitioned away from the Hizb (Hussain 2007), Maajid was imprisoned in Egypt in December 2001 and released in 2006. He left the Hizb in 2007.

Both Ed's and Maajid's transition from Islamism became publicly documented case studies in bestselling books, titled the 'Islamist' (2007) and 'Radical' (2014) respectively. Quilliam's strategy as a think-tank was based on two broad objectives: (1) countering extremism, with a focus on addressing Islamist ideology and (2) promoting a 'liberal' Islam in Britain. As a trend within Islam, 'liberal' Islam was born out the influence of liberal thought during colonialism in Muslim majority countries and seeks the application of the social and political system that resulted from secularisation in Europe. Liberal Islam emphasises private and individual forms of practice and elevates reason above Quran and Sunna as reference points when it comes to norms and behaviour (Ramadan 2004, 27–28). Both Ed and Maajid have articulated and prescribed an interpretation of Islam that conforms to this 'liberal' trend in Islam in their published works (Hussain 2007; Nawaz 2014) and in a number of conceptual pieces published for Quilliam. A subsidiary objective for Quilliam was support for liberal and democratic values in order to counter (1) and promote (2).

With respect to countering Islamist ideology, Quilliam distinguished between Islam as a faith on the one hand and Islam as an ideology on the other. Echoing the analysis in Prevent, Quilliam argued that the ideological formulation of Islam was considered problematic because it was based on political considerations which, although they did not lead to violence, nevertheless created the conditions for violent extremism to flourish. The causal link between Islamist ideology and the transition to violence was stressed. This is explained by the interviewee below.

> People like Ed Hussain … when he brought out the Islamist and Majid Nawaz when Quilliam started there was this whole debate that … it's the conveyor belt theory, you know, people that were involved in ideas and the radicalisation process; that it eventually leads them to becoming terrorists and involved in violent extremism.
>
> (Interview 19, Academic)

The crux of this rationale was the belief that Islamist groups and ideas belonged to the same camp as 'violent extremists'. Hence Quilliam forcefully pronounced the importance of tackling 'non-violent extremism' as a crucial dimension of

'Salvation in this life' 161

Prevent (Nawaz and Hussain 2010). In the early years, their targets were mainly HT, but this changed later to include the majority of mainstream Islamist organisations. Indeed, many respondents mentioned the counter-ideological focus of Quilliam. The former Head of a counter-terrorism unit explains the attractiveness of adopting a counter-ideological approach, which enables the government to extend its reach nationally, as opposed to more local solutions, which are context specific.

> ...that Islamist ideology was going to be targeted and therefore the violence would be dealt with as well because, you know, the ideology understood to be feeding that violence was going to be tackled. I suppose on paper it had the merit, the potential to be adopted nationally anywhere. The great attraction from a policy point of view, of being clear and in theory being able to be deployed anywhere. It had the notion that Hizb-ut-Tahrir in particular and those sorts of groups needed to be tackled as part of the strategy.
>
> (Interview 17, former Head of counter-terrorism unit)

Meanwhile, the quest to construct a Liberal Islam was concretised through a strategy of counter-subversion; Muslim organisations and individuals in Britain were categorised into 'good' and 'bad' Muslims. These tactics were exposed to the public when a document Quilliam had written to the Director of the OSCT at the Home Office, Charles Farr, was leaked into the public domain (Nawaz and Hussain 2010). In the document Quilliam listed a number of organisations they advised that the government should stop working with. Although many respondents claimed that Quilliam's role within the Muslim communities was discredited at the outset because of their affiliation to government as well as their aggressive approach, according to one interviewee Quilliam's approach weakened its relationship with government because they became seen as heavy handed in the delivery of the counter-extremism agenda.

> I think they didn't do themselves any favours in terms of how they presented themselves. Also, they had a tendency to go in for kind of personal attacks on individuals. They were sending out these ... I remember I was getting their updates like three times a day at one point, you know, they'd be sending 'we condemn this individual for this that and the other'. Their tactics weren't well received and then they kind of made it difficult for themselves to be seen as partners of government, they might have been seen as a liability for government.
>
> (Interview 9, ISD analyst)

However, the data shows that Quilliam was very influential in a very short period of time, with a number of reasons cited: being funded by government, instant access to the media, links to influential right wing organisations, the compatibility of its message with Prevent, and the expertise they possessed. Their influence is underscored by the fact that they were consulted in detail on Cameron's 2011

162 *'Salvation in this life'*

Munich Speech on Extremism and the Birmingham Speech in July 2015. This was corroborated by Paul Goodman, editor of Conservative Home in a *Guardian* article (Shariatmadari 2015) and by investigative journalist Nafeez Ahmed (2015b). With respect to receiving Prevent money – this was not controversial since many organisations received Prevent money, including the community organisations like STREET and the MCB. However, it was the level of funding that was particularly distinctive. Reports show that up till 2011, Quilliam received 2.7 million through Prevent (Ahmed 2015b). The two excerpts below corroborate the fact that Quilliam was funded by government to implement Prevent objectives.

> And they were really influential and he was almost like a celebrity within the police, he was invited to all the conferences. Quilliam were heavily funded and nobody knew for a long time where the money was coming from. We did establish later on that they were being paid by government departments like FCO, Home Office, and CLG.
>
> (Interview 16, Representative of NAMP)

> They got the most money from CLG and from the Home Office and Foreign Office to present the public face of Islam so they gave them that money to change the discourse and because they gave them the money it gave the platform that allowed them to go be invited to speak to government Ministers.
>
> (Interview 23, Director of prison intervention provider)

Another factor that explains Quilliam's popularity was the space afforded to them in the popular media, like tabloids such as the 'SUN', which has a readership of several million. The following interviewee explains that this access to media was matched by very accessible and relatable narratives that were effective in getting the Quilliam 'extremism' message across.

> When there was a terrorist incident the popular press would call upon Maajid Nawaz to explain what the problem was. It was done very effective, you know, by Dean Goodson, who was writing in the Times, and in The Sun it was presented in accessible format by Maajid that before the joined Hizb-ut-Tahrir they were regular guys, they enjoyed playing badminton and supported Liverpool football team, that was his football team I think. But they had these wonderful accounts tailor made for The Sun that kind of left out the important bits and thus made it clear that all these terrorist incidences were directly related to problems of the Mosque across the road.
>
> (Interview 17, former Head of counter-terrorism unit)

Third, many respondents believed that Quilliam were influential because they were 'Muslim neo-conservatives' to quote the former leader of a representative organisation.

Now why does the Quilliam Foundation do this? They are Muslim neo-Cons in my opinion.

(Interview 14, former Secretary General of representative organisation)

Quilliam has indeed explicitly identified itself with neo-conservatism, particularly its values-based approach to politics and foreign policy. However, Nawaz stated that his organisation preferred to push liberal and democratic values through a bottom-up approach in contradistinction to the American neo-conservatives' top-down approach (Nawaz 2011). In this respect Quilliam differed only in their approach rather than in the principles of neo-conservatism. However, a few interviewees highlighted the relationship between the neo-conservatives and Quilliam and as a result its ability to influence government. As the former President of a prominent student society put it, there is a 'neo-conservative element within government', which further underscores the influence of neo-conservatives.

> ...that some of these think-tanks perhaps through neo-conservative think-tanks have too much say over the shaping of our policy today. I think that's something to be concerned about. There seems to be a neo-conservative element within the government which is peddling certain narratives, Michael Gove for example being one. That's something for us to be worried about.
>
> (Interview 3, former President of a student society)

This argument is buttressed by the fact that Michael Gove had in fact contributed to the discourse on radicalisation post 2005 with a book (Gove 2006) and was a leading player in the evolution of Policy Exchange, and sat on the Advisory Board for Quilliam. The Policy Exchange is not only neo-conservative but also plays a public role advocating its ideological agenda for the Tory Party. Also, Douglas Murray of the Henry Jackson Society published a book advancing the merits of neo-conservatism. The book is titled: 'Neo-conservatism: Why We Need It'. Interestingly, Douglas Murray was one of the people Gove thanked for helping him write 'Celsius 7/7' (Mills *et al.* 2011, 40). In addition, the former Head of a counter-terrorism unit, from his experience, believes the scrutiny and negative smear campaigns against Islamists, reflect the working of a 'sophisticated' and 'elite' campaign, which is transnational, connected to American and 'pro-Israeli' networks. The influence of right-wing organisations in the shaping of Prevent suggests that Quilliam benefited as a result of their link to these organisations, and their stated agenda seemed to be compatible with the counter-subversion approaches of neo-conservative organisations.

> You know I suppose to a certain extent it is the organisation and the sophistication of the operations. When Daniel Pipes came over it became clear to me what I was witnessing was this very sophisticated movement; it's like an elite campaign; of course it's very pro-Israel in a particular sense and I

164 *'Salvation in this life'*

suppose if you consider the media aspect and that Tony Blair was forging close relations with Rupert Murdoch.

(Interview 17, former Head of counter-terrorism unit)

In contrast to other think-tanks working on counter-terrorism – such as Policy Exchange, the CSC, IPPR, ISD, Centri, Forward Thinking and DEMOS – Quilliam, in the form of Maajid Nawaz, Ed Hussein and Usama Hassan, had Muslims with actual years of experience with political Islam, who could speak Arabic, and were familiar with Islamist theological arguments. Of all the think-tanks vying for influence and power therefore, only Quilliam could claim genuine credible expertise.

Also, they are articulate and eloquent, Ed in particular but both of them. What Whitehall had was as couple of guys that had been there done that and spoke a good game and suited them.

(Interview 4, IPPR analyst)

More important to note, however, is the impact Quilliam had from the beginning. Quilliam were positioned as the official experts on radicalisation amongst the civil service, politicians and the media. Quilliam's status as expert on radicalisation was augmented by the popular and widely read book the 'Islamist'. The former Head of a counter-terrorism unit also identifies this book as being very influential in playing a role in getting Quilliam's view of radicalisation rolled out at as part of a wider national strategy, at the expense of local approaches represented by community experts.

I think Quilliam managed to do more training than anyone else. So you are talking about an elite approach; Quilliam, as an agent of that approach is able to train junior police officers and civil servants; I soon became aware that our very small efforts here were being over-ridden by this national strategy, with Majid Nawaz and Ed Hussain's view of the problem being rolled out, and it was being backed up with a very readable book, the 'Islamist', and other surrounding literature.

(Interview 17, former Head of counter-terrorism unit)

At the time, the lack of knowledge and understanding of radicalisation and Islamism made Hussain's book mandatory reading for civil servants and officials in Whitehall. For example, the Police Officer below mentions the importance of the 'Islamist' as a reference point for senior police officers.

He wrote his book. A lot of senior officers read it. I even wrote an article in the Police Review, because everywhere I went I saw people reading his book.

(Interview 16, Representative of NAMP)

'Salvation in this life' 165

Notably, one possible reason for the success of the Islamist in Whitehall, besides the readability of the book, was offered by investigative journalist Nafeez Ahmed. Ahmed claims to have learned from a senior researcher at the Home Office that the Islamist was 'effectively ghost-written in Whitehall':

> ...the official told me that in 2006, he was informed by a government colleague 'with close ties' to Jack Straw and Gordon Brown that 'the draft was written by Ed but then 'peppered' by government input'. The civil servant told him 'he had seen 'at least five drafts of the book, and the last one was dramatically different from the first.
>
> (Ahmed 2015a)

In any case, seen through the lens of confessional technology, the 'Islamist' should be seen as a biographical and confessional account of Ed's transformation from 'radical' to liberal reformed person. Ed and Maajid's experience encapsulates the repressive hypothesis embodied in the phenomenon of the 'ex-radical/ex-Muslim' syndrome, which epitomises the logic of 'speaking truth to power'. In their public statements and publications and in their discourse more generally, Ed and Maajid could be seen as concretised examples of individuals who had 'confessed' their sins and their bad ways. This confessional logic of ex-Islamists is exemplified in a published Quilliam report, 'In and Out of Extremism':

> The personal stories of Quilliam staff, including Maajid Nawaz and Dr Usama Hasan, have been fundamental to Quilliam's success at deradicalising violent extremists ... Each testimony highlighted the importance of these personal stories when delivering counter-narratives. Upon hearing these personal stories it prompted the then-extremists to rethink their own commitment to the cause.
>
> (Manning and La Bau 2015, 27)

In other words, they have publicly recanted and laid bare their inner secrets, despite the fact that Ed and Maajid had not been violent in their 'extremist' phase. This suggests that the narrative of their experiences was more important than actual facts of what happened. Below are four statements by respondents, two academics and two from the think-tank world, discussing the notion of 'reformed' or 'ex' Islamist/Muslim and its prominence in Prevent.

> I think one of the reasons we had an emphasis on de-radicalisation, because many people didn't come forward to help with Prevent, but those that did were the likes of Shiraz Maher, Shahid Butt, Majid Nawaz, Ed Hussain; these were people who claimed that they were ex-radicals and that they had an antidote to radicalisation and it was called de-radicalisation.
>
> (Interview 26, Forward Thinking analyst)

166   *'Salvation in this life'*

I mean there's even an industry in that context for ex-Muslims who will stand up and say 'yes, I used to be one of them'. It's not just the ex-extremist but it's also the ex-Muslims who are cashing in on money and politics. That's what's happening.

(Interview 12, Academic/freelance consultant on community engagement)

And what we've seen after 7/7 is the rise of the group saying 'well we are extremists, we are reformed extremists so we know even more than they do; we've actually been there, we understand it a lot more'.

(Interview 11, Academic)

Because they said to the establishment, look here we are, we used to be what you fear we're not anymore and we got insight into things that nobody else has.

(Interview 4, IPPR analyst)

Ultimately, the data reveals that a significant reason that Quilliam was afforded this influence on policy by government so early on is the fact that their narrative, conduct and articulated vision embodied a normative model of Muslim identity that the government was actively promoting. This argument was made by the Director of a prison intervention provider, who discussed the fact that the government could not publicly support that organisation; it found it easier instead politically to support Quilliam because they were the 'acceptable face of Islam', that fitted in with 'secularism', not to mention the fact that Quilliam was run by someone who called himself 'Ed' instead of Mohammed.

Because they presented what the government thought was an acceptable face of Islam. The government is interested in who looks like us, talks like us, really into secularism, because we're not really into religion in any shape or form, so who looks like that and better chimes with the public. Those who look like the Muslims blowing people up, we're not accepting those people, like I'm dressing, whatever, we're not accepting those, they're not going to be the public face ... Doesn't even make sense, but he dresses like us; looks like us, he can be an acceptable face of Islam. Same with Majid Nawaz and Ed Hussain – he doesn't even call himself Mohammed, he calls himself Ed instead – became an acceptable face.

(Interview 23, Director of prison intervention provider)

As for the majority of organisations and interventional providers, the funding stream was cut by government with Prevent 2011. Other factors in their diminished position post 2010 included the departure of Ed Hussain from Quilliam; the fact that they had become a bit of a liability for government as a result of a leaked memo and aggressive approach, and the emergence of a more streamlined Prevent policy post 2011, which had less need for their input. Regardless however of their diminished influence post 2010, the data indicates that as the representative of the elite approaches to countering radicalisation, Quilliam succeeded in discrediting and undermining the community approaches embodied by STREET and Siraat, as well as Islamists like the MCB and MAB, whilst simultaneously ensuring that their expertise was incorporated into a more centralised and national strategy post 2009. In many respects, Quilliam encapsulated the confessional: it was run by individuals who were 'ex-radicals' and who publicly confessed their past activities, offered a breakdown of the ideology they previously professed, and were involved in the dissemination of such knowledge publicly.

The Channel Programme: supporting 'vulnerable' people

> When you are talking about de-radicalisation, you are talking about Channel, which is about diverting people away from becoming extremist or terrorist. They would say that Channel is the only long-term solution to preventing this problem.
>
> (Interview 21, Prevent Officer)

As articulated above, de-radicalisation in the UK context is associated with the Channel programme and seeks to support 'vulnerable people' (Home Office 2011, 64). The word 'vulnerable' has developed in conjunction with the discourses on radicalisation and is a central feature in both the Channel identification process and the Prevent strategy. A number of interviewees critically questioned the term and concept 'vulnerable'. The most immediate question relates to the link between the concept of 'vulnerability', normally associated with the young, the disabled and the old on one hand, and violent radicalisation on the other. The academic below questions the relationship between vulnerable youths and violence.

> First of all, the link between vulnerable youths and violence is highly questionable. In particular, when it's also linked to radical ideas; whatever research we have on radicalisation we see that the most active people are by no means vulnerable. Many of them come from the most successful sections, like Ed Hussain, of the Muslim community. What they have, and nobody tries to make sense of it, someone like Ed Hussain is bloody ambitious and he was very clear about this in the Islamist, he wanted to be the leader and now he's using it in a different way but for the same purposes. So who is vulnerable? In what sense they are vulnerable?
>
> (Interview 15, Academic)

This interviewee does not believe that some radicals are 'vulnerable' but that they are instead 'ambitious' and hail from 'successful backgrounds'. Knowledge of the profile typical of those deemed radicals suggests that they are far from being 'vulnerable'. In other words, in order for someone to be susceptible to

168   'Salvation in this life'

radical ideas they need to be educated and ambitious. He thus debunks the notion that vulnerable individuals are typically those most likely to go on to commit terrorism. Another interviewee critical of the notion of 'vulnerability', also asks the pertinent question regarding what constituted 'vulnerability'.

> It's these words like 'support', 'intervention', and 'vulnerable', all of these words are okay if you knew what it actually meant but I don't actually know what it means … Someone who says Osama Bin Laden is cool, is he vulnerable? Just because someone said it, what makes them vulnerable?
>
> (Interview 18, former Chair of community organisation)

There are however a number of interviewees who view the term 'vulnerability' as a legitimate concept in the radicalisation process. The rationale underpinning the notion of 'vulnerability' is that vulnerable people are more 'at risk', in danger and more susceptible to embracing radical ideology or being attracted to extremist groups. Interviewees who were particularly positive with regards to the notion linking vulnerability with radicalisation included two Prevent Officers, two academics based in working on community engagement alongside a local government employee working on Prevent, and some of the think-tank analysts, such as Quilliam and DEMOS. Most of these interviewees were practitioners and, perhaps as a result, more appreciative of its role in the radicalisation process. More important is whether interviewees believed that the relationship between vulnerability and a future propensity to undertake violence could be established and was therefore a legitimate way of pre-empting potential problems. An example of this logic can be seen in the way that a Senior Prevent Officer understands the causes that lead someone down the route of radicalisation.

> What are the vulnerability factors in Keith's life? He's never had a father figure, whatever it is, he's been to Somalia or Yemen, he has post-traumatic stress disorder, I've left the army and I've been made redundant and the right-wing are trying to recruit me and we are getting more and more right wing cases; as you see because of the economy we are getting more and more cases of mental health and people aren't in work. Meanwhile the government's got its head on Al-Qaeda; they're not seeing some of those other risks.
>
> (Interview 22, Senior Prevent Officer)

In this comment we see an expansive view of 'vulnerability'. Vulnerability is associated with a variety of factors; a person's biography, where a person's been, 'traumatic stress disorder', being made redundant, mental health issues, being bullied at school, etc. The word 'vulnerable' according to this Senior Prevent Officer has thus become shorthand for anything that happened in the past that may have played a part in that person's trajectory towards radicalisation. The interesting feature nevertheless in her use of the word 'vulnerable' is the removal

'Salvation in this life' 169

of agency from individuals who have been identified as 'vulnerable'. This understanding of 'vulnerability', which reflects the Prevent conception of 'vulnerability', removes agency from young people attempting to contextualise political, religious, social, cultural and philosophical realities, and instead situates the burden on the evils of ideology and psychological problems. The problem, in other words, is a defect in character or the unfortunate circumstances engulfing the individual. The word 'vulnerable' not only dilutes the seriousness of a crime but also evokes a concern for the vulnerable individual. This logic is explained by a DEMOS analyst.

> It's hard to say; because vulnerability is like a nice sort of forgiving left-wing term for it's not their fault, they are being sucked in by radical preachers and we need to help them become more resilient to being manipulated and I think there's some truth in that for some people. But other people aren't vulnerable at all, they are actively empowered and going out and seeking these opportunities. Vulnerable, I think, has become a short hand, a pleasant non-discriminatory way of talking about it by using a language of vulnerability you are not stigmatising them, you are trying to understand why they are getting involved in this.
>
> (Interview 1, DEMOS analyst)

Whilst he acknowledged that some are not vulnerable and go out 'seeking opportunities', he nevertheless aptly encapsulates the instrumentalising effects of the term, e.g. removing the stigmatisation associated with radical ideas and acts, as well as the fact that it is a 'nice forgiving left-wing term'. The implication of the term vulnerability is that the individual was not to blame, should not be castigated, and instead requires support, care and education. This logic is also buttressed further by the fact that some of the individuals deemed vulnerable are young adolescents. It is more natural and fitting to view young adults (in some cases children) in terms of 'vulnerability' than to see them as being empowered by the adoption of radical ideas and practices.

Implicitly excluded in the use of 'vulnerability' therefore is the agency of those deemed vulnerable, particularly their ability to freely and rationally negotiate and contextualise their wider political, social and religious terrain. Stating that someone is vulnerable in relation to extremism is not only to attribute the blame elsewhere, but also to suggest that the individual was brain-washed, duped and deceived into extremism. In short, the word 'vulnerable' affirms a particular framing of the problem whilst denying others. The overall implication is that 'vulnerability' indicates a pastoral logic embedded in Prevent, and by default de-radicalisation. Indeed, the language of pastoral care is deeply intertwined with the concept of vulnerability. This can be ascertained from the language of the following respondent.

> The impression I get from Channel is that it's nurturing −these kids aren't criminals − just as the schools do and society has an obligation towards

170 'Salvation in this life'

young people and for adults to help nurture them as much as with parenting or teaching.

(Interview 25, Quilliam analyst)

This interviewee employs words like 'nurturing', 'obligation', 'parenting' and 'teaching' to describe Channel. Again, the language used evokes a type of pastoral logic. Also important in this thinking is the idea that the 'kids aren't criminals'. This in fact is one of the striking features of Channel in Prevent – it does not target criminals or even necessarily the individuals involved in extremist groups or activities. It is mainly concerned with individuals showing the potentiality for radicalism in the future. Before discussing how some interviewees believed that future radicalism can be detected, it is important to note therefore that 'vulnerability' denotes a category that describes the vague space spanning non-criminality, 'at risk' of criminality and risky or a threat, which in this instance refers to radicalisation.

However, given the murky continuum between being vulnerable and hence 'at risk' and being considered a threat, it is a notable feature of Channel that non-threat vulnerabilities, such as mental health and social issues, become mixed up with threat-vulnerabilities (that is, extreme views indicating propensity for radicalism). The fact that some individuals who are vulnerable in the non-radical sense get picked up by Channel is explained by an academic who has done Prevent community work.

> ...something say like the Channel Project I know there are community members who may assess and they'll get a report from Channel saying this person looks like they are vulnerable and a person will see that and say: 'no this person isn't vulnerable they might have a mental health issue' developing, lots of other things, they don't need de-radicalisation'. So potentially you have many people going through the system who have no issues anyway.

(Interview 7, Academic/Prevent Practitioner)

The conflation of different forms of 'vulnerability' in the case of Channel, between a general form of vulnerability and 'at risk' of being drawn into a terrorism type of 'vulnerability', is also acknowledged in Prevent 2011.

> During the consultation to the Prevent review we found that the attraction of community cohesion work appears to have sometimes steered people towards Channel who may have been perceived as potentially vulnerable in some broader sense, rather than specifically at risk of being drawn into terrorism.

(HO 2011, 65)

What then are the risk triggers that convey the right type of vulnerability that potentially puts someone on a de-radicalisation intervention? In April 2015, as

'Salvation in this life' 171

part of the Counter-Terrorism and Security Act 2015, the 'Channel Duty Guidance' was issued. It was the first time a 'vulnerability assessment framework' was provided (HMG 2015, 11). It is built around three indicators: (1) engagement with a group or cause or ideology; (2) intent to cause harm; (3) capability to cause harm. This criterion is assessed by considering 22 factors that can contribute to vulnerability (13 associated with engagement, six that relate to intent and three for capability). Despite this however Prevent concedes, 'at present OSCT-funded intervention providers do not have a 'standardised' risk assessment tool; each project has developed and deployed its own risk assessment' (HO 2011, 61).

However, there were two types of broad responses by interviewees. One view states that 'vulnerability' according to Channel corresponds to religious and political ideas and practices, whereas the second view is not antithetical to the first but merely places the emphasis on other factors, situating 'vulnerability' in terms of psychology, the individual, social background and grievances. Again, these two views are not necessarily mutually exclusive and yet, according to where the line is placed, naturally lead to different policy approaches. The second view certainly tries to play down the political and religious context given the sensitivity surrounding claims that government is intervening in the religious and political lives of Muslims. The first view is articulated below.

> What we found is that the way they identified people who are vulnerable was very Islamophobic, to find a better word. So those who visited the mosque regularly, or whose parents were religious, Muslims who belong to a certain school of thought within Islam, whether it was Salafi or Ikhwani; those who were from South East Asia or North African would be identified. There was a phase when Somalis were identified as vulnerable, so now young Somalis are targeted because, you know, especially if they are talking about Somalia or are against African Union intervention there then those individuals would be identified.
>
> (Interview 18, former Chair of community organisation)

According to this view, Channel risk indicators correspond to the articulation of particular views and beliefs associated with religion and politics, in addition to changes in outward behaviour/appearance. In other words, professing a belief in 'sharia' or the 'caliphate', the sudden adoption of certain clothing, the articulation of political views, and the networks individuals associate with flag up that particular individual as a potential terrorist (Gutkowski 2011, 352–353; HMG 2012, 12; Kundnani 2014, 176–181; HMG 2015, 12). This is implicitly acknowledged by ACPO, the body overseeing Channel, but is couched in the language of countering ideology.

In contrast, the second view of what constitutes 'vulnerability' is articulated by both Prevent Officers.

> You are talking about a fine line here. It's about that particular person, how they are, and what they do. It's not about a change of dress, or change of

172 *'Salvation in this life'*

> different things. So, say someone's got a drug problem; if you look at someone like Isa Ibrahim in Bristol; he had a drug problem, he was isolated from his family, and then starts to learn about Islam over the internet and because of that makes homemade explosives and then makes a suicide vest.
>
> (Interview 21, Prevent Officer)

> This is what government doesn't understand; their measurement would seem like I find someone who is radicalised and put them on a de-radicalisation course; I'll get a provider, largely with theological and juris-prudence knowledge, I put them through a mentoring course, and Keith will magically transform and come the other side; meanwhile we haven't dealt with his drug addiction, his dad doesn't sit with him at the dinner table, and he's got a grievance against Kashmir. We are not thought police in that sense.
>
> (Interview 22, Senior Prevent Officer)

This Senior Prevent Officer emphasises general factors like identity, drug addiction and personal experience. She is not dismissive of the other dimension but seems to suggest that a focus on theology and mentoring is futile without tackling the underlying personal and social vulnerabilities. Both conceptions of vulnerability not only frame the problem in a certain light, which actually guides the work of practitioners and intervention providers on the ground with respect to identifying it, but it also serves to legitimise interventions in the lives of individuals, which would not otherwise be normatively and legally possible within liberal structures of governance, which theoretically prizes the sovereignty of the individual in these matters. It is the vocabulary of 'vulnerability' that legitimises the corrective techniques of de-radicalisation.

De-radicalisation interventions: mentoring and psychotherapy

Whilst the majority of respondents associated de-radicalisation with Channel, only a couple of interviewees were able to make more detailed comments about the nature of interventions. However, it is clear from the limited data that de-radicalisation is delivered through the pastoral care of mentorship. The importance of mentoring in de-radicalisation is also supported in the literature (HMG 2012, 21; HMG 2015, 17; Lindekilde 2015; Spalek and Davies 2012). Consequently, this section examines the notion of mentoring as a vehicle for de-radicalisation and how it encapsulates confessional technology.

In Chapter 5 it was stated that Channel makes risk assessments of individuals and places 'extremists' on de-radicalisation interventions. Once Channel assigns individuals to an intervention programme, the premise is that the worldview of the 'extremist' has to be tackled. How is this done? The data shows that de-radicalisation is undertaken through the mentor-mentee relationship. The following respondent, a mentor and Prevent practitioner, identified the link between the

'Salvation in this life' 173

Channel programme and mentoring and described it as the link between the police and the community.

> The individuals, even now at this moment, who go through mentoring, are people from Channel, who are referred through Channel processes. That's where the relationship between the police and the community is. The people who sat on the Project Board for the mentoring came from CTU, came from Birmingham and Coventry City Council, they were the funding bodies but we also got Probation and one or two of us from prisons who were involved in it. So they were the kind of stakeholders and in terms of how it then worked out – so now the projects gone live – you have, say, the police here in terms of Channel and CTU; we have a commission and an organisation called the Centre for Conflict Transformation, CFCT, which is based in Birmingham; they are a third sector community organisation who kind of, I suppose, act as a neutral body through which to receive referrals and they do all the systems and processes so that when you get a referral from the police it goes through the Centre for Conflict; they kind of loosely use the eleven mentors we got on the books to kind of use them as consultants.
>
> (Interview 8, Prevent practitioner)

In her description, de-radicalisation is conceived as a 'community' initiative that involves several bodies and agencies that employ mentors. According to the interviewee (at the time of fieldwork) there were 11 mentors on the books at the CFCT in Birmingham. Meanwhile, another respondent, a senior researcher at Quilliam, highlights the pastoral components of de-radicalisation when asked about de-radicalisation: 'one to one', 'vulnerability', 'didn't have any friends', 'issues' and 'journey'. These words once again show that radicalisation has been couched in the language of 'vulnerability' but also stresses the pastoral features of the mentoring relationships. After all, pastoralist care essentially revolves around the welfare of the individual and their salvation. The language used by the interviewee to describe the signs that mentors examine in the radicalised subject does reflect the pastoral objectives of de-radicalisation interventions.

> It's basically a process of mentoring on a personal one to one basis. Again because of the vulnerability factors a lot of these people became potential terrorists because they didn't have any friends, didn't have a steady job, or had been imprisoned or in trouble with the police before. There are all sorts of reasons why they are angry at society – they don't feel they fit in or feel any sense of brotherhood or sisterhood with people in a different environment. There are many issues to address and these interventions do and lead them away from their previous ideas to better ideas, helping them along their journey.
>
> (Interview 25, Quilliam analyst)

174 *'Salvation in this life'*

The relationship between mentor and mentee is analogous to the relationship between the priest and layperson in Christian penance, which is characterised by the dynamic of the listener vis-à-vis the confessor. In other words, the mentor-mentee relationship should be seen as the secularised version of pastoral power. At the beginning of this chapter, we argued that the 'repressive hypothesis' was a deep-seated practice of 'speaking truth to power' in Western societies. Indeed in the context of de-radicalisation, the 'repressive hypothesis' is manifested in the mentoring of the radicalised subject. The imperative to confess and reveal one's innermost thoughts and secrets is a central technique in de-radicalisation interventions. Hence this first dimension of the confessional logic exists in de-radicalisation interventions, as young 'extremists' are assigned to mentors and are encouraged to speak, argue and confess. In fact my data identifies techniques such as dialectic discussions, rational debate and argumentation as critical components of the process itself. The interviewee below explicitly mentions the discursive dimensions involved in de-radicalisation.

> De-radicalisation, to do it, you need to be able to deconstruct the ideas that formed in that person's mind and give him a better way of understanding the proof and evidences that led him to those thoughts. Plus we have to give him an alternative to taking that course of action. For example, lots of people said they were angry about the Iraq War. Okay well, you as an individual could you change the war in Iraq? Could you go at the time and get Tony Blair to stop? The answer is no. But by blowing up somebody are you going to change the war in Iraq? The answer is no. On top of that you have to give him alternative outlets for his anger.
>
> (Interview 23, Director of prison intervention provider)

The interviewee describes de-radicalisation in terms of 'deconstruct', 'proof' and 'evidence'. These words connote the discursive dialectical technique involved in de-radicalisation interventions. The rationale underlying dialectic argumentation is that rational enquiry, debate and the presumed superior knowledge of the mentor will result in the dislodgement and displacement of the thinking believed to support Islamist ideology. It adheres to liberal assumptions that cognitive change can come about through rational enquiry. More importantly the discursive interaction between the interlocutor and the radicalised subject takes place within the structured and formalised procedure and relationship of mentoring. The academic below views de-radicalisation as 'counter-brainwashing' which occurs through persuasion, debate and discussion.

> I suppose it's like brainwashing really; its counter-brainwashing. They want to convince people that are convinced of something that they shouldn't be that and should be convinced of something else. In a way I am in favour of that. I'm in favour of debate and discussion. If I see a Muslim who has an extreme interpretation, whether extreme in a peaceful way or in a violent

way, I would try and de-radicalise them in a way using discussion and debate.

(Interview 20, Academic)

The de-radicalisation process stresses that cognitive change depends on the discursive interactions characterised by dialogue, debate and language between listener and confessor. As mentioned earlier, speaking 'truth' to power by the radicalised subjects in de-radicalisation interventions is expected to play an important part in reconfiguring the identity of subjects. This is why discursive categories of 'moderate', 'extreme', 'British values', etc. are discursive devices that the subject is expected to embrace in order to become subjected. It is a discourse that guides the subject, 'go here; don't go there'. It is thus the act of verbalisation, alongside the act of proclamation that turns the individual into a subject. It is the performative function of language that turns the individual into a subject.

Furthermore, given the connotation of de-radicalisation with 'brain-washing', something which was evident in a few of the responses by interviewees, a notable feature of the mentoring process that is relevant to understanding de-radicalisation is the idea of 'contract' or 'consent' (HO 2011, 59; HMG 2015, 16). The notion of contract, according to the Director of a prison provider, relates to the fact that intervention programmes only take part with the consent of the radicalised subject. The idea of 'consent' is central to counter claims and accusations that point to similarities between the concept of brainwashing and de-radicalisation. In this way, the mentoring relationship is contingent on the radicalised subject accepting the authority of the mentor and hence the 'contract'.

> Behavioural change business means that if I want to change your behaviour then first and foremost we need to have a contract to say that you are going to accept something I say to you or at least give it credence and dialogue; in the same way that when you are at school you have a contract with your teacher that what your teacher says you're going to take it on board.
>
> (Interview 23, Director of prison intervention provider)

The suggestion here is that de-radicalisation is neither compulsory nor legally mandated but is a by-product of the subject's acceptance. If this were true, then the subject has implicitly conceded that they have a problem or exhibit the symptoms of radicalisation that need to be treated. Insofar as the subject agrees to take part in the mentoring process they consequently affirm their identity as radicalised subjects. Similar therefore to the sinners or the faithful confessing to the priest, radicalised subjects consent to confessing since their liberation is perceived to be hanging on the expertise of the mentor. Again, the fact that de-radicalisation interventions are based on the 'consent' and voluntary acquiescence of individuals is explained below by the researcher at Quilliam. Interestingly he refers to the pastoral logic driving such interventions, the fact that the radicalised subject has not been arrested or changed.

176 *'Salvation in this life'*

> The point with the prison service, same with mentoring, is to try and help turn their life around because generally this country will try to look after the welfare of its people. Remember they are not criminalised; Channel is voluntary and has to be done with the agreement of the parents. They haven't been arrested or charged and the criminal justice system works differently.
> (Interview 25, Quilliam analyst)

Another critical point to consider in the mentoring process that structures interventions is the notion of 'counselling'. Indeed, it is this dimension relating to counselling, psychology and therapy that connects and brings together the aforementioned features inherent to de-radicalisation, such as talking, consenting to take part and mentoring, together. A mentor and Prevent practitioner employs the analogy of counselling to explain the objectives of mentoring.

> It means when you have a referral sitting in with a client, that you're not sitting there indefinitely to talk about life in general – this is something that has an outcome at the end and not to make the process ongoing you need to have an end point. It's more around the basics of what counselling is about. So with counselling, for example, the idea of consent...
> (Interview 8, Prevent practitioner)

This respondent's answer sheds light on the structured logic of de-radicalisation, i.e. it has a beginning and an 'end point' and is compared to counselling. Another interviewee, also employs the language of psychology to tackle radicalisation and speaks of the process in terms of 'stages' that have the aim of inserting 'doubt' into subjects' conceptions.

> ...we also need to tackle the psychology of that individual as well because we don't know about the traumas in their life that might lead them to be the bomber instead of the bomb maker. At least if we can put enough doubt we can stop him becoming the bomber; put some more doubt and stop him becoming the bomb-maker; then put some more doubt and stop him becoming a supporter; and then that takes him back. It goes through a stage process.
> (Interview 23, Director of prison intervention provider)

Continuing the logic of a structured intervention based on consent, with an end in sight, deploying the discursive technique of psychotherapy, the words expressed by the radicalised subject undergoing intervention are recorded and monitored. Seen through the lens of confessional technology, one of the objectives of power in the incitement of discourse is to collate knowledge in order to feed it back into discourse that evokes the methods and language of science, which produces 'truth'. The Prevent practitioner's comments below highlight how this process works through mentoring. She describes de-radicalisation intervention as a formal programme in which 'reports' are written, 'debrief' sessions take place, and information 'passes upwards'.

'Salvation in this life' 177

So there two mentors that go in for example. When you've had an intervention you write up a report and then you have a debrief session with the operations managers from the Centre for Conflict and the idea is that you are aware of everything that happens in the process and you know exactly what will pass upward.

(Interview 8, Prevent practitioner)

The similarities between the techniques of mentoring and psychotherapy and their associations with de-radicalisation intervention are evident (HMG 2015, 17). As argued thus far, this is due to the fact that the rationale, techniques and language employed by all these programmes have a common origin in the Christian confessional. And they are all based on the individual or subject having to discuss, talk and confess. An overview of psychotherapy elucidates this further. Psychotherapy is based on the notion that it provides for a medical, scientific, and objective way of diagnosing the problem experienced by a patient with 'x' symptoms and 'y' problems. Psychoanalysis depends on the expertise of the doctor/therapists/counsellor and their ability to interpret the language used by the patient, in which the patient provides a detailed account and analysis of their past, memories, feelings, hope and expectations – in short, confessing their internal world to the expert (Rose 1999). The objective is that the doctor is able to interpret and diagnose the problem and then offer a prescription that fixes the problem. The patient is offered a chance in this process of understanding and reconciling their issues and in the end being rehabilitated back to 'normality'. Likewise, de-radicalisation interventions are based on programmes with several interlocutors, who shepherd and educate the individual, encouraging them to speak and confess, and have their positions re-examined and minds changed.

Redemption: 'integration into the mainstream'

De-radicalisation is predicated on the notion that intervention agencies and mentors are able to undo years of social, cultural and political conditioning. Is this possible? The simple answer is: we do not know. Channel does not provide access to data with regards to the profile of individuals undergoing interventions, the success rates, or whether those young individuals have been re-orientated in conformity to the objectives of Prevent. This means the public and researchers are unable to know whether de-radicalisation interventions work overall. There are a few other questions that arise: do interventions actually work according to the logic articulated in Prevent, e.g. cognitive change results in behaviour change? What does a successful de-radicalisation look like? And how do we know they were going to commit acts of violent anyway? The dataset is silent on these questions, as is the wider literature. During fieldwork data I was unable to interview 'reformed' extremists who had undergone de-radicalisation or even talk directly to mentors implementing an intervention, so I could not ascertain the phenomenological experience of being 'de-radicalised'. This is a notable weakness in the dataset. Despite the absence of data relating to the de-facto

178 *'Salvation in this life'*

process of de-radicalisation itself, the data does however affirm that de-radicalisation ultimately seeks a transformed self, whose behaviour changes as a result of an internal change of the soul.

The first major challenge for researchers wanting to understand de-radicalisation interventions as a process and not merely as an idea and policy is access to data and an ostensible lack of transparency when it comes to the activities of Channel. This is expressed by the majority of interviewees. This means that we are unable to know if Channel is working and has been successful in implementing de-radicalisation. One respondent noted that, despite the absence of evidence to prove the success of Channel, policymakers are 'proud' of it.

> It's almost like when Prevent first started, everybody is very proud of Channel. I have not seen a single document which is independent, which shows me the tangible results produced by Channel.
>
> (Interview 16, Representative of NAMP)

As a result of the absence of any meaningful and transparent data, some interviewees suggested that Channel is being financed and supported by policymakers off the back of conjecture. And it is risk aversion that bears the fingerprints of political imperatives and pressures and not the mark of the seriously evidence-based research expected of governmental policy. The academic below strikingly articulates the contradiction between a policy imperative that usually evokes the need for evidence to substantiate a policy and the absence of the same logic in Prevent.

> If it was explained to me more, you know, the science, or the rationale, or the evidence for it; nowadays they talk about evidence base policing. Where's the evidence for Channel? Where's the evidence base for de-radicalisation? Where's the evidence base for Prevent? These are not evidence-based or led policies and if you compare it in stark contrast with Islamophobia, the argument against doing anything against Islamophobia is there's no evidence to substantiate action or change. So we look at that and in one breath we can do a lot of things with no evidence whatsoever and in another breath we can't do anything.
>
> (Interview 11, Academic)

Another challenge for policymakers and researchers alike is measuring de-radicalisation. In the words of Prevent:

> It is essential in this area, more even than in other areas of *Prevent*, that data collection is improved against a standard set of criteria.
>
> (HO 2011, 61)

In other words, how do we know when somebody has been successfully de-radicalised? The literature presents the notion of recidivism rates common to crime prevention, which is about measuring re-offending rates of ex-convicts or the number of 'ex' Jihadist who re-engage (Chowdhury and Hearne 2008, 16), but due to the lack of information and the unreliability of this measure, there have been calls, by the likes of Horgan, to find more effective ways of evaluating the success of programmes (Horgan 2009; Horgan and Braddock 2010). Despite the highly publicised claims for success associated with some interventions programmes, Horgan and Braddock (2010, 285–286) concluded that there are major barriers to even the most tentative of evaluations:

- There are no explicit criteria for success associated with any initiative.
- There is little data associated with any of these initiatives that can be reliably corroborated independently.
- There has been no systematic effort to study any aspect of these programmes, even individually, let alone collectively.

Notwithstanding the absence of any robust way to evaluate de-radicalisation interventions, there is nevertheless still something intuitive about the notion of long term prevention. But even if this may be true, measuring 'cognitive change' is fraught with serious challenges. One respondent explains this inherent ambiguity in the exercise of establishing successful de-radicalisation.

> There will always be ambiguity and I don't know the answer to that; because remember the people that go through Channel, how do we decide they're 'clean'? What, are you going to peer in their heads and see if they've changed their minds?
>
> (Interview 1, DEMOS analyst)

Whereas this comment represents the sceptical view on how to measure de-radicalisation, the respondent below argues for the use of recidivism rates in measuring de-radicalisation, and that they should also encompass an assessment of 'vulnerabilities'.

> All we can look at is what the vulnerabilities were beforehand and what they look like after. So when they started, they had a drug addiction, a mental health problem, and some family problems and when they come out they still got two of four of those indicators and say there's been some progress. That's all you can do is benchmark with an individual before and after and that's what you'd do with any programme. So if you were looking at repeated criminal offenders you'd say: twelve months on how many have re-offended? Six years on how many have reoffended? Ten years on how many have re-offended? And at the moment we have seven convicted terrorist and none of them have reoffended. Now we don't know what reoffending rates in the country are. Again, apart from the two in prisons, the others are in work or education.
>
> (Interview 22, Senior Prevent Officer)

180 *'Salvation in this life'*

Furthermore, another difficulty in analysing Channel is the clandestine nature surrounding the profile of individuals who have undertaken a de-radicalisation intervention. The interviewee advised me that interviewing individuals who had been on intervention programmes would benefit my investigation of de-radicalisation but that he also mentioned that I would not have access to them.

> But the people you really want to talk to are punter A, B, and C who went through the programme: how do they feel and what happened? I don't know their names and you're not going to get it in Google. A lot of them wouldn't have known they were channelled and those that did probably don't talk about it much. But if you ask to the government they will tell you there are hundreds of those.
>
> (Interview 4, IPPR analyst)

As a result, not only do we not know whether de-radicalisation interventions have been successful but we also do not know the actual reality of the process itself. What, for example, is the phenomenological experience of de-radicalisation? Does it operate the way formulated in the Prevent conception of de-radicalisation in terms of cognitive change first? Again, the absence of data surrounding the actual process in the UK means we can only speculate. This provokes the following questions: Why persist with de-radicalisation if we cannot establish whether it has worked? And caring for vulnerable individuals may be important, but why does it have to be done under the auspices of a counter-terrorism policy? What is the overall goal of de-radicalisation?

There are two broad perspectives on the issue of the overall objective of de-radicalisation; the first perspective is articulated in Prevent and by policymakers that de-radicalisation seeks to get individuals to abandon violence and to do that requires a change in the worldview of the radicalised individual. The second perspective articulated by some interviewees is that the change of subjectivity and behaviour is less to do with violence and more to do with the adoption of the 'mainstream' worldview. The first perspective is encapsulated in the view expressed below.

> It's quite simple, they have to renounce violence. We know from their own testimonies that they are convinced that violence, including terrorism, is an illegitimate means of achieving the end. So they might say that we could attack British taxpayers as they are legitimate targets because of the Iraq War and that they are Kufar and we have to wage Jihad against the Kufar. A lot of individuals say things like that and after a successful intervention when they've realised from religious experience, general experience, and practical arguments, they renounce those ideas and say it's never right to kill innocent people.
>
> (Interview 25, Quilliam analyst)

'Salvation in this life' 181

The idea expressed here is that 'arguments' will lead the militant individual to renounce violence. This idea of deconstructing the thoughts that lead to violence is also explained by the interviewee below.

> What I or we class as radicalisation is somebody has the wrong understanding of those five things, not necessary all five, but enough of those five to justify unjustly killing people or unjustly harming people.
>
> (Interview 23, Director of prison intervention provider)

The five categorises mentioned above have been discussed in Chapter 2 but in essence they relate to concepts like 'Jihad', Sharia', 'Caliphate', 'takfirr' and 'ummah'. With de-radicalisation interventions therefore, policymakers and experts aim to rearticulate and reshape the individual's understanding of these terms. Thus both interviewees explain the fact that the problem with radicals was their understanding of central terms and ideas.

> I had a few objections to the definition of Islamist though. It said the Islamists believed in Sharia, Caliphate, and Jihad. Well I disagree with that. I believe in those terms but I have a modern understanding of them whereas I agree that extremists exploit those terms and have a medieval understanding of those three points.
>
> (Interview 25, Quilliam analyst)

According to this perspective de-radicalisation is concerned with changing the worldview of the radicalised subject with respect to their understanding and interpretation of certain classical notions in the Islamic tradition. Whilst this approach seeks to suppress a particular Muslim identity, e.g. politicised Muslim identities, it does not necessarily require, in theory, the adoption of 'British values' or liberal values. The dividing line in this instance is violence.

However, the second broad perspective views the objective of de-radicalisation as integration into mainstream society (see Chapter 2). One of the definitions evidenced in the data is reflected in official definitions of de-radicalisation in the literature: 'dissuade somebody from the use of violence or/ and reintegrate *into mainstream society'* (UN Counterterrorism Implementation Task Force 2008, 5). The two interviewees below explicitly associate de-radicalisation with a 'return to the mainstream'.

> So when you are talking about de-radicalisation as a dictionary definition, what you're saying is we are talking about moving people towards what mainstream society believes.
>
> (Interview 10, Investigative journalist)

> I understand Islam to be de-radicalisation, again with all the reservations about using the word, but bringing people back from the margins if you

182 *'Salvation in this life'*

wish from the extremities of practice – whether it be religious, political, social, ideological – bringing them back to the mainstream fold.

(Interview 27, President of Prevent funded think-tank)

The key question here is what is meant by the 'mainstream'. While some interviewees could not define what the 'mainstream' meant in practice, the following three interviewees associated the 'mainstream' with either 'Liberal secularism', 'British values' or 'values compatible with the Prevent strategy'.

... if you feel someone isn't well integrated and believes Britain is the enemy and that kind of narrative and that's somebody you consider to be radical, then de-radicalisation is about pacifying this person to try and make him understand that actually, Britain and the West doesn't have a problem with Muslims and British society and values are great.

(Interview 26, Forward Thinking analyst)

To answer your question, a journey to radicalisation and backwards, where to a point you are considered by the government to be a saint and don't pose a threat and you hold Islamic values that are compatible with the Prevent strategy.

(Interview 16, Representative of NAMP)

I think the agenda is to stir disaffected young people into the mainstream viewpoint. Getting them to sign up to those elusive British values we were talking about, getting them to sign up to liberal secularism.

(Interview 24, former Chief Inspector/Prevent Board member)

These comments suggest that the purpose of de-radicalisation for policymakers is getting Muslim youngsters to adopt particular modes of subjectivity through pastoral care. In these examples the 'mainstream view' is represented by discursive categories like 'British values' and 'secular liberalism'. As articulated by the respondents above, policymakers want to affirm, through de-radicalisation intervention, a particular Muslim identity in conformity with society and, according to one respondent, the Prevent strategy. Indeed, overall this view of de-radicalisation – the second perspective on the objective of de-radicalisation – is more convincing. The first view is contradicted by the fact that the majority of the individuals deemed 'extremist', from the little we know, are young, non-violent, with little connection to actual militant groups. In addition, it has become clear through the analysis of data in Chapter 5 and this chapter, that de-radicalisation does not attempt to tackle terrorism but works to produce alternative Muslim subjectivity. This fact is explained by a Prevent Officer.

The difference is whether you consider that person crossing the line into criminality. People have this idea sometimes that Prevent wants to lock

'Salvation in this life' 183

people up and stop committing terrorist acts; it's not the case, we want to get to them before they get that far and realign their thinking, in many ways, and give them a balance in life.

(Interview 21, Prevent Officer)

The important points raised in the comment above are 'get them before they get that far', 'realign their thinking' and give them a 'balance in life'. These notions support the idea argued in this chapter that de-radicalisation interventions are a form of pastoral power. This pastoral logic exhibits the logic of risk management ('get them before they get that far'), care ('realign their thinking') and redemption ('balance of life'). To do this, Prevent has employed the discourse on radicalisation, which problematises Muslim identity in terms of explaining terrorism and integration as a problem of religious and political practices (Chapter 4) and, through Channel, identifies the individuals that exhibit such problematic ideas and behaviour (Chapter 5), in order to apply corrective solutions to individuals categorised as 'extremist' through pastoral care (Chapter 6), with a particular focus on theological and political revision.

The outcome is a socially sanitised and politically sanctioned Muslim identity. It is in this way that the radicalised subject is expected to adopt 'British values' (good) and 'secular liberalism' (even better) and abandon extremism (e.g. Islamism, which is synonymous with bad). This is what a de-radicalisation point/position would ideally resemble. Hence from the point of view of normalcy, 'normal' adolescence is constituted by privatised religious practice, depoliticisation and self-regulated citizenry.

References

Ahmed, N. (2015a). 'The circus: how British intelligence primed both sides of the "terror war"', *Middle East Eye*, www.middleeasteye.net/columns/circus-how-british-intelligence-primed-both-sides-terror-war-55293733#sthash.e0OwoGOg.dpuf.

Ahmed, N. (2015b). 'How violent extremists hijacked london-based "counter-extremism" think tank', *Alternet*, www.alternet.org/world/how-violent-extremists-hijacked-london-based-counter-extremism-think-tank.

Besley, T. (2005). 'Foucault, truth telling and technologies of the self in schools', *Journal of Educational Enquiry*, 6 (1): 76–89.

Chowdhury, N. and Hearne, E.B. (2008). *Beyond Terrorism: Deradicalization and Disengagement from Violent Extremism*. International Peace Institute, New York, http://ipacademy.org/media/pdf/publications/beter.pdf.

Foucault, M. (1982). 'The subject and power', *Critical Inquiry*, 8 (4): 777–795.

Foucault, M. (1987). ' "The ethic of care for the self as a practice of freedom": an interview with Michel Foucault on January 20, 1984', Raúl Fornet-Batancourt, Helmut Becker, Alfredo Gomez-Müller and J.D. Gauthier, *Philosophy & Social Criticism* 12: 112–131.

Foucault, M. (1988). *Technologies of the Self: A Seminar with Michel Foucault*, edited by L. Martin, H. Gutman and P. Hutton. Amherst: The University of Massachusetts Press.

184 *'Salvation in this life'*

Gove, M. (2006). *Celsius 7/7*. London: Weidenfeld & Nicolson.

Gutkowski, S. (2011). 'Secularism and the politics of risk Britain's prevent agenda, 2005–2009' *International Relations*, 25 (3): 346–362.

HMG (2012). *Channel: Protecting Vulnerable People from Being Drawn into Terrorism. A Guide for Local Partnership*, ACPO, www.acpo/police/documents/TAM/2012/201210TAMChannel/Guidance.pdf.

HMG (2015). *Channel Duty Guidance, Protecting Vulnerable People from Being Drawn into Terrorism, Statutory Guidance from Channel Panels Members and Partners of Local Panels*, www.gov.uk/government/uploads/system/uploads/attachment_data/file/425189/Channel_Duty_Guidance_April_2015.pdf.

Home Office (HO) (2011). *Prevent, CONTEST 2011*, www.homeoffice.gov.uk/publications/counter-terrorism/prevent/prevent-strategy.

Horgan, J. (2009). *Assessing the Effectiveness of Current De-Radicalization Initiatives and Identifying Implications for the Development of US-Based Initiatives in Multiple Setting*, National Consortium for The Study of Terrorism and Responses to Terrorism, www.start.umd.edu/start/research/investigators/project.asp?id=56.

Horgan, J. and K. Braddock (2010). 'Rehabilitating the terrorists? Challenges in assessing the effectiveness of de-radicalization programs', *Terrorism and Political Violence*, 22: 267–291.

Hussain, E. (2007). *The Islamist: Why I Joined Radical Islam in Britain, What I Saw Inside and Why I Left*. London: Penguin.

Kundnani, A. (2014). *The Muslims Are Coming! Islamophobia, Extremism, and the Domestic War on Terror*. London: Verso.

Lindekilde, L. (2015). 'Refocusing Danish counter-radicalisation efforts: an analysis of the (problematic) logic and practice of individual de-radicalisation interventions', in *Counter-Radicalisation: Critical Perspectives*, edited by C. Baker-Beall, C. Heath-Kelly and L. Jarvis. Abingdon: Routledge.

Manning, R. and La Bau, C. (2015). *In and Out of Extremism, the Quilliam Foundation*, www.quilliamfoundation.org/wp/wp-content/uploads/publications/free/in-and-out-of-extremism.pdf.

McNay, L. (1994). *Foucault: A Critical Introduction*. Cambridge: Polity Press.

Mills, T., Griffin, T. and Miller, D. (2011). *The Cold War on British Muslims: An Examination of Policy Exchange and the Centre for Social Cohesion*, SpinWatch, www.thecordobafoundation.com/attach/SpinwatchReport_ColdWar12.pdf.

Nawaz, M. (2011). *A Global Culture to Fight Extremism*, Ted Talks, /www.youtube.com/watch?v=EZwxKPv1CwA.

Nawaz, M. (2014). *Radical: My Journey from Islamist Extremism to a Democratic Awakening*. London: WH Allen Ltd.

Nawaz, M. and Hussain, E. (2010). *Preventing Terrorism: Where Next for Britain? The Quilliam Foundation, Leaked Memo to Government*, www.scribd.com/doc/34834977/Secret-Quilliam-Memo-to-government.

Rainbow, P. (1984). *The Foucault Reader*. New York: Pantheon Books.

Ramadan, T. (2004). *Western Muslims and the Future of Islam*. Oxford: Oxford University Press.

Rose, N. (1999). *Governing the Soul: The Shaping of the Private Self, Free Association*. London: Free Association Books.

Shariatmadari, D. (2015). 'Non-violent extremists thinking and jihadism are linked', *Guardian*, 2 August 2015, www.theguardian.com/politics/2015/aug/02/maajid-nawaz-how-a-former-islamist-became-david-camerons-anti-extremism-adviser.

Spalek, B. and Davies, L. (2012). 'Mentoring in relation to violent extremism: a study of role, purpose, and outcomes', *Studies in Conflict & Terrorism*, 35: 354–368.

UN Counterterrorism Implementation Task Force (2008). *First Report of the Working Group on Radicalisation and Extremism that Lead to Terrorism: Inventory of State Programmes*, www.un.org/terrorism/pdfs/radicalization.pdf.

7 A new framework for engagement

The most immediate benefit of viewing de-radicalisation through the concept of the technologies of the self is how we understand it. In some respects, my account of de-radicalisation echoes the critical constructivist and post-structuralist works of David Campbell (1998), Iver Neumann (1998) and Stuart Croft (2012) which emphasise the fact that identity and security are co-constitutive. However, unlike these authors, the focus of my book has been on the micro-politics of identity rather than the macro and externalised version of identity formation between states. In fact, the wider conclusion of conceptualising de-radicalisation as technologies of the self is that it is about 'who we are' as much as about disciplining the conduct of subjects. The attempt to fix a national political identity and socialise subjects in conformity to it is not merely the objective of security. Rather, the existence of security is contingent on identity constructions. It is in this sense that identity and security cannot be ontologically separated, which is controversial given that the role identity plays in security is contested (Jarvis and Holland 2015, 115). Notwithstanding the challenging questions open to exploration in this field, the technologies of the self integrate the idea and practice of de-radicalisation into the more elaborate schema of Foucauldian governmentality. It is a more comprehensive, coherent and analytically fecund theory than the current Prevent framework of de-radicalisation.

Remarkably, the literature was devoid of theories on de-radicalisation. The closest to such a theory were Foucauldian interpretations of de-radicalisation by Aggarwal (2013) and Lindekilde (2015) and yet neither account is relevant to the UK context. The overall lack of theoretical development is surprising given that the de-radicalisation thesis claims explanatory and prescriptive powers. For example, it claims that it can explain human behaviour (the causal relationship between thought and action) and transform behaviour (the experience of change), which manifest in both the renunciation of violence and the socialisation of militants back into mainstream society. But the technology of the self provides a theory that not only accommodates the claims of de-radicalisation but also offers more with respect to salient debates in security studies on issues relating to complexity/parsimony, continuity/change, ideas/material and agency/structure. The way the technologies of the self respond to the aforementioned issues is elaborated below.

A new framework for engagement 187

Despite the immense complexity of deradicalising someone, government and academic accounts are parsimonious: they situate de-radicalisation merely as an instrument of counter-terrorism and have primarily focused on the need to tackle Islamist ideology. In contrast, the technologies of the self introduce more complexity to de-radicalisation. They allow us to debunk the prevalent notion that de-radicalisation is concerned with merely mitigating the possibility of violence on British soil. Although this is undeniably one objective amongst others, and indeed a necessary and desirable goal for policymakers, employing the concept of the technologies of the self situates de-radicalisation as a technique deployed by government in order to ensure that the Muslim populations within the nation-state are disciplined, that citizens acquire the appropriate conduct, and that individuals adopt and invest in modes of subjectivity that are deemed sanitised and certified by political authorities. From the standpoint of neo-liberal governmentality, acceptable subjectivity begins with the notion of the ideal liberal citizen, who is not only democratic, non-violent and tolerant, but also active, responsible and self-regulating.

The preoccupation of policymakers with the ideas and practices of citizens beyond issues relating to violence is reflected in the way that certain forms of identity are being suppressed and affirmed. This risk management logic at the heart of de-radicalisation and Prevent strategies has to be contextualised within wider narratives, in which Islam is being constructed as an essentially fundamentalist religion and Muslims as a threat to the security and identity of the nation state. The technologies of the self is an individuating power that represents one pole of governmentality, whereas the other pole is concerned with the collective population. Hence the reason why governmentality is conceptualised as the government of 'all and each'. Conceptualising de-radicalisation as technologies of the self therefore enables us to view it as an instrument of government that seeks to deal with the multifarious challenges embodied in 'the Muslim question' and construction of the majority identity, and not merely as a strategy to fight terrorism.

An additional layer of theoretical complexity implicit in using the technologies of the self is the role of civil society in shaping conduct on behalf of government. After all, the Prevent strategy delegated the responsibility for tackling radicalisation to Muslim civil society, not to mention the fact that de-radicalisation interventions in the UK primarily target non-violent youths in civil society and not in the enclosed environment of prisons. The prevailing view in social sciences literature sees civil society as a sphere located between state and market – a buffer zone strong enough to keep both state and market in check, thereby preventing either from becoming too powerful (Habermas 1991; Fukuyama 1999).

However, the technologies of the self also support a view of civil society that posits a sphere which is not just independent and external to the state and government but internal to, as well as an extension of, the state and political institutions. In other words, civil society is something which forms part of modern governmental rationalities. To say that civil society belongs to political

188 *A new framework for engagement*

rationalities does not deny its external reality but instead presents another perspective. It is only by viewing civil society in this way that we can begin to reconcile the paradox in which the strategy of de-radicalisation has sections of civil society as its target whilst simultaneously accomplishing its objective with the help of the very thing it targets. Put in another way civil society is tasked with the job of controlling, disciplining and modifying the bad apples at the bottom of its own barrel. It is this self-regulating and self-correcting mechanism that connects de-radicalisation, civil society and disciplinary technology.

Another theoretical benefit gained in employing the technologies of the self is the distinction between whether de-radicalisation represents continuity or change in governmental policy. It sheds lights on the workings of governmentality with respect to interventions and programmes that operate in society outside juridical spaces and frameworks. Indeed, the non-juridical dimension of de-radicalisation interventions remains one of the striking features of UK de-radicalisation. I have hitherto demonstrated the way governments seek the modification of behaviour in their citizenry outside the juridical realm through wide ranging measures, e.g. discourses, strategies, policies, programmes, interventions and pastoral power. Therefore, understanding de-radicalisation through the lens of the technologies of the self contextualises de-radicalisation in relation to similar interventions in other policy domains.

In this respect, de-radicalisation interventions share a similarity with programmes that help individuals improve their well-being by overcoming threats to their health, like obesity and smoking found in the policy area of Health, or 'back to work' initiatives found in Welfare and Employment. Whilst undeniably constituting a change in certain respects, this represents more continuity; the critical difference is that the nation, and by extension the European project, is invested in cultural universalism through the objectification of its antithesis, Islam, and so a lot more is at stake here than back to work schemes for job seekers. The difference therefore between de-radicalisation and other corrective programmes, and where this type of technique represents a change in the delivery of government rehabilitation programmes, is that de-radicalisation overtly incorporates theological and political components in de-radicalisation efforts.

Furthermore, the technologies of the self present a symbiotic relationship between the role of ideas and material in the de-radicalisation process. The whole enterprise of fighting radicalisation and extremism is built on the premise that ideas have agency and that ideology is the root cause of our new security challenge. By implication therefore, counter-ideology gets militants away from violence. However, the literature on de-radicalisation argues against the primacy of counter-ideology in interventions. In fact, the literature shows that ideological factors play little or no role in persuading individuals to enter or leave such groups and movements. This highlights the disjuncture between the largely ideological focus of current de-radicalisation programmes and the factors found to motivate individuals' entry into and exit from terrorist organisations.

A new framework for engagement   189

Although I have not been concerned with the actual process of de-radicalisation in my investigation, the literature on the process of de-radicalisation nevertheless forces us to question the influence of ideology as a primary factor in explaining the journey towards and away from radicalisation. Similar to contemporary security thinking regarding the importance of ideas, the technologies of the self also valorise the role of ideas and discourse in the formation of the self and the implementation of policy. However, unlike current thinking on de-radicalisation, the technologies of the self offer a more holistic account that reconciles discursive dimensions with material domains, describing the interplay between radicalisation and its concretisation in institutions and programmes. In doing so, the technologies of the self encompass the discursive production of 'radicalisation' that has distinctively characterised the British experience in relation to fighting terrorism and which much of the literature on de-radicalisation has evaded and overlooked.

However, the importance of discursive technology does not mean that radicalisation does not exist in the real world or that there is no such thing as de-radicalisation. Nor does it mean that the only thing that exists is meaning, language and discourse. A distinction must be made between the idea that 'nothing *meaningful* exists outside the discourse' on the one hand, and that '*nothing* exists outside of discourse' on the other. The second statement is a claim that no material world exists out there and that is patently not the case. But to say nothing is 'meaningful' is different; it is to say that you could make sense of the world only within the framework of discourse and interpretation. Therefore, without the constitutive and instrumental role of discursive production in the Prevent strategy, the meaning of radicalisation as body of knowledge could not be exchanged and secured. It is through discourse that the interplay between representations of difference – what should be regarded as a threat and what is legitimate – that the dissemination of that knowledge, in conjunction with power, occurs.

The role of agency is really important. This is another area where the concept of the technologies of the self moves the debate along, even if only slightly. The positivist framework does not afford space for subjects to have any agency. It forces the conceptualisation of de-radicalisation to take a deterministic view of human behaviour and relegates the influence of structure on subjects, reducing the radicalisation process to questions of psychology, identity and ideology. This is obvious in definitions of de-radicalisation as 'cognitive' and 'behavioural' and in other definitions that posit de-radicalisation as a process of integrating 'militants into mainstream society'. The suggestion in popular conceptions of de-radicalisation is that 'mainstream society' and radicalised subjects are at polar ends of the spectrum, completely divorced from one another. It is reflected in the discourse of Prevent itself, the concept of 'vulnerability' being a case in point.

Therefore, the technologies of the self present a more sophisticated account of the debate surrounding agency. They allow the subject to act and make decisions, albeit that the space for action is limited. The subject was presented in Chapter 3 as internal and not external to structures and as a by-product of society

190 *A new framework for engagement*

and history, not as a disengaged subject floating abstractly in a transcendent way. Foucault's account of the subject, as presented in his later works, had to be included in order secure the agency of the subject in our context, the Muslim subject, who although subject to scrutiny, objectification and regimes of domination, has the capacity to act in different ways, to reject subjectification and resist in a multitude of ways – as many do and many others are trying to negotiate – just as much as many end up accepting and silently embracing regimes of normalisation.

Whilst this book has not included examples of Muslim agency, and perhaps my account of de-radicalisation ostensibly appears too silent on Muslim agency, I nevertheless tried to maintain the capacity for agency theoretically out of the belief that, although regimes of domination and processes of normalisation are impossible to escape, governmentality can only guide and shape conduct – it cannot generally determine it. In any case, my concern has been with the task of ontological description rather than normative statements. As a result, the technologies of the self provide a better account of the relationship between structure and agency.

Tackling neo-Jihadi terrorism: a new framework for engagement

In this book I have shown how de-radicalisation is framed and understood in the UK. I have also demonstrated that, in policy terms, de-radicalisation exhibits a tangled logic in which it performs the functions of counter-terrorism, counter-subversion, community cohesion and crime prevention. Insofar as de-radicalisation encompasses all four logics, then it unequivocally represents an incoherent policy that moves the concern of policymakers far beyond terrorism. It is this particular framing of de-radicalisation that causes confusion and leads to very bad policy. Put in crude terms, de-radicalisation in the UK does not actually address terrorism. And yet government has a responsibility and duty to protect its citizens and keep the UK safe. The scourge of terrorism must be countered. But if we are serious about stemming the tide of political violence and if de-radicalisation is going to succeed in the UK, a multi-pronged strategy is needed.

I propose an alternative framework that policymakers should consider in their efforts to counter the turn to political violence by a minority of young British Muslims, which includes: (1) re-framing the problem (2) bespoke interventions targeting terrorists only (3) empowering youth; and (4) investing in the research on exit from political violence. Contrary to Prevent, this framework sees de-radicalisation as a holistic strategy and not as an intervention. For individual level interventions the focus needs to be on disengagement. The current entanglement of four different policy areas will need to be unbundled and each given its distinctive remit. Individual interventions to disengage violent extremists are but one instrument among several other interconnected political, social, economic and cultural measures required to address the turn to political violence, as well as wider 'hearts and minds' considerations.

A new framework for engagement   191

Addressing the question 'what is to be done?' about neo-Jihadi political violence is complex and to deal with the wider discursive, political, economic and social problems required to tackle properly and substantially the conditions that generate violence would require another book. Due to space constraints, therefore, the following must be read in terms of broad brushstrokes that illuminate a different way of seeing and doing things, rather than a detailed analysis/prescription.

Reframe the problem

- Rethinking counter-terrorism: proportionality and re-calibration, not distortion
  There needs to be a rethink of our counter-terrorism strategy. Counter-terrorism thinking is still stuck in the mindset of the post-9/11 paradigm, even though the threats to our country have evolved. As outlined in Chapter 1, the characteristics of the 9/11 security paradigm are: a pre-emptive logic that is driven by the need to act in the present to prevent an imagined worst-case scenario in the future; shaped by a particular construction of risk, one which subordinated the threat posed by nation-states whilst overly emphasising the threat posed by non-state actors, as well as the power of ideational factors like ideology in causing violence. This discursive framing has led to major political and social restructuring of Western societies. It has also consumed a huge proportion of the intelligence services resources, evidenced by the fact that current spending on counter-terrorism surpasses that allocated to combating the Communist threat at the height of the Cold War. And yet the Cold War period was significantly more dangerous to international security than present-day Jihadi violence – a period which saw the deaths of millions in developing countries, the division of the world into two camps and the real prospect of nuclear war.

  Policymakers have to reconsider what constitutes a 'threat' in light of new threats to our national security in 2017. These include: the conventional threats posed by certain nation-states to British interests, a post-Brexit Europe, the rise of populism, the growing threat of far-right terrorism, the growing proliferation of cyber-wars, the dislocating effects of a Middle East in the throes of realignment and the mutations visible in the Neo-Jihadi movement. The fourth wave of Jihadi violence, embodied by Daesh, represents a subtle shift away from the terrorism of Al-Qaeda. Daesh is the violent side of a niche counter-cultural and transnational movement yearning for an 'Islamic State', pumped by online hype and which has offline impact, motivated by the political interests of certain countries, who are instrumentalising the internal theological and political differences between Islam's two major groups to legitimise their power struggles in the Middle East. In other words, the current fourth wave is less concerned with the West and more preoccupied with its political and cultural project in the Middle East. This does not mean there won't be attacks in Europe. But it does mean that realities on the ground have shifted. Terrorism should thus be placed within a narrower and more contained framework. Instead of hyper securitisation,

192 *A new framework for engagement*

terrorism should be tackled by law enforcement agencies and traditional counter-terrorism forces. A new counter-terrorism strategy would therefore seek to attain a balanced approach between protecting British citizens whilst simultaneously mitigating the threat posed by Neo-Jihadi violence in a proportionate manner, so that resources are recalibrated elsewhere to meet the new challenges that face Britain.

- Political violence, not radicalisation
  We need to see neo-Jihadi violence through the lens of political violence and not radicalisation. Viewing the turn to political violence by some Western Muslims through the concept of radicalisation does not help us. Radicalisation is the vehicle by which policymakers and an acquiescent media made sense of the 'problems' represented by its Muslim population. Radicalisation assumes that there are pre-given radicals, extremists and vulnerable people. These are abstractions. Its trajectory as an analytical category has been mired by contention and plagued by simplistic claims of linear causality with an over emphasis on ideology, so that it has come to be regarded as an ahistorical and de-contextualised process that is synonymous with violence. Rather than a scholarly and academic attempt at understanding the phenomenon of terrorism, the radicalisation discourse became circumscribed by the demands of counter-terrorism policy. Radicalisation is useful for specifically understanding social movements and how some individuals become active and are motivated into political and social action. It does not explain the transition to violence. This does not mean that radicalisation doesn't exist in the real world. It does exist. Instead it means that the concept is inoperable, for reasons indicated earlier in this book.

  Radicalisation is nothing new if, by radicalisation, we mean the socialisation of young men into violence. A known example includes numerous British young men, like one of Britain's celebrated writers, George Orwell, who travelled to Spain in order to fight for the communists in the Spanish civil war. All acts of terrorism are acts of political violence in order to defend the 'nomos' or to create a new 'nomos'. By viewing terrorism through the lens of political violence, we get the closest to understanding it and defeating it.

- Identity, not ideology
  Neo-Jihadi political violence is about identity and emotions; it's about who you are and where you belong and less about ideology. You can have extremist ideas but this does not necessarily make you violent and, by the same token, you can be violent without having extremist ideas. While there could be a relationship in some instances, on the whole, this is not borne out by the evidence. The role of ideology has to be qualified, being a factor in different ways for different individuals, and even used differently across generations. Many of the young men going to fight in Syria-Iraq today are not ideologues or intellectuals. And perhaps even more surprisingly, neither

are they religious. The well-publicised fact about one of the would be fighters ordering 'Islam for Dummies' before heading out to the Middle East is a striking illustration of this. Ideology and Islam do not push these young men to go and fight abroad or to undertake violence at home. These factors serve other functions in their trajectory towards violence, such as providing legitimisation for their action or being deployed as validation of in-group membership.

Neo-Jihadi violence is about social identity and coming to the defence of what is perceived to be a beleaguered community in different conflicts around the world. They do not see themselves as terrorist but as soldiers and warriors. Psychologically, Jihadists seek self-purification and redemption through acts of sacrifice for the sake of Muslims in Palestine, Kashmir, Iraq, Syria, Chechnya, Somalia and other parts of the world. And this is not merely directed at the West. A lot of this political violence is directed at corrupt despotic domestic rulers or against sectarian rivals. Some of the first wave of Jihadism was undertaken against the 'near enemy'. Many of the young Sunni Muslims flocking to the Syrian Civil/international War since 2011 did so in order to fight what they perceived to be an unjust regime. Others flocked to Iraq in order to take part in sectarian conflicts following the disintegration of the country. Questions of justice, self-esteem and resistance to perceived oppression, cannot be divorced from their actions, counter-intuitive though it seems to us. Understanding the significance of social identity over that of ideology would move our counter-terrorist efforts away from policing thought crimes in our social institutions.

- Groups/networks, not individuals
  Terrorism is a group phenomenon. Individuals who commit violence are criminals. Political violence requires a group and a network. Not only in terms of training, know-how, connecting you to conflict zones, but even for the so-called 'lone wolves' phenomenon, it is the group that provides the discourse and symbols of meaning, and acts as the focal point of identification with an in-group pitted against 'evil' outside groups. Della Porta (1995), Sageman (2008), Atran (2010) and Wiktorowicz (2005), and social movement theorists have all shown that the turn to political violence is instigated by small groups of friends and families. It is your social group and who you play football with that shapes the individual. It is the strong social bonds amongst friends and family that socialise individuals into a Manichean world view and pushes them inexorably towards violence. Despite this fact, supported by empirical data, the radicalisation models favoured by policymakers are formulated with the individual in mind, with de-radicalisation also targeting individuals and not groups.

- Sacred values, not religion
  It is sacred values that people are willing to die for, and not just Islam or religious fanaticism. Human beings are meaning-seeking creatures. Contrary

194 *A new framework for engagement*

to rational choice theory and utilitarian models of cost-benefit analysis, sacred values are not up for sale. This in part explains the consternation of many liberals, who view humans as rational animals seeking their self-interest. Those with sacred values sacrifice their self-interest and life for the sake of the group and the defence of sacred values, something that also puzzles Darwinists and evolutionists. This is why individuals have died for religion but also for the tribe, the nation, the environment, animals, freedom, communism, and so on and so forth. Religion does not, therefore, have a monopoly on sacred values and neither is it the sole instigator causing violence. The current wave of neo-Jihadi political violence is motivated by two goals: the creation of a political utopia inspired by a modernist and hybrid version of revivalist born-again Islam; and second the defence of Muslims in different parts of the word (deliberately killing Muslims in the process to do this). This globalised Islam sees Muslims as more akin to a race than a group subscribing to the faith of Islam. This movement is more a by-product of modernity, globalisation and nationalism than of Islam. The struggle should not be formulated in terms of McGlobalisation vs. Jihad, in other words between Western modernity and violent Islamism, but instead as McGlobalisation vs. McJihad. It is not Islam but a modern and globalised political movement that constitute the sacred values of neo-Jihadism.

- Politics and not just culture
It is not just through the lens of culture but that of politics as well that we should view political violence, identity issues and world events. Whilst culture does play an important role, it is not alone in providing a context or explanation as the discourse suggests. Since Samuel Huntington's formulation of the 'clash of civilisations' (1993), we have analysed politics and economics through the lens of culture. We are thus living in the era of the 'culturalisation of politics'. The 'culturalisation of politics' consigns politics, history, economy, class, gender, sociology, international relations, colonialism, the state and many more to mere footnotes in the analysis of phenomena, placing in its stead 'culture' as the primary explanation for motivations, actions and events. Due to its focus on individuals and tendency to claim universality, liberalism uses culture to tame the political, individualising problems as well as rendering culture as a natural site of conflict. The offshoot of culturalisation is de-politicisation – significant issues that demand political solutions are replaced with therapeutic or behavioural solutions. It is little wonder that political analysis evades radicalisation discourses, not to mention that there is a glaring absence of politics in discussions surrounding de-radicalisation.

- The role of wars, regional rivalries and Western foreign policy
Political violence undertake by Western Muslims is stoked (not the same as caused) by conflicts and wars in the Middle East, Africa and Asia. Between 2005 and 2007 the role of foreign policy in the radicalisation process was

fiercely contested. Muslim representatives and sections of the British Left argued that foreign policy was a primary cause of radicalisation. The New Labour government was keen to marginalise the role of foreign policy in accounts of radicalisation, given Tony Blair's association with the Iraq War. Whilst the detractors are right to point out that foreign policy in itself does not cause radicalisation, the War on Terror, the question of Palestine, the wars in Afghanistan and Iraq, interventions in Syria and Libya, drone attacks on Somalia, Yemen and Pakistan, in a period of just 15 years have created the macro and political enabling environment for political violence to ferment. Our policies and those of other states in the region, have of course created a physical space, a theatre of war in which terrorists can convene. And they also allow a narrative to be spun regarding the suffering and humiliation of Muslims globally, even if the role of local corrupt regimes and sectarian rivalry in the region has contributed more to these conflicts.

Political violence has been exacerbated, sustained and expanded by war and conflict in these countries, spilling over into Europe. Political violence is able to thrive in conditions of anarchy and power vacuum, in places where the nation-state has collapsed, and where people, who still affiliate along tribal and denominational lines, are vying for power and control. In these conflicts, the centralisation of violence is absent and other groups with access to arms are able to mount a political challenge. Terrorism remains heavily concentrated in five countries – Iraq, Nigeria, Afghanistan, Pakistan and Syria. These countries accounted for 78 per cent of lives lost in 2014 (IEP 2015, 2). This complicated state of affairs is exacerbated by the interventions of regional and global powers, which includes the involvement of Western powers, who have galvanised and mobilised Jihadi movements to further their interest in Afghanistan in the 70s and 80s, in the Balkans in the 1990s and in Syria in the 2000s. Understanding the complicated history and politics driving third and fourth wave neo-Jihadi political violence is key to undermining it. Whilst implicitly considered in Prevent – commonly referred to by policymakers as 'perceived grievances' – the strategy nevertheless sweeps these material realities and very significant facts under the carpet, hiding our analysis behind the problems of 'ideology' and 'vulnerability'.

Bespoke interventions targeting terrorism only (not counter-subversion, crime prevention or community cohesion)

- The Prevent strategy: what next, abandon or re-configure?
  Prevent does not work. Ten years after the first Prevent strategy was made public, it has failed to stop the move by some towards political violence. It had been in place for over five years and yet this did not stop hundreds of young Muslims going to Syria post 2011. The three strands that form the Prevent strategy – counter-ideology, supporting vulnerable people and

196 *A new framework for engagement*

having institutions identify radicals – does not tackle terrorism nor stem the tide of future outbreaks of political violence. What emerges from the data is that de-radicalisation is not about tackling terrorism and radicalisation but is more about the production of citizenship, the construction of a mainstream British identity and the promotion of a specific subjectivity for subjects deemed problematic. In effect, it re-educates deviant individuals and disciplines a block of people called the 'Muslim Community'. Now, for some, and perhaps controversially, this is a good thing. Some may hold the view that a problematic minority should be acculturated to the values of British political, social and cultural society. Others may also believe that there is nothing wrong with supporting 'vulnerable people'. But this has little to do with protecting our country from attacks, keeping citizens safe or forging a new politics of belonging. Prevent misses the point. It focuses on ideology instead of emotions, individuals instead of groups, and ideas instead of behaviour. A policy to tackle the threat of violence from neo-Jihadi political violence is necessary but in its current guise Prevent is not fit for purpose.

• Disengagement, not de-radicalisation

Interventions need to target individuals who have committed terrorism or have been proven to belong to a network/group planning to attack. Interventions should not aim to de-radicalise the young, the vulnerable, and those who have extreme or wacky ideas. We need to disengage militants from violence, not de-radicalise the views of young people. How does putting a young Muslim of, say, 15 years, identified by his school and vetted through Channel, on a de-radicalisation programme protect Britain from terrorism? De-radicalisation in Prevent assumes that people are brainwashed and indoctrinated and so the way to resolve this is by de-programming and counter-ideology. It is foolish to believe that de-radicalisation will resolve the current wave of hyper-terrorism.

De-radicalisation in Prevent moves the focus significantly beyond terrorism. This has led to a focus on what people are saying and thinking and charges of 'thought-crime'. Given that it is not a crime to have sinister, extreme or wacky thoughts, why place particular emphasis on certain ideas? Many interviewees believed that the focus on ideology was not merely confined to the problem of violence but also includes the perceived problem of the subversive threat posed by Muslim mobilisation, the threat to community cohesion as a result of illiberal values and the inability of 'vulnerable' Muslim youth to effectively think through ideology and make the right choices. The important point to note here is the wide repercussions such a valorisation of ideas has in counter-terrorism policy.

Combined with a pre-emptive logic, this results in the net being cast far and wide. We have moved into extremism which, combined with the pastoral logic of 'vulnerability', means we've arrived in a confusing place where we can't distinguish between threatening radicalisation and non-threatening radicalisation. We have moved the line too far back in a way that is unprecedented in the history of UK policymaking: we have gone from terrorism, to violent radicalisation, to radicalisation, to violent extremism, to non-violent extremism, to just extremism in a short space of time. The line should be placed where someone has done something illegal. It is about behaviour not thoughts.

- Important factors in disengagement
Counter-ideology is important for public debate and for dialogue with militants in interventions. But how this works in actual reality has been convoluted by the Prevent conception of de-radicalisation. The preoccupation of policymakers with the threat of ideology consequently gave the impression that the solution to radicalisation resided with alterations to the worldview of the radicalised subject, in which tweaking an individual's beliefs on certain issues would result in behavioural change.

    More influential than counter-ideology for disengagement efforts in the UK however, is the vital role played by charismatic individuals (from within the movement/group); the support of wider family members (identity is contingent on our social groups and thus family and friends play a huge role in either joining or leaving violence); material dimensions in terms of employment and skills training to ensure transition to normal life; the support of what is seen as 'traditional' modes of Islam (and not 'progressive' Islam); programmes that are well structured and sustainable for long periods of time (a few years may be required – as seen with right-wing disengagement programmes in Germany, the process can be long); and the leeway to accommodate the differences amongst individuals – some of whom feel more burnt out than others and some more disillusioned while others yearn for a normal life, some grow out of it, and some simply fail to walk away.

- Conventional 'hard' edge counter-terrorism: intelligence and interrupting networks
It is important to stress the invaluable work done by conventional 'hard' measures of counter-terrorism in protecting Britain. Thus far, counter-terrorism professionals have been successful in keeping Britain safe from terrorism, excluding the tragic death of Lee Rigby in 2013, which is regarded as a low-impact (in terms of numbers killed) and low scale attack (small operation). Key to these operations is solid intelligence and the capacity to disrupt violent extremists' networks. Intelligence is the blood-line of counter-terrorism agencies. But collating intelligence must be left to the professionals and not delegated to care workers, teachers and youth workers. This is not only bad practice and counter-productive but forces public employees to confront ethical questions and it results in poor intelligence. Prevent has deployed its resources to map the Muslim population and has laid down a vast infrastructure of surveillance within institutions of the state.

198 *A new framework for engagement*

But this spreads the net too wide and risks undermining the legitimate imperative to gather information. It has the effect of casting the role of citizenship as an obligation to inform; it increases suspicion and criminalises the most benign behaviour. It also avoids catching the right suspects, since neo-Jihadists operate amongst family and friends in small groups. Alongside the appropriate technologies needed for intelligence is the necessity of disrupting the networks and groups that connect young Muslims to other networks abroad.

- The use of the internet amongst neo-Jihadi groups

There has to be a coherent strategy for fighting online jihadism. There is a fine line between the rights of individuals to access and consume what they want online and the point at which that right infringes the security of others. The legal debate between freedom and security is a serious one that needs to be weighed properly and any response must be measured. The focus should be on violent groups active online. But it is important to note that the internet nevertheless remains the logical place for neo-Jihadis to be: it is a space in which information and propaganda is disseminated outside mainstream channels, using mainstream tools. The internet acts a locus in which individuals can obtain all sorts of material, training manuals and videos. Neo-Jihadis rely on uploading a stream of shocking videos depicting the humiliation and suffering of Muslims in order to induce a traumatic effect. These videos create a sense of moral outrage and anger and are successful in motivating youth to take up direct action. After all, for politically violent groups, 'propaganda by the deed' is extremely important in order to induce fear, attract recruits and raise the profile of their cause.

The internet is the ideal place for such objectives, not least because it fits with the news and material consumption of young people, who on the whole spend a great deal more time online than watching TV. Also, given the horizontal and de-centralised structure of the neo-Jihadi movement, the internet allows 'like-minded' people to connect and propagate mini-worlds with their own distinctive cultures and capacity to mobilise offline in the real world. There has been much talk about the influence of the internet on 'lone wolves', those who self-radicalise without interaction with an organisation or exposure to ideology. No matter, however, how important the internet may be for propaganda and cultivation of a 'pop-jihad as a lifestyle' (Coolsaet 2015), it is not the engine of political violence but rather an echo chamber that both reinforces made-up minds and creates virtual communities of belonging. A strategy to disrupt online Jihadism is vital.

Empower the youth

Policy and programmes in the area of youth empowerment should not be run by the police or embedded within existing crime prevention infrastructure but delivered by schools, civil society and the employment sector.

- Providing work and skills
  The prime vehicle for the transformation of one's socio-economic condition is employment. The easiest way to eliminate the experience of discrimination is by providing youth with opportunities to acquire skills, receive training and access jobs. Many of those who join ISIS in this current wave, unlike earlier Jihadis of the 70s and 80s, are on the whole less educated. The majority hail from the urban slums of European capitals, where many spend their days involved in petty crimes and local gang culture. There seems to be an easy transition from urban gang culture to radical Islamist violence. Many of them have little education, are unskilled for the job market and face a lifetime of unemployment. This situation forces many individuals into a life of crime, whilst others sink into an abyss of boredom and low self-esteem. In a situation characterised by little hope and alienation, many young Muslims see the Jihad as a way out and as an opportunity to embark on an adventure. The Jihad, to quote Scott Atran (2010), is 'an egalitarian equal opportunity employer'. The most effective way to undercut the appeal of neo-Jihadi lifestyle is to provide skills training and to help disempowered youngsters into employment.

- The power of hopes and dreams
  Youth generally favours action and challenges over words and the mundane. We have seen what the idealism, energy and dynamism of the young can do. Young people are not only spearheading technological and business innovation but have been the engine of social and political change in the Middle East with the Arab uprisings in 2011. We therefore need to encourage the youth to dream and we need to create the opportunities that would allow them to realise their dreams. Consider, for example, the counter-cultural appeal of 'Pop-Jihad' for many young disenfranchised Muslims: there is the idealistic utopia of establishing a new society and state, picking up a gun and fighting what they see as a noble cause, resisting oppression, the chance to enact collective ritual with a group of like-minded individuals, the thrill and adventure of travelling to another part of the world, getting married and feeling like they are part of something greater. This picture appeals to the young generally and not just specific groups of young Muslims. Whilst the reality is far removed from this rose-tinted picture of the Jihad, the unemployed and alienated youth in the cities of London, Paris and Brussels see it as an alternative option and way out of the dire predicament they face at home. We need to override this picture and expose the pernicious realities of the Jihad.

  In many respects, America is more suited to tackling the radicalisation of youth than Britain and Europe generally. Many young people in America still subscribe to the American Dream and, regardless of whether it is true or not, it is a powerful motivation for many Americans who believe that if they work hard they can accomplish their dreams. In Britain and Europe, we are a lot less sanguine about our prospects. We see the power of a

200 *A new framework for engagement*

dream in the way that millions of immigrants travel far and wide against their wishes and risk everything in the pursuit of a better life. It is the hope and dream of something better that drives them. It also motivates billions of people every day around the world to go to work, take risks and attempt the impossible. Hopes and dreams are a powerful thing. This becomes a problem when the young lose hope and have no dreams. The real driver behind fourth wave neo-Jihadi violence is, to quote Rik Coolsaet, the 'no future subculture' (2016). We need to cut the appeal and traction of ISIS and neo-Jihadi Violence by generating a more powerful narrative about Britain's commitment to providing opportunity, success and challenges for young people. This, of course, has to be backed by policy. But a narrative in our schools and culture that speaks to the hopes and dream of the young has to be cultivated.

- The importance of heroes and role models
Muslim role models should be encouraged in mainstream venues. There is a notable shortage of Muslim role models and inspirational heroes in main-stream consciousness. Their importance cannot be overstated. The youth do not, on the whole, see politicians, intellectuals and religious figures as role models. Role models tend to be cultural figures like sports people, celebrities, musicians, artists, actors and in some cases political/human-itarian activists. A most influential figure was the late boxer and heavy-weight legend, Mohammed Ali, as was political/religious activist Malcom X. These figures are American, with global appeal and more British role models are harder to come by. More, though, are becoming visible: Zain Malik, Nadya Hussain, Mo Farah and Amir Khan.

Role models provide a shining example of what to do, how to be and how to act. They provide inspiration, awe and motivation. And many who feel like they belong to socially beleaguered groups that are outside the priv-ileged dominant group in society find in their role models paragons of virtue and beacons of light that confer on them a sense of confidence and dignity. The symbolic and cultural power of Mohammed Ali globally, for example, emanated from the perception that he was carrying the plight and oppression of Black Americans and the less developed world, on his shoulders. Every punch he landed on his opponents was seen as a victory of David against Goliath.

The same aura surrounded Osama Bin Laden, who must be understood more as a figure in the cut of Che Guevara than as a religious leader. He was seen by many of the young in the Muslim world at one point as a counter-hegemonic figure who abandoned his wealth and the comforts of an easy life for the struggle against powerful Empires. He was seen by some of the young at the time as a warrior striking at the belly of the imperial leviathan. Today, the disempowered young would-be Jihadi sees members of the Jihad as charismatic, rebellious and therefore 'cool' individuals. The 'Jihad Cool' association must be replaced by the 'coolness' of other Muslim role models,

A new framework for engagement   201

which requires mainstream air and space. Policymakers and Muslims should actively promote positive, successful and empowering role models to youth.

- Promoting a creative culture
One key strategy for winning hearts and minds is investing in the cultural sphere. Nation-states are not merely civil political entities that demand the civil allegiance to institutions of the state but are also 'imagined communities' that call for a cultural identification with the nation. These feelings of identification cannot be constructed outside of culture, or outside of representation, which depend on the dense, complex and multifaceted web of symbols and meaning. Culture is extremely important for re-imagining who we are and for indigenising the Muslim presence into the fabric of British cultural life in a way that is palatable to dominant social imaginaries and which also empowers Muslims in an organic and authentic way.

A growing counter-culture and alternative lifestyles movement has emerged amongst young Muslims in many European capitals. It has its own music, designer clothes, language and magazines. The Jihad should therefore be seen within this cultural paradigm; it is thus an extension of the attempt of the wider diaspora in European societies to embrace new experiences and lifestyles and develop a new culture. But instead of focusing on the cultural displacement of Muslims, this trend must be viewed within the context of what Zygmunt Bauman calls 'liquid Modernity' (2000); this concept explains the fact that identity, culture, society and politics are no longer fixed in late modernity: we now have fluid identities in an age dominated by individualism, the breakdown of communities and the deep penetration of market values into our social fabric.

In this new environment, the young seek status in alternative ways: rather than having to work your way up the dominant social hierarchy, you can attain status by belonging to a niche group with its own values. So you gain status by belonging to a group – 'I'm a vegetarian hipster', 'I'm a liberal environmentalist, 'I'm a Jihadi Muslim'. You then gain further status by demonstrating excellence in the traits important to your particular group. In the case of neo-Jihadi groups this entails external conformity to dress and behavioural codes and willingness to sacrifice one's self for the cause. This is not, then, the radicalisation of the Muslim population but a generational revolt of a sub-category of youths or, to quote Olivier Roy (2015), 'This is not the radicalization of Islam, but the Islamization of radicalism.'

Muslims should be encouraged to strike out in new ways through being a creative cultural minority. To thrive in Britain, it is not possible to think of a Muslim presence without nourishing creative cultural expressions which are alternative to popular culture but at the same time able touch it. There is scope for outside the box articulations of diverse cultural and artistic styles in a way that is rooted in spiritual, ethical and diverse ethnic traditions (which are usually ignored in mainstream youth cultures) and yet synthesised and

202 *A new framework for engagement*

expressed in a way indigenous to wider British culture and society. There is already a 'Muslim Cool' Scene, but it is overwhelmingly marginal. Till now, there has been little or no space in which to manifest the creative contribution that has emerged in polymorphous cultural spaces. Doing so goes to the very heart of the problems that policymakers believe have been plaguing us – political identity, cultural displacement and the politics of belonging.

Investing in the research on exit from political violence

* The importance of primary data
  The field of terrorism and political violence is in very bad shape. The study of exiting political violence is even worse. The vast bulk of the literature on de-radicalisation/disengagement, save for two studies, uses secondary data, most of which is recycled. Nearly everything we know about exit from political violence is descriptive. It is also disseminated in information form through think-tank reports found online. Current approaches to investigating de-radicalisation therefore are not evaluative, rely on personal accounts and are not peer-reviewed, and there isn't a single case of counter-factual assessment found in the literature. What, for example, would have happened to the individual had they not undergone intervention?

  Primary data must be collected. There are of course many obstacles to being able to interview terrorists – from access to terrorists, to the confidentiality of information and also the ethical challenges involved in such a process. However, unless qualitative data is compiled from individuals who have been 'deradicalised' it will be difficult to draw any inferences. In the UK, we still do not know about the experience of individuals who have undergone de-radicalisation. As a result, a major area of research for the future will be the collation of data on Channel in all of its dimensions: the process from beginning to end, the experience of subjects undergoing de-radicalisation, the experience from the point of view of public servants and an actual in depth investigation into the process of de-radicalisation in order to understand how individuals become de-radicalised. Until data is collected on Channel, we will continue to know very little about de-radicalisation beyond the platitudes of policymakers and media vignettes.

* Quantifying the success of interventions
  Another area worth pursuing in terms of further research is trying to find out how de-radicalisation programmes can be evaluated. This is undeniably one of the biggest challenges of intervention programmes: how do we know when someone has genuinely deradicalised? It is the difficulty of establishing a reliable way to gauge de-radicalisation that prevents practitioners from claiming the success of intervention programmes. The challenge stems from the claim of 'cognitive change' embedded in conceptions of de-radicalisation. It is impossible, for example, to look inside an individual's head to ascertain whether they have really changed their world-

view; and more often than not, most individuals will play along with the requirements of an intervention programme in order to complete it, or to earn early parole in the case of prison programmes. This is why academics like Bjorgo and Horgan (2009) have advocated focusing on behavioural dimensions in intervention programmes because at least this is an indicator that can be observed. Also, the current focus on recidivism rates, which is borrowed from the field of crime prevention, merely informs us about the rate of re-offending. It remains an unreliable way of evaluating the success of an intervention programme. Given that policymakers would like to be able to point to the successes of their policies, as well as prove to the electorate that counter-terrorism is working, research investigating ways of quantifying success is likely to gain some endorsement from policymakers. Important questions are: what does success look like? How do we quantify it?

- Identifying factors involved in disengagement/exit from violence
  There are few, if any, conclusive causal factors that can be established in terms of the process of leaving violence. Current de-radicalisation interventions are complex and inter-disciplinary: effective execution of deradicalisation interventions requires an understanding of political and theological thinking in the classical Islamic tradition with respect to violence and techniques of psychotherapy, like counselling, knowledge of psychology and mentoring skills; a knowledge of international and Middle Eastern politics, supported by a wide-ranging rehabilitative package, material incentives, medical knowledge and an awareness of the local community the subject hails from, amongst other things. Further research would then have to examine all these factors individually and in tandem to establish which is the most effective. Intervention programmes will have to be observed in a real life context; individuals undergoing interventions have to be interviewed and longitudinal data sought in order to follow the participants' development over a long period of time. The question remains: what made an individual disengage? Was it the counter-ideology? Was it maturity and changing life circumstance in the life of the individual? Was it more utilitarian factors like the promise of work, money and a better life? Ethnographic fieldwork and qualitative data will be important in answering such questions.

References

Aggarwal, N. (2013). 'Mental discipline, punishment and recidivism: reading Foucault against de-radicalisation programmes in the War on Terror', *Critical Studies on Terrorism*, 6 (2): 262–278.

Atran, S. (2010). *Talking to the Enemy. Violent Extremism, Sacred Values, And What It Means To Be Human*. London: Penguin.

Bauman, Z. (2000). *Liquid Modernity*. Cambridge: Polity Press

204 *A new framework for engagement*

Bjorgo, T. and Horgan, J. (2009). *Leaving Terrorism Behind: Disengagement from Political Violence.* New York: Routledge.

Campbell, D. (1998). *Writing Security: United States Foreign Policy and the Politics of Identity.* Manchester: Manchester University Press.

Coolsaet, R. (2015). *Jihad as a Lifestyle, Freedom from Fear,* http://f3magazine.unicri.it/?p=1088.

Coolsaet, R. (2016). 'Facing the fourth wave foreign fighters, what drives Europeans to Syria, and to Islamic State? Insights from the Belgian case', *The Egmont Papers* 81, Royal Institute for International Relations, www.egmontinstitute.be/wp-content/uploads/2016/02/egmont.papers.81_online-versie.pdf.

Croft, S. (2012). *Securitizing Islam: Identity and the Search for Security.* Cambridge: Cambridge University Press.

Della Porta, D. (1995). *Terrorism in Context: Left-Wing Terrorism in Italy,* edited by Martha Crenshaw. University Park, Pennsylvania: The Pennsylvania State University Press.

Foucault, M. (1988). *Technologies of the Self: A Seminar with Michel Foucault,* edited by L. Martin, H. Gutman and P. Hutton. Amherst: The University of Massachusetts Press.

Fukuyama, F. (1999). *Social Capital and Civil Society.* The Institute of Public Policy, George Mason University, www.imf.org/external/pubs/ft/wp/2000/wp0074.pdf.

Habermas, J. (1991). *The Structural Transformation of the Public Sphere: An Inquiry into a Category of Bourgeois Society.* Cambridge, MA: MIT Press.

Huntington, S. (1993). 'The clash of civilizations?', *Foreign Affairs,* Summer 72: 3, www.svt.ntnu.no/iss/Indra.de.Soysa/POL2003H05/huntington_clash%20of%20civlizations.pdf.

The Institute for Economics and Peace (IEP) (2015). *The Global Terrorism Index 2015,* http://economicsandpeace.org/wp-content/uploads/2015/11/Global-Terrorism-Index-2015.pdf.

Jarvis, L. and Holland, J. (2015). *Security: A Critical Introduction.* London: Palgrave Macmillan.

Lindekilde, L. (2015). 'Refocusing Danish counter-radicalisation efforts: an analysis of the (problematic) logic and practice of individual de-radicalisation interventions', in *Counter-Radicalisation: Critical Perspectives,* edited by C. Baker-Beall, C. Heath-Kelly and L. Jarvis. Abingdon: Routledge.

Neumann, Iver B. (1998). *Uses of the Other: The 'East' in European Identity Formation.* Minnesota: University of Minnesota Press.

Roy, O. (2015). 'France's oedipal Islamist complex', *Foreign Policy,* http://foreignpolicy.com/2016/01/07/frances-oedipal-islamist-complex-charlie-hebdo-islamic-state-isis/.

Sageman, M. (2008). *Leaderless Jihad: Terror Networks in the Twenty-First Century.* Philadelphia: University of Pennsylvania Press.

Wiktorowicz, Q. (2005). *Radical Islam Rising: Muslim Extremism in the West.* Lanham, MD: Rowman and Littlefield.

Conclusion

This book has attempted to advance a conceptualisation of de-radicalisation as the analytical category and the theoretical object that has the capacity and purchase to map a coherent concept on to the phenomenon in the real world; a phenomenon which is unique in its conceptualisation and implementation in contradistinction to other places − one which is characterised by a diversity of terms and meanings, and a whole range of other family resemblances of associations; and which is also rife with the contradictions and paradoxes in both discursive and policy domains. This necessity of investigating the ontological framework of de-radicalisation is magnified when we consider the vast amounts of political, emotional and financial capital expended by the UK government on the production, distribution and execution of de-radicalisation since 2011 − the pace and scope of which intensified even further after 2015.

This book was thus provoked by my consternation − particularly given the importance policymakers have bestowed on de-radicalisation and the fact that the Prevent strategy has effectively morphed into and is subsumed under de-radicalisation − about the way that Prevent, the media and the wider research field has addressed (or failed to address) the conceptual framework of de-radicalisation. The current understanding of de-radicalisation as 'cognitive change', 'behaviour change', 'integration into the mainstream', 'rehabilitation', 'dialogue', 'counter-ideology', 'crime prevention' and tackling Islamist radicalism, amongst countless other understandings, is insufficient, confusing and misleading. The current aporia has left the signifier 'de-radicalisation' floating without a stable signification, and yet at the same time, paradoxically, connected to a palette of competing, conflicting significations. This book took the plunge into the academic quagmire in order to salvage a concept that might be able to tell us something about a particular phenomenon in the UK.

The book has also sought to make sense of the glaring contradictions and paradoxes characterising de-radicalisation: the absence of a coherent and rigorous research field to inform policy; the non-existent empirical evidence for policy development; the lack of data on actual UK Channel interventions; confused and conflicting conceptual and policy logics; the hegemonic future orientated logic characterising the radicalisation discourse, which is concerned with the *potentiality and possibility* of threats rather than *actual threat*; the tolerance

206 *Conclusion*

of policymakers to the substantial gap between what is said and done, between perception and reality, and between counter-terrorism policies that focus on countering extremism versus those that target radicalisation versus those that actually counter-terrorism; the incomprehensibility of the nebulous concept 'extremism' and its conflation with radicalisation and general conservatism; the role of British values in a counter-terrorism policy; the restrictive way it has defined Britishness along liberal lines; the young age of subjects being reported to Channel; the disconnection of young 'radicals' from wider terrorist networks; the focus on pre-crime and policing thought-crimes; focusing interventions on individuals despite the fact that the path towards violence on the whole requires groups; and the confusion of conflating radicalisation with concepts of 'vulnerability' and 'at risk'; employing all citizens and employees as, effectively, agents of security; all these feature amongst a panoply of other tensions.

One of the primary goals of the book, then, was not only to reconcile the aforementioned fissures in our conceptualisation of de-radicalisation, but also to provide a concept that enriches our understanding of the phenomenon of de-radicalisation, to contextualise it, place it genealogically in place and time, and situate it within wider social and political relations. Such an enterprise goes against current attempts to impoverish and distort it, even if by neglect rather than design, which leaves our understanding of de-radicalisation floating abstractly in differentiated domains and spaces. By re-orientating our conceptual gaze, this book sought to bring something else into view, open a new path for making sense of a strategy and policy that not only targets a particular group, despite its claims to universality in its application, but also re-configures both the epistemic apparatus and the social, political and ideational forces of relations governing the paradigmatic structures of British society. De-radicalisation matters because it belongs to a language game that instrumentalises state techniques in order to correct and rehabilitate not only individuals but everyone else in society. Without the right conceptual armoury that allows for a different epistemic prism and language to be applied analytically, current discursive, spatial and material realignments occurring through Prevent would remain undetected and invisible to the everyday gaze of citizens.

Conceptualising de-radicalisation as the technologies of the self emerged out of the limitations of the inductive method in making any ingress into conceptualising de-radicalisation. The ontological question – 'what is it?' – had to be arrived at discursively, interpreting the data emanating from my discussions with experts who work in and intimately know this field, through the Foucauldian interpretive analytics. Employing a post-structural ontology therefore meant I was able to analyse how UK de-radicalisation is framed discursively and what relationship, if any, it had with the phenomenon in the real world. In the process, I discovered the various strands of discourses it encompassed, the extent of the conceptual confusion and the fact that it was painting an alternative picture of a phenomenon called de-radicalisation, differentiated from the language, discourse and research that existed on it. The technologies of the self are hence an apt and a rich concept because they encapsulates the complex interplay between

Conclusion 207

discursive, epistemic, relational, institutional and material domains operating within the infrastructure of UK governmentality to shape and guide the modern self. The technical application of the micro-physics and apparatus of power in order to transform selves affects the Muslim and non-Muslim subject equally, albeit it targets Muslims in a particular way within the wider context of paradigmatic ideals formulated by the political and neo-liberalism.

With respect to paradigmatic norms then, this book argued, perhaps ambitiously, that there were different dimensions shaping the norms of our society, and that one of them was the Schmittian 'political'. Drawing on the notion of the political was attractive not only because it laid the foundations for understanding the preconditions of the nation-state, but also because it offered analytical purchase in explanations of collective identity, the power of sovereignty post-9/11 vis-à-vis Juridical Law, and the pre-emptive logic driving domestic securitisation of all institutions, agencies and domains. In order for the political and national community to exist, politics has to be exclusionary and antagonistic. Schmitt shows that every act of consensus is based on exclusion, since the nation presupposes the collective agency of the 'we'; it reinforces the fact that identities are constructed through difference and hence the exclusion of Muslims from the British nation symbolically. It is the 'political' that allows practices like citizenship and identity to acquire significance and therefore provides the normative blueprint for everyone bounded by the sovereignty, law and power of the nation-state.

Meanwhile, the second paradigmatic norm, neo-liberalism, was conceived as a practice of government that seeks alignment between the functions of government, the management of society, the normative values promoted to citizens and a market-based logic. Specifically, neo-liberalism seeks a de-politicised subject and market-consumer based values, as well as self-regulating and responsible citizenship. It is in this sense that 'radicalisation' represents an aberration of the neo-liberal ideal or what constitutes normality. If, in other words, radicalisation is about too much religion, politicisation and a problem of identity, normality is defined as de-politicisation, liberal values and particular forms of conduct. This is why British identity and values are valorised as an antidote to the radicalisation malaise. The technologies of self depend on the criterion of normal and deviant, of good and bad, and hence the significance of discursive production in the technologies of the self.

Thus, seen in this light, it became clear through the technologies of the self, that the ultimate goal of de-radicalisation in the UK is not necessarily the reduction of violence (for many of the subjects were never violent to begin with) but a type of ideological and religious revisionism, which contextualises world politics, foreign policy and theology in a way that is endorsed by political authority. The underlying objective of Channel is consequently designed to tackle problematic Muslim identity, which is believed to be impregnated with theological and political excess that potentially risks being converted into violence in the future. Policymakers have chosen to cull Muslim surfeit by shaping the subjectivity of Muslim youngsters through the instruments of discursive, disciplinary

208   *Conclusion*

and pastoral power. In terms of intervention programmes, de-radicalisation seeks to inscribe a form of Muslim subjectivity compatible with the nation state and neo-liberalism: modern, secular and liberal, consumerist, self-regulating, individualistic and apolitical. It is Muslim identity − not terrorism − that has been problematised in the UK counter-terrorism policy.

It is in this sense that de-radicalisation is the logical endpoint of the problematisation of identity that has spanned a couple of decades. At the heart of these debates and concerns has been the 'Muslim Question' or 'what to do with Muslims?' but, more importantly, they have provoked profound questions for both the Muslim subject and, perhaps ironically, wider and deeper questions about personal, political and cultural identity, which have become a ubiquitous feature of our condition in late modernity. Where we end up in response to the 'Muslim question' is irrevocably entangled and adjoined with the direction we take and where we end up as a country. This relationship between minority and majority has not only been underscored by the logic that once Muslims have been de-radicalised, a Muslim can be included in the national majority. Rather, this relationship of power is interlocked and intertwined; one of the by-products of all of this concern with deradicalising Muslims − of which those of who are deemed radical number a mere few hundred in a population of over 60 million − has been questions about the cultural and political identity of these isles. De-radicalisation is therefore not only about the remaking of subjectivity of the problematic radical 'Other' (individuals), not to mention disciplining the Orientalised Other (the British Muslim community in the singular), but perhaps more importantly, it is about the remaking of the British self in relation to the uncertainty about British political identity amidst the wider pressures posed by globalisation, the fragmentation of the nation, Scottish Independence and Britain's exit from the EU. If the BREXIT vote has shown anything, it has shown that issues about identity and culture, for millions of people in this country, remain of utmost importance. Culture, today, is what people are willing to die for.

Beyond the ethereal and existential questions about culture lurk the concrete and material effects of the existing epistemic and discursive paradigm. Its impact can be gleamed from the spatial restructuring that has occurred since 2005: the social engineering of communities, the Otherising of a population grouped together under an expedient administrative label, the rendering of everyday mundane spaces, like primary schools, hospitals and the internet into hotspot locations of surveillance, and the installation and greater visibility of cameras and associated (in)security paraphernalia, to name but a few examples. Alongside such special realignments has been the instrumentalisation of human bodies: children become potential suspects; teachers, administrators and other types of public managers/employees become security and intelligence agents/informants; Muslims begin to define themselves in relation to a whole range of categories ('radical', 'vulnerable', 'at-risk', 'extreme', 'moderate', 'liberal', 'good', 'bad', etc.), with many deploying these categories strategically in order advance their careers, obtaining funding for their organisations, rebelling and protesting,

Conclusion 209

mobilising and resisting, seeking new coherent and empowering ways of living and actively pursuing alternatives, amongst countless other responses.

But this dual deployment of discursive and disciplinary technologies has also been accompanied by a new reality, a striking symptom of the current discursive paradigm − a new type of citizenry. This new type of citizen has to regulate their own minds, feelings and dispositions according to a narrow bandwidth of acceptable mental prisms and beliefs permitted by the normative paradigmatic neo-liberal blueprint. Everyone is not only watching everyone else, they also have to scrutinise their own minds for signs of potential 'extremism'. This hegemonic 'Overton window' (a metaphor used in the policy-making world to denote the range of ideas acceptable to the public at a particular period of time) has pushed a whole spectrum of thinking, values and ways of being beyond the pale − unrelated to religion − which now make you an anomaly, an oddball, someone who stands in need of correction. Mainstream conservative positions, various political opinions, everyday mainstream practices like debates at Universities, dissent over foreign policy, as well as countless other examples which would form a list so long it would indubitably implicate the majority of the British population − let alone the diminutive and impotent 5 per cent Muslim population. The paradox of all this for every British citizen has to be explicitly stated: de-radicalisation and Prevent is in gross violation and breach of British values.

But a question remains: are Muslims stuck with the identities they never owned, but must forever assume? A serious challenge for Muslims now is how to understand and respond to the epistemic and normative paradigms that dislocate and disrupt the integrity of identity formations in all their multivalent and polyvalent expressions. Having to constantly question your ideas and beliefs, scrutinise your behaviour and psychologically feel the Kafkaesque hands of power on your shoulders, places the Muslim subject in an immense pressure cooker. Whilst the fact that this pressure is being asserted politically and culturally in top-down fashion is undeniably coercive − it nevertheless presents a positive opportunity, counter-intuitive as this might seem, for Muslims to undertake a more explorative and reflexive direction. Many have taken up the challenge and, contrary to the image of a docile subject at the mercy of the tumbling currents of events, Muslims are striking out in exciting and creative new ways.

Lest we forget, the category of British Muslim − and the radicalised Muslim subject that springs out of it − is a recent invention. The lines in the sand can still be washed away by the waves gushing out of a new 'Overton window'. The question, however, is whether or not we should wait for the owl of Minerva to spread its wings at the fall of dusk.

Appendix

Table A.1 Details of fieldwork interviews

No.	Organisation	Date of interview	No.	Organisation	Date of interview
1	DEMOS analyst	08/12/11	2	Director of an organisation (countering extremism on campus)	14/12/11
3	Former President of a student society	19/12/11	4	Institute for Public Policy Research (IPPR) analyst	20/12/11
5	Director of company (received Prevent funding)	21/01/12	6	Academic/Director of a research programme on radicalisation	03/02/12
7	Academic and former Prevent practitioner	21/02/12	8	Prevent practitioner	21/02/12
9	Institute for Strategic Dialogue (ISD) analyst	27/02/12	10	Investigative journalist	01/03/12
11	Academic	20/03/12	12	Academic/freelance consultant on Prevent community engagement	20/03/12
13	Former Vice-Chair of community organisation	11/04/12	14	Former Secretary General of leading representative organisation	17/05/12
15	Academic	21/05/12	16	Representative of National Association of Muslim Police (NAMP)	30/05/12
17	Former Head of a unit working in counter-terrorism	31/05/12	18	Former Chair of community organisation	12/06/12
19	Academic	25/11/12	20	Academic	21/12/12
21	Prevent Engagement Officer in Lancashire	05/02/13	22	Senior Prevent Engagement Officer in Lancashire	05/02/13
23	Director of prison intervention provider	07/02/13	24	Former Chief Inspector and Prevent Delivery Board member	18/02/13
25	Quilliam Foundation analyst	25/03/13	26	Forward Thinking analyst	26/03/13
27	President of think-tank (received Prevent funding)	10/04/13			

Appendix 211

Table A.2 Definitions of de-radicalisation

Author	Definition	Features
UN	Programmes that are generally directed against individuals who have become radical with the aim of re-integrating them into society or dissuading them from violence.	• Programmes • Individuals • Reintegration into Society • Dissuade from use of violence
UK Home Office	This support is sometimes described as "deradicalisation", a term which is used to refer to cognitive or behavioural change and sometimes to both. There are analogies between this work and other forms of crime prevention.	• Support for the 'vulnerable' • Individual process • Cognitive Change • Behavioural Change • Analogies with Crime Prevention
Horgan	Reducing the risk for engagement (and/or re-engagement) in terrorism and illicit activity.	• Reducing risk • Terrorism • Illicit activity
Ashour	A process of relative change within Islamist movements, one in which a radical group reverses its ideology and de-legitimises the use of violence to achieve political goals.	• Islamist Movements • Collective Process • Ideology • Delegitimising violence
Demant et al.	The opposite of radicalisation and becoming less radical with respect to behaviour and beliefs. Belief change entails increase in the confidence in the system, a desire to be a part of society, and the rejection of non-democratic means.	• Opposite of Radicalisation • Becoming less Radical • Behaviour • Beliefs • Belief change = support system, society and politics
Rabasa et al. (Rand)	A process of abandoning an extremist worldview and concluding it is not acceptable to use violence to effect social change. Recognition that social, political, and economic transformation will occur slowly and in a pluralistic environment.	• Abandoning Extremist Worldview • Rejection of violence • Accepting of political, social, and economic structure • Accepts pluralistic environment
International Crisis Group (ICG)	Prison based effort to persuade terrorists and their supporters to abandon the use of violence.	• Prison programmes • Persuade terrorist • Abandon violence
Quilliam Foundation (QF)	Ideology behind extremism is questioned and refuted and replaced by a more traditional, pluralistic understanding of Islam.	• Ideology • Extremism • Refutation • Acceptance of Liberal Islam

Index

Page numbers in *italics* denote tables.

9/11 terror attacks 28, 36, 101

Abuza, Z. 68
Active Change Foundation (ACF) 6,
   142–3, 147, 159
'Age of Neutralizations and
   Depoliticizations, The' (Schmitt) 90
agency 81–2, 83, 168–9, 189–90
Aggarwal, Neil 84
Ahmed, Nafeez 162, 165
Al-Qaeda 30, 122–3, 141
'Al-Qaeda influenced Radicalisation: a
   Rapid Evidence Assessment provided
   by Situation Action Theory' (Home
   Office) 122–3
Algeria 3, 67
Alibihai-Brown, Ali 33–4
Anderson, Benedict 35, 38
antagonism 93
Asad, T. 40
ascetics 76
Ashour, Omar 7, 54, 63, 64–5, 67, 68,
   70–1, 84, *211*
Atran, Scott 199
audiences 28
Austen, J. L. 27
Awan, A. 32, 107

Bauman, Zygmunt 201
Beck, Ulrich 32
'Beliefs, ideologies and narratives of
   violent radicalisation' (Change Institute)
   68
biopolitics 86–8
Bjorgo, Tore 7, 66–7, 68, 203
Braddock, K. 179
brainwashing 174–5

Brighton, Shane 38–9
'Bringing it Home' 142
Brown, Wendy 95
bunch of guys theory 38
Butler, Judith 10, 81

Cameron, David 1–2, 3, 34, 36, 44, 104,
   161–2
Campbell, David 186
Cantle Report 34
Casanova, J. 39–40, 42, 44
central sphere concept 89, 90
Centre for Social Cohesion (CSC) (later
   Henry Jackson Society) 151
Change Institute 68
'Channel Duty Guidance' 171
Channel Programme 2–3, 6, 8, 13, 72,
   128–9, 153, 172–3, 207; evaluation of
   177–80; lack of transparency 178; as a
   link between community and
   intervention providers 147–50; support
   for vulnerable people 167–72
Charlie Hebdo attacks 1, 34, 40
Chishty, Mak 1
'Choosing Our Friends Wisely' (Policy
   Exchange) 144
Christianity 44, 156–7
civil society 187–8
cognitive change 4, 12–13, 59, 62–3, 64–5,
   69–70, 174–5, 177, 179, 202
'Communication on prevention,
   preparedness and response to terrorist
   attacks' 22
community cohesion 34, 38, 64, 73, 131–2
confessional technology 15–16, 77, 78–9,
   156–85; Channel Programme 167–72,
   172–3; conceptual framework of the

Index 213

confessional 156–9; contract and consent notions 175–6; counselling notion 176; evaluating the effectiveness of interventions 177–80; mentoring and psychotherapy as de-radicalisation interventions 172–7; Quilliam Foundation 159–67; redemption 177–83; salvation in this life notion 157–8; vulnerability 167–72, 173, 179
constructivism 10, 135, 186
CONTEST 2, 23, 125
Coolsaet, R. 22, 200
Copenhagen School in Security Studies 27–8, 45n1
counter-brainwashing 174–5
counter-ideology/extremism 53, 59–60, 73; counter-ideology and disengagement 197; role of counter-ideology in de-radicalisation 62–9
counter-radicalisation 4, 24, 58, 85, 122, 126, 129, 143
counter-subversion 73, 161
counter-terrorism 21–2, 191; conventional 'hard' edge counter-terrorism 197; focus on de-radicalisation 2
Counter-Terrorism and Security Bill 2, 13
crime prevention 4, 53, 61–2, 73
Croft, Stuart 28, 33, 186

Danish cartoons affair 40
data *see* research
de-politicisation 95, 183, 194, 207
de-programming 4, 58, 196
de-radicalisation 196–7; analysis of research data on de-radicalisation 51–75; as an area of study and research 6–7; challenges of investigating de-radicalisation 7–12; conceptual confusion 4, 69–70, 71–2; conceptual framework 58–62; concern underpinning interventions 5; contradictions and paradoxes 205–6; counter-ideology, role of 62–9; definitions 3–4, 52–3, 54–8; features of UK interventions 3; importance of 12–14; interventions 172–7; interviewees' interpretations of de-radicalisation 52–3, 54–8; material provisions 68; as a muddled policy 72–3; multiple conceptions, implications of 69–74; non-juridical dimension of 188; and policy-makers 5–6; practices of 11; process of 4–5; programmes 2–3; purpose of 5;

relationship with radicalisation 72; theories 186; *see also* technologies of the self
Dean, Mitchell 85, 95
Demant, F. 64, *211*
Denmark 25, 84–5
deontology 76–7
Department for Communities and Local Government (DCLG) 38, 125, 126
Derrida, Jacques 10
dialogue 4, 58, 63–4, 159, 175, 205
disciplinary technology 15, 77, 78, 125–55; British values and extremism in Prevent 135–41; community approaches to countering radicalisation 141–6; Prevent, assessment of by interviewees 129–34; sectors and institutions as radicalisation hotspots 147–54
Discipline and Punishment (Foucault) 81, 88
discursive technology 15, 77, 78, 100–24, 189; expertise and knowledge, contested boundaries of 105–11; Foucault's notion of truth 100; radicalisation as a body of knowledge 118–23; root-causes and process 111–18, 119–20; threat narratives, construction of 100–5
disengagement 4, 65–7, 69–70, 180–1; *see also* engagement strategy and implications
Douglas, Mary 32
Dreyfus, Hubert 97

Egypt 3, 59, 64–5, 67
engagement strategy and implications 186–204, 196; bespoke interventions targeting terrorism only 195–8; disengagement in preference to de-radicalisation 196; engagement, new framework for 190–5; heroes and role models, importance of 200–1; identifying factors involved in disengagement from violence 203; identity and neo-Jihadi political violence 192–3; important factors in disengagement 196–7; intelligence and disrupting extremists' networks 198; internet use among neo-Jihadi groups 198; investing in research on exit from political violence 202–3; politics and terrorism 194; Prevent, failure of 195, 196; primary data, importance of 202; promotion of a creative culture 201–2; quantifying the success of interventions 203;

214 *Index*

engagement strategy and implications *continued*
reframing the problem 191–5; sacred values and terrorism 193–4; terrorism as a group phenomenon 193; terrorism as political violence not radicalisation 191–2; wars, regional rivalries and Western foreign policy 194–5; work and skills provision for young people 198; young people's hopes and dreams, power of 200; youth empowerment 198–202
English Defence League (EDL) 41, 42, 139
episteme 12, 20, 77
ethics 76–7, 82, 86–7
'EU Plan of Action on Combating Terrorism' 22
'EU Strategy and Action Plan on Radicalisation and Recruitment' 22
European Commission Directorate General (DG) for Communication 22
evaluation 6, 132–3, 177–80, 202–3
exception *see* state of exception concept
expertise 105–11, 164; community expertise, marginalisation of 145–6
extremism 23–4, 58; counter-extremism 53, 59–60; non-violent extremism 126, 137–8, 140, 143, 145, 160–1; and Prevent 135–41

Farouk, Umar 150–1
fold concept 83
foreign policy 25, 40, 105, 115, 116–17, 136, 194–5
Foucault, Michel 10, 11, 14–15, 20, 76, 77, 79–80, 80–2, 85–6, 89, 91, 93, 94, 96, 100, 156, 157, 158, 190
Freud, S. 80
Fukuyama, Francis 91–2

Geller, Ernst 35
Githens-Mazer, J. 24, 25, 26, 32
Global War on Terror (GWT) 28–9, 33, 101
globalisation 36–7
Gove, Michael 163
governmentality 77–8, 90–1, 187, 188; and biopolitics 83–9; definition 85–6; ethics and government 86–7
Gray, John 35
Gutkowski, S. 43
Gutkowski, Stacy 32, 43

Habermas, Jürgen 42

'Hague Programme' 22
Hall, Stuart 81
Hallaq, Wael 91
Harvey, David 94
Heath-Kelly, C. 26, 30, 32–3, 38, 39
History of Sexuality (Foucault) 79–80, 88
Hobsbawm, E. 35
Holland, J. 27
home-grown bomber theory 22, 101
Home Office *211*
Horgan, John 6–7, 54, 58, 64, 65–6, 68, 69–70, 71, 84, 179, 203, *211*
human behaviour 12–13, 63, 186, 189
Huntington, Samuel 194
Hussain, Ed 159–60, 164–5, 166, 167

identity 186–7; confessional technology 78–9, 156–85; fluidity of 80–1; and neo-Jihadi political violence 192–3; political identity 34–5; problematic Muslim identity 33–9, 114–16; securitisation of Muslim identity 28–33; and threat narratives 102, 104
ideology 31; counter-ideology 53, 59–60, 62–9, 73, 188–9; as a primary cause of radicalisation 112–14; takffiri ideology 63, 109, 112, 181
'In and Out of Extremism' (Quilliam Foundation) 165
integration 33–9, 44, 73, 115; and mainstream society 181–2; re-integration 60–1; threat narratives 102–3
intelligence gathering 8, 23, 127, 133, 134, 197
International Crisis Group (ICG) *211*
internet 198
interventions 172–7; bespoke interventions targeting terrorism only 195–8; concern about 5; evaluating the effectiveness of 6, 132–3, 177–80, 202–3; as a form of pastoral power 180–3
Islam 37; association with radicalisation 24; calls for reform of 44; expert knowledge of 109–10; as the first step to terrorism 114; 'liberal' Islam 160, 161; as the orientalised other 39–44; political Islam 137–8; 'reformed' or 'ex' Islamists/Muslims 165–6; and risk 32–3
'Islamist, The' (Hussain) 160, 164–5
islamophobia 42, 178

Jackson, Richard 11
Jarvis, L. 27
Jenkins, Roy 33, 34

jihad 63, 109, 112, 181; *see also* engagement strategy and implications

knowledge 78, 105–11, 145–6; radicalisation as a body of knowledge 118–23
Kuhn, Thomas 89
Kundnani, Arund 127

language: designative theory of 54–5; language-game concept 55–6
Laqueur, Walter 30
liberal democracy 34–5; *see also* neo-liberalism
Lindekilde, Lasse 84–5
logistical life concept 87–8
London bombings, 2005 21, 22, 30, 34

McCauley, C. 25
Manningham-Buller, Eliza 117
market rationality 94, 95
Massumi, B. 29–30
media 106–7
mentoring 84–5, 172–7
modernity 32, 40, 201; multiple modernities notion 42
Moskalenko, S. 25
Mouffe, C. 92
multiculturalism 33–9, 103–4
Murray, Douglas 163
Muslim Association of Britain (MAB) 141–2
Muslim Contact Unit (MCU) 141
Muslim Council of Britain (MCB) 117, 126–7, 140, 142–3, 144–5
Muslims 2, 13–14; association with radicalisation 24; failure to integrate, narrative on 36; and globalisation 37; 'good' or 'moderate' Muslim notion 136–7; intelligence gathering 133–4; 'Muslim question' in a European secular context 39–44; perpetually changing signifiers 36; problematic Muslim identity 33–9, 114–16, 207–8; redesigning Muslim communities 134; 'reformed' or 'ex' Islamists/Muslims 165–6; Salafi Muslims 138–9; securitisation of Muslim identity 28–33; threat narratives 100–5

nation-state 90–2; reason of state 93, 94
national community 35, 207
Nawaz, Maajid 144, 159–60, 163, 164, 165, 166

neo-conservatism 162–3
'Neo-conservatism: Why We Need It' (Murray) 163
neo-liberalism 84–5, 89, 92, 94–6, 207
Neumann, Iver 186
Neumann, Peter 21, 30
'New Security Challenge, The: Radicalisation and Violence – A Critical Reassessment' (research project) 23
normalisation notion 89, 96–7, 190
Northern Riots 34

Obama, Barack 1–2
Office for Security and Counter-Terrorism (OSCT) 57
ontology 9–11, 76, 92
Overton window metaphor 209

paradigm metaphor 89, 96
Parekh, Bhiku 35, 40–1
Philosophical Investigations (Wittgenstein) 55–6
Policy Exchange 71, 143, 144, 145, 163
political concept 89, 92–4, 207
political liberalism 35–6
post-structuralism 10–11, 12, 186, 206
power 78, 82; bio-power 87–8; of the body as machine 86–7; disciplinary technology 78; governmental power 85–6; normalisation notion 89, 96–7; pastoral power 156–8, 183; repressive hypotheses 158
'Power and the Subject' (Foucault) 82
pre-emption 29–30, 33
Prevent 2, 23, 43, 125; British values and extremism in Prevent 135–41; community approaches to countering radicalisation 141–6; conception of de-radicalisation 3–4, 62, 64, 72–3; and counter-ideology 68–9; criticism of 127; delivery of 126; evaluation, absence of 132–3; failure of 195; financial support and publicity for organisations 130–1; objectives 126; ontological framework of radicalisation governing Prevent 111–18; Prevent II 125, 126–7; Prevent III 128; and the problematic Muslim identity narrative 38–9; reputation of 13; sectors and institutions at risk of radicalisation, support for 147–54; Select Committee review of 127–8; use of, by civil servants for career progression 130
Preventing Extremism Together (PET) 125

216 Index

'Preventing terrorism; where next for Britain?' (Quilliam Foundation) 144
'Preventing Violent Extremism Together' (working groups) 23
'Preventing Violent Extremism: Winning Hearts and Minds' (DCLG) 125
prevention 29
prisons 16n1, 84
private space 1, 2, 40
propaganda 13, 198
psychotherapy 172–7

Quilliam Foundation 16, 54, 71, 134, 143, 144, 145, 146, 151, 159–67, *211*; access to media 162; credible expertise 164; funding from Prevent 162; and neo-conservatism 162–3; and 'reformed' or 'ex' Islamists/Muslims 165–6

Rabasa, A. 64, *211*
'Radical Islam on UK Campuses' (CSC) 151
radicalisation 7–8, 191–2, 207; advent of radicalisation as a term and concept 21; association with Islam and Muslims 24; awareness training 13; as a body of knowledge 118–23; community approaches to countering radicalisation 141–6; conceptual framework 24–5; definitions 20–1, 23–4, *211*; discourses on the truth of 31; diversity of meanings 25–6; home-grown bomber theory 22; ideology, threat of 31; integration agenda and the politics of belonging 33–9; 'Muslim question' in a European secular context 39–44; and politics 25; relationship with de-radicalisation 72; research projects 23; risk 32–3, 43; root-causes and process 111–18, 119–20; sectors and institutions as radicalisation hotspots 147–54; securitisation and the radicalised other: new security paradigm 26–33; as a security challenge 20–50; and violence 24
Rainbow, Paul 97
re-integration 60–1
re-socialisation 4, 60–1
redemption 177–83
rehabilitation 4, 5; religious rehabilitation 84
Reid, Julien 87–8
religion 9, 193–4; religious rehabilitation 84; role in public life 39–44
repressive hypothesis 158, 165, 174

research 6–7; analysis of research data on de-radicalisation 51–75; case study method 51; challenges of investigating de-radicalisation 7–12; conceptual framework of de-radicalisation 58–62; counter-ideology, role in de-radicalisation 62–9; data, use and organisation of 79; de-radicalisation, interviewees' interpretations of 52–3, 54–8; exit from political violence 202–3; and the expert industry 108; identifying factors involved in disengagement from violence 203; interviews 51–2, *210*; multiple conceptions of deradicalisation, implications of 69–74; primary data, importance of 202; quantifying the success of interventions 203; radicalisation as a body of knowledge 118–23
Richards, A. 26
RICU (Research, Information and Communications Unit) 13, 73
risk 32–3, 43, 147; identification of 147–54; and identity 116; and neo-liberalism 95
Rose, Nikolas 80, 83, 95, 96, 158
Roselle, L. 28, 100–1
Roy, Olivier 37, 41, 201
Rushdie affair 34, 36, 40

Sageman, Marc 37–8
salvation in this life notion 157–8
Sayyid, S. 37, 42
Schmid, Alex 57
Schmitt, Carl 29, 89, 90, 92, 93, 207
Searle, John 27
secularism 39–44, 45n7, 166
security 186; concept of security 26–7; integration agenda and the politics of belonging 33–9; 'Muslim question' in a European secular context 39–44; new terrorism 30–1; prevention and pre-emption 29–30, 33; risk 32–3, 43; securitisation and the radicalised other 26–33; securitisation theory and process 27–8; state of exception concept 29
Sedgwick, M. 25
sexuality 87–8
social movement theories 37–8
sovereignty 29, 86, 92, 93
Spalek, Basia 30
speech acts 27, 28
'SPOOKED!' (Kundnani) 127

state of exception concept 29, 33, 93
Strategy to Reach, Empower and Educate
(STREET) 6, 141–2, 143, 144, 147, 159
'Structure of Scientific Revolutions, The'
(Kuhn) 89
students 150–2
Sufi Muslim Council 134

takffiri ideology 63, 109, 112, 181
Taylor, Charles 34–5, 40, 42, 44, 54–5
technologies of the self 14–15, 76–99,
186–7, 206–7; and agency 189–90;
central sphere concept 89, 90; civil
society, view of 187–8; de-radicalisation
as a corrective technique of
normalization 97; de-radicalisation as a
governmentality technique 88–9;
definitions 76, 80; dimensions of 76–7;
distinction between subject and
individual 82–3; fold concept 83;
Foucault's ethical turn 82; as
governmental policy continuation or
change 188; governmentality and
biopolitics 83–9, 90–1; nation-state
90–2, 93, 94; neo-liberalism, as an art of
government 94–6; normalisation notion
89, 96–7; paradigm metaphor 89, 96;
political concept 92–4; regulatory norms
89–97; theory of the subject 81–2
teleology 77
terrorism 11, 21–2, 26; new terrorism
30–1; threat narratives 101–2; *see also*
engagement strategy and implications
'Terrorist recruitment: addressing the
factors contributing to violent
radicalisation' 22
theory of the subject 81–2
think-tanks 6, 54, 71, 108, 143, 145–6
threat narratives 100–5

'Threat of Radicalisation on British
University Campuses' (Quilliam
Foundation) 151
truth 10, 31, 78–9, 80, 158; *see also*
discursive technology
Tyrer, D. 37

'Understanding vulnerability and resilience
in individuals to the influence of Al
Qa'ida violent extremism' (Home
Office) 122
United Nations *211*
universities 150–2

values 182; British values and Prevent
135–41; sacred values and terrorism
193–4; shared values 126–7, 135, 145
violence 24, 59, 113–14; disengagement
from 65–7, 69–70, 180–1, 196–7, 203;
link with vulnerable youths 167–8
vulnerability 115–16, 155, 173, 179;
Channel support for vulnerable people
167–72

Wendt, Alexander 10
Wiktorowicz, Quintan 30, 37–8
Wittgenstein, Ludwig 20, 55–6
Workshop to Raise Awareness of Prevent
(WRAP) 148
worldview 3, 4, 5, 59, 60, 61, 64, 69,
172–3, 180, 181, 197, 202, *211*

young people: heroes and role models,
importance of 200–1; hopes and dreams
200; promotion of a creative culture
201–2; risk identification 150–5; work
and skills provision 199; youth
empowerment 53, 56, 61–2, 73,
198–202

Taylor & Francis eBooks

Helping you to choose the right eBooks for your Library

Add Routledge titles to your library's digital collection today. Taylor and Francis ebooks contains over 50,000 titles in the Humanities, Social Sciences, Behavioural Sciences, Built Environment and Law.

Choose from a range of subject packages or create your own!

Benefits for you
- Free MARC records
- COUNTER-compliant usage statistics
- Flexible purchase and pricing options
- All titles DRM-free.

REQUEST YOUR FREE INSTITUTIONAL TRIAL TODAY

Free Trials Available
We offer free trials to qualifying academic, corporate and government customers.

Benefits for your user
- Off-site, anytime access via Athens or referring URL
- Print or copy pages or chapters
- Full content search
- Bookmark, highlight and annotate text
- Access to thousands of pages of quality research at the click of a button.

eCollections – Choose from over 30 subject eCollections, including:

Archaeology	Language Learning
Architecture	Law
Asian Studies	Literature
Business & Management	Media & Communication
Classical Studies	Middle East Studies
Construction	Music
Creative & Media Arts	Philosophy
Criminology & Criminal Justice	Planning
Economics	Politics
Education	Psychology & Mental Health
Energy	Religion
Engineering	Security
English Language & Linguistics	Social Work
Environment & Sustainability	Sociology
Geography	Sport
Health Studies	Theatre & Performance
History	Tourism, Hospitality & Events

For more information, pricing enquiries or to order a free trial, please contact your local sales team: **www.tandfebooks.com/page/sales**

The home of Routledge books

www.tandfebooks.com